DATING AGAIN

A GUIDE TO DATING JUST WHEN YOU
THOUGHT YOU WERE DONE

ROBERT M. FLEISHER

UPHILL BOOKS

Copyright © 2018 by Robert M. Fleisher

All rights reserved.

No part of this book may be reproduced in any form or by any electronic or mechanical means, including information storage and retrieval systems, without written permission from the author, except for the use of brief quotations in a book review.

First Edition: 2018

ISBN 978-0-9828441-2-0 e-book

ISBN 978-0-9828441-3-7 paperback

Published by Uphill Books • An imprint of Uphill Publishing

www.uphillpublishing.com

CONTENTS

Acknowledgments   vii
FOREWARD   ix

PART I
STARTING OVER

1. You Are Not Alone   3
2. In the Beginning   6
3. How Did You Get Here?   8
4. Are You Lonely or Alone?   12
5. Are You Ready for Love?   14
6. Dating ... Again!   18
7. Aging and Dating   21
8. Is Age Just a Number?   24
9. Why Is it So hard to Date Again?   26

PART II
THE HOW-TO OF INTERNET DATING

10. Signing Up for Internet Dating   33
11. Setting Up Your Dating Profile   36
12. Profile Taboos   40
13. Picking Your Username   45
14. Posting Your Photo   49
15. Winks and Flirts   55
16. How Come They Look So Old?   59
17. Choosing the Perfect Internet Date   61
18. Instant Karma: Instant Messaging   64
19. Dating on Tinder   67
20. Why No Callback?   71
21. What's GU Mean?   74
22. The Candy Store   77
23. I'd Never Do Internet Dating   79

24. Home Alone	83
25. The Community	88

PART III
WHO'S LEFT FOR YOU TO DATE?

26. The Seven Categories of People You will Meet on the Internet	93
27. The Lecher	94
28. The Widow and Widower	96
29. Single People Are Not All Created Equal	99
30. The Separated Dater: Good or Bad?	101
31. The Divorced	104
32. The Predator	109
33. Dating the Dysfunctional	113
34. Dating a Tranny	120
35. How to Tell If Your Date Is a Shrew or a Wife-Beater	123
36. Do You Want to Date a Gun-Carrying Guy?	125
37. Do You Investigate Before You Meet?	127
38. Avoiding the Gold-Digging Date	129
39. The Medicine Cabinet and Dating	132
40. Beware the Fraudulent Dater	134

PART IV
ALL THE FISH IN THE SEA

41. What Are You Looking For?	141
42. Love at First Sight	145
43. Dating the Cream of the Crop	147
44. Cognitive Dissonance	150
45. The Oblivious Nature of Some People	155
46. Poor Girl, Rich Girl	157
47. Are All Single Women Horny?	159
48. Rich Guy, Poor Guy	162
49. Are All Single Men Horny (a.k.a. Lechers)?	164
50. Compromise and Compatibility: The Controller	168
51. Desirable Traits: Picking the Perfect Mate	172
52. Looks and Dating	176

PART V
THERE'S A FIRST FOR EVERYTHING

53. The First Phone Call	183
54. The First Date	187
55. What to Talk About	190
56. Rejection of Acceptance	193
57. The First Good-Bye: Hug, Kiss, Handshake, or Wave?	198
58. Never Talk About Money	201
59. The First Kiss	204
60. The First Naked	209
61. First Sex	211

PART VI
SEX AND DATING

62. Sex and Dating in America	217
63. Men Are From Mars and Women … Who Knows?	221
64. Do Women Have An Estrous Cycle?	225
65. Do Men Have and Estrous Cycle?	228
66. Praying at the Altar of the Jade Temple	230
67. Do You Just Settle?	233
68. Praying at the Mount of the Crimson Mushroom	236
69. Performance Anxiety: It's Mostly a Guy Thing	238
70. Astroglide, KY, Viagra … Oh, My!	242
71. Sexual Injuries	245
72. 1ooth Sex	248
73. Forbidden Fruit: The Key to Perpetual Love	250
74. Date Rape	253
75. Recreational Drugs and Dating	257

PART VII
DATING, DISEASE, AND INFIRMITY

76. Dating and Disease	263
77. The STDs	266
78. Does Dating Cause Cancer?	277
79. Does Kissing Cause Cancer?	280
80. HIV/AIDS	282
81. Preventing STDs When Dating	285
82. Tuberculosis and Dating	287

83. Can You Catch Ebola When Dating? — 289
84. Deformity, Disability, and Dating — 291
85. Menopause and Dating — 294
86. Andropause and Dating: Bummer! — 297
87. Will You Still Love Me Tomorrow ... When I'm Sick? — 300

PART VIII
THE MECHANICS OF DATING

88. Guess Who's Coming to Dinner! — 305
89. The Magic of Dating - The Magician — 309
90. Monogamy or Not Monogamy ... That is A Question — 312
91. Marriage ... When Dating Goes Too Far! — 316
92. The Heart, the Brain, the Sex Glands — 318
93. The Odd Couple — 321
94. Your Ex Thinks You're a Jerk! — 323
95. The Battered Man and Dating — 325

PART IX
DATING BEHAVIORS

96. WHERE TO GO, WHAT TO DO? — 331
97. Dirty Dancing and Dating — 332
98. Meeting Their Friends: Who Pays? — 335
99. Introductions — 337
100. Getting to Know You ... on the Vacation — 341
101. The Cruise — 344
102. The Dinner Date — 346
103. On the Road Again: Dating While Away From Home — 348

Afterword — 351
About the Author — 353
Also by Robert M. Fleisher — 355

ACKNOWLEDGMENTS

I would like to thank my friends and family who have been so supportive of my writing. Perhaps they've never read anything I've written, but they told me how much my books inspired them, and it kept me writing. The stories and adventures shared by the many folks who have entrusted their secrets to me have helped enormously in formulating the advice and in developing the basis for this book. Thank you!

FOREWARD

In the beginning ... God created man and woman, and He said this was good.

— GENESIS 1:27

What was He thinking?

This book is dedicated to *e-daters*. We have email, e-commerce, e-tickets, e-files, and more; you get the point. Why not e-dates? Besides the traditional ways to meet new mates, for one reason or another, people have come to the Internet to finding a date, mate, lover, or companion. Online dating (a.k.a. Internet dating, a.k.a. e-dating) is the way to meet people. The future is now.

This book's primary purpose is to help you navigate and find success in the dating world. You find yourself in need of dating advice. A how-to dating guide would be helpful. After all, you want to find true love. To be single, divorced, or widowed and dating *again* is frightening. You are in search of a lasting relationship. You want a

FOREWARD

love life. You want to find the right person. You've come to the right place.

This book's secondary purpose is to let you know that *you are not alone*. We all share similar experiences. As a community, it's important to understand that the tribulations of dating are universal. Offering ideas, cautions, and advice is what this book is all about. Get ready for some interesting stories and great ideas to find the perfect mate and avoid the date from hell!

How did you get here?

Let me count the ways. You may have never found Mr. or Ms. Right and are still looking. You may have found yourself in the dating pool unexpectedly after a divorce or the death of a mate. Or you may have experienced the dissolution of a meaningful or committed relationship. Your mate left you, and you had to be committed. Just kidding.

I

STARTING OVER

1

YOU ARE NOT ALONE

BECAUSE OF THE personal nature of the subjects of dating, companionship, loneliness, and life, you may not wish to talk about your experiences, feelings, or thoughts with family and friends, especially if you happen to be dating a goat or other small farm animal. Remember, they still have laws against that – I think. By understanding the dating experiences I describe, you'll see that you're not alone.

Why are you here?

Connecting with another is a basic human need. That's why *you* are here, unless you're a friendly voyeur having fun peeking into others' lives. Sure, there are those who've given up on dating, but if possible, most of us would like to find someone to share our lives with.

Why is it so hard to get along?

Other human needs include complaining, arguing, getting upset, and blaming. To share your life with another who exhibits too many of these less-than-pleasant traits, results in a paradox: *I want to love someone, but who the hell wants to spend a lifetime with that jerk?*

The glue that keeps us together!

God or Mother Nature (depending on who you believe) created the *sex drive*, a way of getting us to put up with all sorts of poop (I'm trying to refrain from using any of George Carlin's seven dirty words). This setup presents some difficulties for the over-40 dating set. From the guy's point of view, if you can't or won't have sex with him, then why should he put up with all the negativity? From the woman's point of view, if you act like an ass, why should she give you any sex?

Giving guys shit (sorry, no foul language from now on) or acting like an ass to your gal is why most relationships fail. At best, they're held together by the need for *sex* and *security*, the two glues that bind relationships.

When the glue doesn't hold, what happens?

Once the sex drives of guys or gals diminish, once the security of the relationship fails, once the guys no longer spew forth testosterone and the gals' estrogen levels decline, they can grow apart. Or they may only be interested in cuddling and putting up with poop and ass-like behavior.

Is it sex or security they want?

It's been said that guys want sex and women want security. However, there are many men who are terrible providers, and there are many women who are powerhouse providers. There are guys who have limited interest in sex, and women who love their sex. Though there is some truth to male/female stereotypes, the reality is that there are many people out there you may find to be a good match. You just have to be careful or you could end up with the wrong stereotype.

Be smart.

The last thing you want to do is get hurt in a breakup, or get a divorce if the relationship culminates in marriage. Wait, maybe it's the second divorce – or is it the third? You get the picture. Smarter this time is the way to go, even if it means holding out for a better match.

So where do you go from here?

Your first step in the instructions on dating is to turn the page. You may want to start at the beginning, or you can jump around to find a chapter or section that catches your attention. Have fun, and good luck in your search for a better tomorrow.

2

IN THE BEGINNING

YOUNG PEOPLE HAVE a distinct advantage when dating. They can still meet people in the nightclub scene. Older people don't do well in nightclubs because they no longer have the hearing of a dolphin, the eyes of an eagle, or the mobility of a mongoose. That said, you can understand that meeting people at a nightclub means you can't tell what they look like in the dim lighting, you can't hear much of what they say, and you look terribly uncool dancing, even though you think you still have it.

As you get older, you look for the *real* qualities of life, such as intelligence, truthfulness, honor, dignity, and wild sex. Or maybe not. It depends on how well you've taken care of yourself and what you now want out of life. More people than ever are divorced, widowed, or single and set in their ways while still hoping for that perfect Mr. or Ms. Somebody.

Even geriatrics no longer sit at home. They want to date, too. While this book isn't geared toward the centenarians, there must be information out there discussing losing your dentures while French kissing, the physical difficulties of oral sex ("I've gone down, and I can't get up!"), and what to do if you soil your pants on the all-important first encounter. It's never too late to date.

3

HOW DID YOU GET HERE?

WE ALL HAVE our stories to tell – the stories of how circumstances suddenly thrust us into the dating world after many years of marriage or commingling. Before we can begin healing and the journey of dating, it's best to tell your story, but not to your dates. They often find your stories filled with anger, frustration, hate, and bitterness. Let's face it: no one wants to date someone harboring wrath. Tell your story to your shrink, your bartender, your best friend, or your pet. Here's one guy's story. You can use it for comparison, and maybe you won't need to tell your story once you realize the universality of the experience.

"I was 58 when my wife left me – 58! I still can't believe it. While I felt young and vital, the number scared the hell out of me. Who wants a 58-year-old guy? As it turned out, a whole bunch of 65-year-old women. You see, it appears that everyone wants to date someone a few years younger. Now it was my turn to find a new mate, companion, lover, or at least a date for the next Saturday night.

"Many factors come into play in the dating game – many of the same ones that came into play in youth. Everyone still wants the best mate he or she can find with the following traits: most handsome, most beautiful, most popular, caring, loving, loyal, truthful, successful, and rich. Rich is very important – and sexy. Being sexy is very important, but not as much as it was in our youth. And don't forget funny, someone who can make us laugh ... but not by taking off his or her clothing.

"Like a precious gem, this ideal mate is valuable because he or she is so very hard to find. I suspect that even in our youth, most of us realized we had to compromise. Back then, we tried to pick the prettiest, most handsome, most popular mate we could find.

"What we *want* and what we *get* often differ based on what we bring to the table. If all you bring to the table is some stale bread and moldy cheese, you end up with pretty much the same.

"Alas, with all this knowledge and the fact that I brought to the table a decent spread, I set my standards high. Upon this pedestal, I planned to place the most important quality: *a good soul*. Oh, how the shallowness of youth passed me by.

"It's been seven months since my wife of 34 years left me. She moved out, leaving me with two houses: a beautiful suburban home with a pool, and a dream house at the shore no more than 100 feet from the beach. There are views of the ocean from almost every room. This is no stale bread. I have a dream car, sometimes referred to as a "chick magnet." No moldy cheese in this package. How did I get these material things? I worked way too hard for many years. Working too much can ruin a relationship.

"Material things have no correlation with being a good person, a good friend, a good lover, or even a good financial planner. Material things look impressive to those who expect a direct correlation between "things" and "goodness." Actually, sometimes those with the most "stuff" are the biggest jerks, often letting success go to their heads.

"How long can I expect to have these nice things? Divorce does something humbling to those who've worked a lifetime to achieve their station in life. It forces one to take an involuntary vow of poverty. Can you imagine how devastating it would be to lose half your net worth in the stock market? Now that you have a point of reference, I will tell you that it feels about a million times worse if you were betrayed. Can you imagine a business partner stabbing you in the back and the court telling you to give him half of everything? It's not pleasant.

"Anyway, you have to get past this. So take pictures of the nice house and the cool car you used to own, and when you go on dates show them to the person you want to impress. It may also be a good idea to avoid taking a first date to your new refrigerator box that you've lived in since the divorce. Sure, you may have a nice big-screen TV ... box. Not the TV, just the box, recently added to your main refrigerator carton.

"As I collected the words for my tale of woe, I was having my biweekly manicure and pedicure. I had never partaken in this kind of high-style living in years past, and I never had a manicure, let alone a pedicure, until my brother introduced me to the indulgence that most women appreciate. It was right after my breakup, and it was his way of consoling me in my time of despair. He said it would take my mind off the breakup. How?

"You must understand that my brother is a mafia hit man. A manicure is not what you'd expect, and neither did I. Actually, he isn't a hit man, but he does look the part, in that he is big and strong, and you would never guess he gets manicures.

"So here I am at the nail salon, and for the first time in my life, I think I understand the true meaning of vulnerability, rebounding, and being needy. A young Vietnamese girl, one-third my age, rubs my feet and calves. I am in love! No, she's not gorgeous. And how rich can she be on two-dollar tips, even working 12-hour days? Is she good in bed? Who knows? Is she popular? It's hard to tell since she doesn't speak much English. I elicit polite smiles as I ask her deep philosophical questions like, "How are you?" and "Busy today?"

"I offer a compliment. "You are very good!" I'm hoping she'll massage a bit above my kneecap (the fantasy is so nice), or perhaps she'll rub my toe against her breast, and I'll experience the joy of a fleeting pulse of blood to my groin. While I never had a foot fetish, I do have a new respect for all sorts of perverts."

What a story. Does it sound familiar? We all have our own personal stories, and as such, we all embark upon the single world with trepidation. We have all the same questions: Will I ever love again? Will I meet someone nice? Will I meet someone hot? Will I live alone forever? Will I be lonely? I could go on and on, but you get the point, and, hey, you have your own questions.

Let's begin the search for a companion, a new mate, a lover, a spouse, a friend – even a goat is starting to look like an option when you are really down, but trust me, it isn't all that bad.

You do have to get over the shock, anger, fear, and depression that come with lost love, whether by betrayal, by death, or by choice. If you go into the dating scene and you aren't ready, it may prove to be very difficult, even impossible, to connect with anyone on a meaningful level.

Activity Suggestions – List the most meaningful relationships you've had. How long did each one last? How did each one end?

4

ARE YOU LONELY OR ALONE?

IN THE WORDS of John Lennon in a letter to his distraught cousin, Leila, that I procured, he asked, "Are you lonely ... or alone?" There is a world of difference, and you have to recognize the difference if you wish to make sensible choices in your dating life.

Loneliness can lead some to choose less-than-ideal partners out of desperation and depression often associated with lonesomeness. Judgment, when looking for that perfect mate, may be clouded and result in more desperation and depression if you end up with the wrong person.

Being alone isn't all bad, especially if you were in an empty or abusive relationship. You must distinguish what you're truly feeling with your partner and what you need. You may be the type that needs to be with someone no matter the cost, but if you can choose wisely, you'll find more happiness.

Lennon went on to write, "Prayer is always answered ... so be precise and careful when you wish/pray for someone/something. You don't have to SEARCH for a SOUL MATE ... he will find you! What you have to do is BE PREPARED! We are all 'magnets' ..."

These are interesting words from someone with considerable

insight. You can live by them – or acknowledge he had a period in his life when he used psychedelic drugs and abused his first wife. So you might be better off if you figure things out for yourself.

Since you are, at present, alone, you need to be there for a while to see how you adjust. Some relationships fail because one or the other person is so needy in terms of a companion that he or she doesn't give any space to the other party. Others need lots of space. You need to find someone compatible.

With Internet dating, there is ample opportunity to find people to chat with if you are looking for something to do. A companion is found when you meet and enjoy each other's company.

Try not to fall into the trap of staying alone for convenience. It's not healthy to take anything to the extreme and becoming a hermit is no exception. Learn to enjoy time alone, and make sure you put forth the effort to find companions and friends, as well as lovers. When the right one comes along, you'll know, if you have a clear mind and respect for yourself and others.

Activity Suggestion – On a scale of 1 to 10, with 1 being the loneliest, how lonely are you? If you score below 5, you may want to discuss this with a friend, counselor, or clergy member.

5

ARE YOU READY FOR LOVE?

DEPENDING ON YOUR PSYCHE, age, looks, the date of your separation, and a multitude of other factors, you may or may not be ready for *love*. That's not quite right. You're always ready for love. It's *commitment* you may not be ready to grasp. That's not even right, as some are not ready for love or commitment; they are just ready for baseless, raw *sex*. No, that, too, is flawed thinking. The fact is you may or may not be ready for any of these things at any particular time, as your *wants*, *needs*, and *desires* may vary from time to time.

The problem arises when your wants, needs, and desires are not in sync with those you meet, much like they weren't in sync, for example, in the marriage that resulted in divorce. The good part is that at this stage of your life you aren't bound by a contract that will see half or more of your net worth go to your mate from hell, at least not yet.

It is the very nature of divorce and what it can do to you psychologically, physically, and financially that makes many divorcees gun-shy. This applies to both men and women, and more so to the breadwinners, but everyone is affected in various ways.

The dependent partner (psychologically or financially) may be looking to marry for security, while the independent partner may prefer to enjoy the status of dating without commitment and still be happy. Those who were badgered in a relationship (physically or mentally) may also prefer to remain single.

Your job is to find someone looking for the same things you want. This is often not easy to determine on a first date. The sadness arises when you spent time learning all about the potential mate, fall in love, and then realize this person isn't the one for you because you both are in different places in life.

If you want to have ammunition on your side, you can use common sense to predict what type of person you'll meet. The mere knowledge that one has been spurned by a spouse who engaged in an adulterous affair is an indicator that he or she may need time to think about *ever* getting married again. The same applies to someone who was physically abused. While not a hard and fast rule, a relationship with those types of people may go nowhere. However, some spurned individuals run to another relationship for the security they feel when they are with someone.

Remember, all your dates won't necessarily work out, and you may get hurt. However, in the words of that famous bard, Alfred, Lord T., "'Tis better to have loved and lost than never to have loved at all."

The big question, then, is, should you waste your time with one who is not in the same place that you find yourself in?

Good question! Only you can answer it. If you have an abundance of people around you who can't wait to be with you, then you can be picky. If you've been searching for that special someone for years, and he or she comes along and is not ready to settle down, you may want to enjoy each day as it comes and not pressure this person to tie any knots.

If you have a great time with that special someone, and would like to spend the rest of your life with him or her, remember that those wonderful feelings of love, passion, lust, and desire will most likely not last beyond the honeymoon phase, after which you might realize you'd have been better off having a fun time with that wonderful person for as long as it could last. For you see, having a second divorce cannot be all that much fun. Don't jump into, or out of, relationships just because of insecurities.

What about the serial dater or the person who doesn't want to have a monogamous relationship? This is a personal choice. With all of the diseases running rampant in the dating world, a monogamous relationship is the better choice from an infectious-disease point of view. However, know that a monogamous relationship may also lead to a dull existence for some individuals who prefer to date many people.

Some guys find dating many people to be very difficult, as not having enough time, energy, money, and sperm to go around makes this task near impossible, especially as you get older and have less of those things anyway. Unless you are a good juggler, CEO type, or just plain amazing, it is difficult to get a bunch of people to *just* date you. But there are those who can pull this off and even consider it a dream come true.

Some men and women with a lot of money have the forethought to avoid risking their wealth and sanity in the bonds of holy matrimony. Being successful and worldly, they know that "many ships in many ports" can offer great pleasure in contrast to a mundane existence fraught with all the vagaries that define the human condition. They don't need marriage for financial security. They can certainly pay all of their bills, and if they become disabled, they can pay a nurse to take care of them. And many women and men have no interest in becoming caretakers for someone they've known only a few years. They'd just as soon enjoy being taken care of while all is well and be able to get out when necessary.

Your e-dating experiences offer you many chances to find that perfect mate. Just remember, it still takes a lot of effort on your part to figure out if someone is the right person for you. Yes, those looking for second marriages or love affairs in later life have different needs, wants, and desires. They are not looking to have kids at this stage of life. They are all looking for happiness as they define it for themselves.

Activity Suggestion – Think long and hard about where you are in life. Should you waste your time with someone who is not in the same place? Reread this section before answering this very important question.

6

DATING ... AGAIN!

THERE ARE four big reasons why you may find yourself dating again. It's either *death, betrayal, incompatibility* where *your lover wants out*, or *incompatibility* where *you want out*.

We talk about dating after the death of a lover in a later chapter. For now, let's explore the other lost loves that you have no control over: betrayal or incompatibility where your lover wants out.

Betrayal.

For those who have lost love, not to death, but to another lover, the sorrow may be just as deep, especially if the relationship was of long standing and had not devolved into a bad experience; you probably never saw the end coming. We are talking about what you may feel when your lover leaves you for another: an act of betrayal. For some, the burden is heavy, and they can only think of their lost love. They experience a type of mourning, which may be worse than the death of a lover. We have no control over death. But with betrayal, you question what went wrong.

When your lover leaves you for another, you feel alone, hurt, and jealous. You may even blame yourself. You sure as hell will want to blame your lover. You will have many questions. Why didn't your lover act better? Why didn't you act better? Why did you neglect your partner all those years? The list can be long, but you need to deal with these issues before you begin dating again.

No matter who's to blame, you may try to win back your lost love, and for some, that works out. For others, it just makes matters worse. Don't try for too long. There comes a moment when you have to recognize that it's over, and it's time to move on.

Betrayal needs much healing and support from friends and family. For some, a therapist may help resolve the various issues associated with understanding and managing the hurt of betrayal before they consider dating again.

Your lover wants out.

Sometimes your lover leaves because he or she has had it with the relationship for one reason or another, *without* already being in the arms of a new lover. It still hurts, especially if you never saw it coming. And so many never see it coming. They missed the part about neglecting their partner, withholding sex, their loss of affection, and the myriad of reasons relationships get stale and fail.

All the same rules of dating after a death apply to dating again after your partner walks out for whatever the reason. It is best to heal and move on with your life.

Some jilted lovers will never date again. Hey, if that works for you, fine. However, for a full life, it makes sense to find another love that can bring happiness to an otherwise empty existence. Once you do find your new, and better, love, you may feel a great deal of satisfaction and even an odd type of spite. Many times, you will look back on the loss as a good thing that brought you to a better place. While the task of dating again may seem daunting, the object of this book is to make the effort go better than doing it all alone.

You want out.

Some of you are the ones to leave your lover. The reasons are usually the same, though if *you* leave, there may be other issues, like addictions and abuse, added to the usual reasons like boredom, neglect, and lack of sex.

Because *you* are the one to leave, you will likely feel less depression, anger, sorrow, and jealousy. These feelings are replaced with guilt for leaving. But you will also likely get over the guilt rather fast, and dating is less of a burden for you since you were ready for a new adventure.

Activity Suggestions – Make a list of things you would like to get from dating again that were missing from past relationships. Make a list of things that make you anxious about dating.

7

AGING AND DATING

SOMETHING INTERESTING HAPPENS when you involve yourself in dating as you age. Actually, lots of interesting things happen to you as you age, but that's a story for another time. Suffice it to say, dating in youth is much different than dating as you get old, or, shall we say, older.

While your taste for fine wine, beautiful art, and the host of niceties that life offers doesn't decline, your ability to attain some of these things changes dramatically. If you are lucky and prudent, at some point in getting to the older stages of life, you can attain things like fine art, a Corvette, a beautiful young woman (only if you have the Corvette), wonderful vacations, and more. Of course, there are things that, in time, you may no longer be able to get – like your way home from the mall, the taste for spicy foods, and the elusive erection.

Let's get right to the point. Unless you have not planned properly or have perhaps invested poorly, you can still drink fine wine and buy nice clothing. What does change with advancing age is your choice in dates if you find yourself widowed, divorced, or just remaining single.

While you still admire the beauty of youth and can appreciate a handsome guy or a stunningly beautiful woman, they are not realistically in your league. Sure, you may be able to attract a 10 with enough money or a promise of fame or notoriety, but will this mismatched mate really love you? Do you care? I think you know the answers. You see it, at times, where a beauty is on the arm of some old guy, and you can't help but think, *I guess he has a lot of money.*

A lady of wealth and station may also be seen with a stud by her side, but this is a less common occurrence because women are usually less shallow than men. In either case, you don't first think that they are a mismatched couple because the older one is great in bed.

Most 60-year-old folks are not going to attract model-like mates unless they are perusing the dating sites that attract prostitutes, gigolos, and the forlorn. Do they exist? Well, yes, they do. The selling of sex is one of the most lucrative markets on the Internet, and if that's what you want, google it.

Assuming you are not looking for love in all the wrong places, it's time to compromise your appreciation for beauty and become realistic. Your date may not be exactly what you want or what you experienced in your youth. And that's okay if you can adjust to this reality.

And on that note, take care of yourself while you still can. You never know when you are going back into the dating game. Your chance of attracting a nice mate is much easier if you look good, have good health, and have retained your mind in good working order. There are so many assaults and challenges to our well-being as we age that it's only with vigilance and decent genes that we survive in basically good shape.

Some hints you surely know but ignore: stop smoking, stop drinking so much alcohol, stop eating so much food, limit red meat, exercise at least a little, brush your teeth, take showers regularly, avoid fried foods – you get the point. Stay fit and trim, and your pool of companions will be in the upper percentile.

Activity Suggestions – What age range are you looking

for in your dates? How much older or younger are you willing to go? When you consider what age range you are going for, does your age for dating worry you? What things can you no longer do as a result of the effects of aging? Now think of some steps you can take to improve your chances. For example, are there things you can do to look younger? What can you do to get back into shape?

8

IS AGE JUST A NUMBER?

EVERYWHERE I TURN, they're either too old or too young. Goldilocks has got to be out there, but finding "just right" has been elusive so far. Finding a lover my age that's in good condition is like finding a rare antique living in an undiscovered attic, sheltered from the ravages of time.

Someone *younger* seems better on the surface, but too young and you can't relate on so many levels. And you can forget the ones who want to have your child. Don't get me wrong, guys. You may want to go through the motions of having a child, but there is no way you want to have any other part of the outcome, like changing diapers, running alongside a two-wheeler, or funding yet another college education.

You women have a similar dilemma: all the guys are too old or too gross. Sure, there are plenty of out-of-shape, nerdy, sex-starved lechers waiting to be led to the boudoir. That isn't happening anytime soon for you classy ladies. Even in the throes of desperation, you'll pass.

While age is just a number, there are many adjustments required when you go about dating as an older individual. Your wants, needs, and desires may not have changed over the years, but you may need to adjust your tastes, since the people you will find are now past their prime as well. There are many well-preserved specimens from which to choose; however, they are just harder come by the second time around.

What about the younger set in the process of dating again? They, too, will notice many of the same issues come into play. A thirty-something guy or gal who's been out of the dating world for even a few years may be surprised at the changes he or she encounters. It can be an ego bust to realize a 21-year-old may have no interest in someone 10 years older. While your mind's eye wants twenty-something, his or her mind's eye may not be interested.

9

WHY IS IT SO HARD TO DATE AGAIN?

MOST FOLKS LOOKING to date *again* are doing so because they have divorced or have become widowed. While as young adults, dating was an ongoing process to find the *right one*, now it has become a search for *another right one* from an entirely different pool of candidates. Back then, most of us dated a variety of potential mates until we made our choice. After that commitment, we didn't think much about the possibility that we would have to repeat the process. After all, wasn't it until death do us part? Oh, yes, for some it was death that took them apart. For others, it was the death of the relationship that caused the parting of ways.

In either case, you now find yourself alone, and perhaps even lonely – big difference. You can be alone but happy and fulfilled with many activities and people in your life. Or you can be alone and lonely without those things. You want to venture out and connect with someone on a higher level. Yes, you want to have sexual relations with someone new after 10, 20, 30, or even more years of being with the same person. You may not even want the sexual relations, but the possibility that your new mate just might want to indulge puts you in a state of confusion, anxiety, and basic fear of engagement (not the type that comes with a ring).

There are a few simple steps to dating *again* and moving forward.

Step 1: Meeting someone. Even meeting someone new can evoke a level of anxiety in those who were never the life of the party. The wallflower may actually remain alone for fear of socializing. This is not good. You really want to work on first getting out and talking with strangers you meet at various venues, like the supermarket, museums, coffee shops, and of course, online dating services.

If your level of anxiety is overwhelming and keeping you a shut-in, consider getting some professional help with a therapist. Who knows? You might even meet a nice, shy mate in the therapist's waiting room. (Go to someone who has a busy practice.)

When you worry about the reality of dating anew, the small talk, the meeting over coffee, the phone conversations, and even the first date, remember, these are nothing compared to eventually hopping into bed. This has got to be a stunning step forward into the unknown – and actually the known. Yes, you know what's coming. Oops, not that word.

Step 2: Getting naked. At this stage in life, getting naked in front of others is just not a natural thing, nor a matter of modesty. The fear of getting naked can actually be paralyzing for some. If years of change have altered your body, you may never want to become involved in a relationship that requires showering with another person, let alone one that requires sex. If this is the case, you should be up-front and let your date know early on that you are not looking for a sexual relationship. Either way, there are others out there with the same feelings, and you can find them if you let your dates know that you are looking for a friendship with or without the possibility of nakedness.

If you haven't taken care of yourself (e.g., eaten right and exercised), this may put you at a disadvantage. You may have feelings of embarrassment that actually keep you from seeking a new mate. You need to get past this. You will realize there are others out there who will appreciate your body no matter what the shape. If you still have issues about how you look, you may work toward correcting the situation by diet and exercise. Besides helping yourself find a new mate, you will be doing something important for your health.

Step 3: Doing the nasty. This is an urban word meaning "sex" taught to me by World Heavyweight Champ Joe Frasier. For some people, the sexual encounter, especially the first one, has got to rank right up there with things that can make you throw up. If you are, or were, a "player," you may actually enjoy the hunt. If, however, you are like most 40, 50, 60, or even 70-year-old daters, this is not a fun experience. Just like when you were a teen, "Do you really want to go all the way?" remains an important question. And it becomes more of a question of *"Can you?"* than *"Do you want to?"* For the ladies, you don't want to come off as a slut, and for the guys, oh, wait ... there *is* a double standard. You don't want to come off looking like a nerd in the bedroom.

It is important to pace the relationship. The older your generation, the more you want to give the relationship a few dates before becoming intimate. Even if you were from the free-love generation, being too promiscuous looks, well, too promiscuous. You have nothing to lose by waiting a few dates (three to five to make sure you really like this person) before engaging in the nasty. Waiting much longer than that, or sleeping together too early, sends the wrong message. If you really like this person, you don't want to scare them off.

Step 4: Managing anxiety. Beyond the fear of meeting, being naked, and finally engaging in sexual behaviors, there is always the *performance-anxiety* issue. This affects both men and women, though men are more at risk because they are required to come to the bedroom with an erection. If he can't bring one along, that's a problem, unless he is dating a severely farsighted lady who might mistake a cucumber for his body part.

Both men and women worry about how good they are in bed when engaging in sexual relations with a new partner: you may find yourself asking, "How will I compare to his other mate?" or, "How do I compare to her life experiences in bed?"

You certainly want to come off well, and the comparison has much to do with who your new partner was with before, and how good you can perform under duress. Most people should understand that the first encounter, sexually speaking, may not go well, and that is not uncommon. Compassionate people will not have an issue with that *first time*; uncaring people will.

So now you met, got naked, and had sex. The *next* anxiety is all about "will they call back?" And that is another story to be explored next time.

Activity Suggestions – Are you afraid of performance or appearance when it comes to sex? Would you desire sex if you were not afraid? What could you do to improve your performance and reduce your anxiety? Read a sex manual? Watch an instructional video? Watch porn? What could you do to improve your appearance? Diet? Exercise? Plastic or bariatric surgery?

II

THE HOW-TO OF INTERNET DATING

10

SIGNING UP FOR INTERNET DATING

MANY PEOPLE ARE reluctant to use Internet dating services. They may be afraid of technology. Others don't like to put themselves out there for all to see. However, the world has changed, and if you don't want to be left behind, get online.

My niece decided to sign me up for JDate, an ethnic online dating service. If you have ethnic dating services available, and assuming you like, respect, or gravitate toward your ethnicity, go for it; while the pool of possible matches may be smaller, you will already have something in common with your potential dates.

If you are fed up with your ethnicity, try a new one. You may meet some very interesting people or just realize you like your own kind. Remember, life is a journey. Also remember that just because you are on a journey, it doesn't mean you won't pay dearly for choosing incompatible cultural differences.

Being a neophyte, I picked another service before my niece told me about her actions on my behalf. I felt a need and a desire to explore cyber relations that would hopefully lead to a connection that is most necessary after a traumatic loss. Betrayal is a trauma that requires a new interest, and if you think you can be satisfied with stamp collecting, do it. However, if you need to feel desirable, sexual, and whole again, you need to get online.

I picked TruLove.com. Don't ask me why. I just think the model on their website really looked like she wanted me to join, and she was so hot. Yes, early on, right after a loss, you don't think rationally, thus your choices and decision-making skills may be compromised. As it turned out, I soon realized that the hot model couldn't actually see me as I typed away on my computer, entering the information to join their dating service.

TruLove.com – what a great domain name. There is something exciting, almost sexual about contacting potential lovers online. I guess I'm not the only one to have this thought, as cybersex and Internet dating are some of the most lucrative online businesses ever.

First, I had to learn how to navigate the dating site. Even though I'm fairly tech savvy, it still required time to learn. But it wasn't that hard to get the hang of it, and as I found out, there are some rather inept dullards lurking on the web. If they figured out how to do this kind of thing, so can you.

Pretty soon, a decision must be made as to whether one should join these various dating services for a fee or just use their free service. How can anyone resist something free? Actually, I learned rather soon that you have to *pay to play* unless you plan on merely looking at pictures of potential mates and getting letters from them that you can neither read nor respond to unless you pay to join.

These services are really not that expensive, and you will pay if you want to get anything out of it. There is no free lunch. Well, there is if you get a guy to take you to lunch and he isn't so cheap as to ask you to split the bill. Yes, there are many cheapskates out there so the phrase "no free lunch" probably still works.

It does make sense to test the waters before you pay to join any particular dating service. You go for the free trial, since this test gives you the opportunity to make sure that the potential mates on the website don't live in faraway places. In one service I tested, the only people contacting me were weirdos living in states miles away. You won't have much opportunity to meet a nice selection of dates nearby if the dating service is too new and doesn't have tons of members. Once you find a service that offers a nice selection of members, pay your dues.

There are some truly free Internet dating services out there. One is plentyoffish.com. If you don't find a date, at least you might find a good fish sandwich. For some reason, when I tried this site, I didn't get many contacts. There are lots of people on this site, yet they seem to be relatively complacent. It's likely that comes from the service being free. If you pay for being on the dating site, you probably want your money's worth, so you use it.

There are so many sites with so much variety that it is ridiculous, sort of like how we have hundreds of television channels to choose from. While variety might be nice, it makes life that much more confusing. Now you can join dating sites to meet specific ethnic groups, married women who cheat, baby boomers, midgets, people with intractable diseases who can be together without worrying about catching something that they already have. The list is endless.

Activity Suggestions – List five dating sites you will visit this week. Rank them 1 to 5 after a week of exploration. Pick the one you like best, and join.

11

SETTING UP YOUR DATING PROFILE

PROFILES ARE how you and all the other members of Internet dating sites describe yourselves. Writing your profile is both an art and a science. The science is the easy part. You figure out what year you were born and do a simple math calculation to come up with your age. For your weight, you use the scientific method: stand on an accurate scale and see what the reading indicates. This number is called your weight. You probably noticed that you don't have to understand advanced mathematics nor be a rocket scientist to come up with these very objective answers for your profile.

It is the art of the profile that takes a little more creativity. Perhaps *lying* is a better word than *creativity*. One honest (after the fact) date explained to me that others told her about *the rule of five*: you must subtract five from everything. That's right; you state that you are five years younger and five pounds lighter than you are. This bothered me because I am usually honest, and honesty is the one trait that most users on Internet dating services cherish in their profiles. So, what does this mean? That everyone is a liar?

Well, yes. This isn't so bad, as long as you know to conduct your search for a new mate by looking for someone who is five pounds lighter and five years younger than you actually desire. You have to learn to navigate in the trenches. It's not always that easy, and you have to expect to date a few toads before you find that prince or princess you so long for.

I did not succumb to lying. Of course, I'm lucky, standing over six feet tall and weighing in at 170 pounds, but I still understand the mentality of all this. If you happen to weigh a few pounds more than you would like, you may as well post your *ideal weight*: the weight you desire, even if it isn't what you weigh. But don't get carried away. No one wants to meet someone who wrote down what they weighed when they were eight years old.

This rule of five still scares me. While I haven't yet encountered a request for this much information, I sure don't want to subtract five from the size of my penis, or it will come out looking like it did when I was eight years old.

You want to come off looking like a good catch, so read through several of the profiles from others, and you will surely find people who got it right. They probably paid a professional public relations firm to write their profiles, so don't be afraid to steal some of their unique lines, phrases, and characterizations to enhance your profile. Oops, did I say steal? Let's say borrow. Remember, everyone is looking for honesty and trust.

Many services offer an opportunity to state what you do for a living, how much money you make, and your level of education. Remember, some people are only out for what they can get, and others seek the security of a rich and successful companion. Be careful what you reveal to strangers on the Internet. You don't want someone to use you for your money. And surely, you don't want to be a kept man or woman (actually that's not such a bad idea if you can find the right mate who just so happens to be very rich).

There are secret codes that help you find the good catches. A profile, for example, may indicate the person has an advanced education at the graduate level in medicine, which is a subtle way of stating that the person may just be a doctor. Still, you must consider that this person is exaggerating (or lying) and what's really meant that he or she *has* a doctor who has an advanced medical education. While some may argue that it's just a subtle exaggeration, I see a big difference.

When someone checks off the highest income level (usually around $100,000), which is not actually very high in today's inflationary world, it is not that impressive to someone looking for the über-rich mate, but it sure beats anyone who checks off that he or she makes half the government poverty level. Since you are starting over, you may just want to look for someone a step above that homeless creep you hooked up with last time around.

Another subtle indicator of wealth involves noting that one's interests include investing. I've noticed several women include investing as an interest in their profiles, and it does pique one's interest to know that a prospective mate has a few bucks, or why else would she be interested in investing? Caveat emptor! These people may want to invest your money after they dump you.

Many people come off as being very active. They must think everyone loves this attribute. We all would like some vitality in our mates, but this may not be such a great thing to list unless you really want to date a marathon runner. I was actually turned off by a few women who listed their numerous activities with such gusto that I got tired just thinking about what their schedules must be like.

The bottom line: you can exaggerate a little, and lie even less, but don't come off being what you are not, or you will disappoint all involved. Truth is really the best policy.

You will find many people don't post their pictures, and as noted in the section on photographs, you probably don't want to contact these people. You'll save a lot of time if you include little tidbits of advice in your profile: *I do not respond to those who don't post their pictures.* Another tidbit goes like this: *I do not respond to IM. I cannot type witty remarks that fast and they did invent the telephone a few years ago.* IM is instant messaging, a pastime your kids love, but for the life of me, I don't get it. These two warnings should save you from many wasted walks down empty trails. If someone does contact you with no picture but an intriguing profile, and you want to give chase, go for it. However, there are so many others, why waste your time?

There's a world of single people out there waiting to meet you. There's a lid for every pot. You can find some very nice and interesting people if you are careful and savvy in your selection process. Now get online and go for the gold! That's a figure of speech, you know.

Activity Suggestions – List three of your best traits you would like to put on your profile. List three traits you would most like to find in your new mate. List three deal breakers: things you absolutely cannot stand or must have, like no smokers, or the person must be a sports enthusiast, concert lover, or theatergoer. The list is long. Pick three.

12

PROFILE TABOOS

AFTER READING a bunch of Internet dating profiles over a long period of time I noticed a theme, of sorts, that can best be described as *poorly executed*. You may need to rethink the way you present yourself. After all, who you meet is an important matter whether you just date, have a new friend, or end up marrying. The following are real-life profile descriptions found on dating sites.

I like to have fun but know when to be serious.

Don't we all want to have fun? Isn't this a given? Then why do 80% of profiles state that they want to have fun?

I like going out but can stay in and snuggle just as well.

Again, I think we all like to go out and then snuggle when we get home. Maybe state things that are not so obvious!

I can even stand in the doorway and be happy.

I know you really want to cover all bases, but do you really need to mention this position, too?

My glass is half full.

Then why are you on medication for depression? Why is there broken glass all over your kitchen floor?

I value loyalty, truthfulness, and goodness, but I want a man with an edge.

Men with an edge are pigs! Don't expect loyalty and truthfulness.

I love sports as long as they don't interfere with my gardening.

Are you trying too hard to be accepted?

I love scuba diving in my above-ground pool.

Don't tell us about all the activities you don't really like to do.

The basics. Some of these profiles are absolute turnoffs. I hope you can tell if your own profile is guilty of being poorly written and fix it before life passes you by. Spelling and grammar mistakes say something about you on a subtle level. I know you think everyone will excuse you, thinking you were just in a rush, and some will, but the quality guys and gals who speak English properly will not give you a pass. Have your fifth-grade teacher edit your profile to make sure it's well written.

Here's some more help. Get a profile name that exudes greatness and is an amalgamation of all things good. I just saw one that said *Mizery13*. Is this a joke, or is this a very depressed person? Maybe *Happy Girl7* says it better.

What about that cleavage? Now here's a subject that needs to be addressed. There are so many "come hither" photos. I suppose there are some women who believe in the "sex sells" mantra. They are actually onto something – sex does sell! What they may be missing is that *they* are actually selling sex, perhaps to their detriment if they are looking for a meaningful relationship rather than a roll in the hay.

It is rather funny to see how many photos are taken with women bending down to put on their shoe. *What the ...?* I suppose they weren't ready for the photo, and since they had no others, they posted these ... or is it because when you bend over to adjust your shoe, your cleavage explodes forth from your tight shirt that just so happened to have the top three buttons undone?

If you're going to take a photo half dressed, why leave us

wondering about the rest of the package? Take a shot adjusting your garter belt and thong! Maybe I'm old-fashioned, but I think looking like a hooker may send the wrong message, though I'm sure it works. Just don't complain about attracting the players.

Exhibitionism works both ways, too. Do you really think a guy who posts photos of himself in his muscle shirt, or without a shirt, is the type of guy who is interested in a quality relationship? While most of us have some level of exhibitionist tendencies, it is not one of those traits that breeds quality kinds of people.

Interestingly, those who can't seem to walk with head held high, based on their intrinsic worth, tend to go to the extreme. There are those folks who need to find something to substitute for substance. There are those who do the "gym thing" to develop admirable bodies, while others opt for showing "the goods" (cleavage, etc.), and others take it to another level by going the ink-and-piercing route. Yes, they paint their bodies with assorted tattoos and pierce their faces to the extreme. Then they enjoy the stares that they somehow think of as admiration while they are often getting stares of "What were you thinking?"

Here is a simple test to see if you learned anything today. Read through the following profiles and see if there is anything that you feel sends the wrong message or that could have been better constructed by using the hints offered in this section.

The guy's profile test. *My friends all say I'm miserable, rude, boring, and not to be trusted. I don't like having fun and would much rather stay in the house sulking. I don't even own a glass, but if I did, there would be no bottom, hence it would be empty. I watch a lot of TV after hours of watching porn, the later being my preference. For a first date, I think we should meet at a public water fountain. That way no one has to pay for coffee in case we realize we are not a match. I had a dog, but he left home because I used to forget to feed him one too many times. But he was loyal (like me) ... when I remembered to feed him. Well, that's about it, so take a look at my photos of me in my*

Speedo. I think you may especially like the one showing the tattoo that covers my back with the picture of me on my friend's Harley. (Well, not actually my friend. It was at the curb outside this biker bar, and I just got on it for the photo.) Well, that's all I can think of to tell you so, so long for now, and I hope we can meet really soon, and maybe get married if the sex is good.

Yours truly,
Satan666

The girl's profile test. *My friends all say I'm a great shopper at retail outlets. While they often think of me as being catty, I take that to mean feline in appearance. I like to have fun, and if you want to find me, check out the beach to find me just chilling. The last book I read was* Jane and Tom Go to School. *I like the part about Jiff, the dog, running. To quote: "Run Jiff, run." I think it's the plot that gives me chills ever since I first read those words in second grade. A real classic. With lights down low, I like to snuggle, but don't think snuggle means sex – because it doesn't. It means: to snuggle. My Champagne glass is always mostly full, and I'm working on that issue at AA. Here's a picture of me putting on my shoe – forget the shoe, take a look at my boobs. I got a good deal on them, 3.5K by an Indian surgeon – can't pronounce his name. I'd give you his number, but he had to go back to India suddenly. Anyway, as you can see, I do well with 36 double Ds. Just make sure you look at all my photos because, as you will see, I shop at all the finer stores. Well, that's it for now. I hope we can do one of those simple first dates at a high-end steakhouse. I find that high-calorie food helps me maintain a tight fit in my Victoria Secret push-up bras. FYI, I am interested in marriage as long as you don't expect sex too often. Once a month is a compatible number for me. Whaddya say?*

Sincerely,
Bitch4U

Okay. Read through these sample profiles again, take notes, and compare them to yours. Make changes as needed.

Activity Suggestions – Write a ridiculous profile that is 100% not you. Now that you have that out of your system, try your hand at a mock profile for actual use. Show both profiles to a friend to get feedback. If he or she likes the ridiculous one better, realize this friend is not your friend.

13

PICKING YOUR USERNAME

HOW ABOUT ALIASES, usernames, or whatever you want to call them? These are the names used to identify members of the dating site without revealing their real names. When you join, you give the company your personal details and choose a username that shows up online. So, the first contact you have with others when e-dating is when you see their pictures and usernames while searching for a mate. You'll need this information to contact them or to show interest in connecting.

The wrong username can turn others off before they've even looked at your picture. Some of the goofiest names can be found posted online. I suppose everyone is trying to be noticed, but you really don't want to come off as a dork, especially if you happen to be hip and just didn't think about how stupid your username sounds.

Names like *theoneforu* or *lookingforthatspecialu* or anything that too obviously shows what you want or that you are lonely are not cool. How about *coolromanticone*? If you have to tell them you are cool and romantic, at best you are not cool.

Would you use *wanttobekept* or *likesdiamonds* as a username? I hope not; it makes you look like a gold digger. And anyway, gold diggers are usually more intelligent than to reveal their motives so clumsily. Don't pick a stupid username.

Then there are the names that sound animal-like. Some of them are okay, like *feline36*, or *catwoman21*, or *bluejay11*. They conjure the kind of image that attracts. Men like feline features and beautiful, birdlike associations. On the other hand, you don't want to use animal names that are unattractive. So stay away from animal names that could never do you justice, like *chipmunk60*, *littlepiggy56*, *aardvark17*, *elephantlady*, or any others that give the impression you might just use that name because you look like that particular animal. Those names don't create a reason to look at your picture.

Men usually don't understand that "macho" isn't the best way to attract a mature, sensitive lady, so they are more prone to use names like *gorillaguy2*, *allyoop44*, or *musclehead19*. All that's going to attract are loose women who have nothing on their minds other than hard sex. I guess I should mention that my username is *apeman69* for that very reason. Just kidding.

You may have noticed how often numbers are attached to the usernames you see on the Internet. That is because they either have some significance to the person, or the users needed to add a number to the catchy names they picked because a hundred others already used that catchy name. So if you pick *coolme* and 10 other people already have that name, you may have to settle for using *coolme11*. Of course, now that you read this treatise on picking names, you won't be picking a popular name like *coolme*.

Certain numbers work well, like 36, which immediately makes men think of firm, plump breasts. Yes, I would contact *marla36c*, yet *sally30a* has the reverse connotation. I'm not contacting her, and I might never find out that she lives in apartment 30A. Choose wisely. Guys should note that adding the number 7, 8, 9, or 10 to your username (as in *9inchescharlie*) does not have the effect you think it will.

Stay away from names that could be used to describe your physical shape, especially if you are not in good shape. *Pudgeball44* doesn't get many responses. *Chubby, fatso, stringbean,* and *lankylad* are not the names to use.

Stay away from names that make you seem old, like *busybubby, grandpa89,* or *goodwithmywalker94*. Even if you are 94 and good with your walker, that's not the first impression you want to make. The thirty-something e-daters will pass you by.

Never include your age in your username, and never use any number that may give the impression it has something to do with your age. If you live at 75 Winter Road, it is very easy to have a username like *winter75*. However, the first thing people will think of when they see this name is that you must be 75 and in the winter of your life, even though that may have nothing to do with your reality.

Just be conscious of what your name may sound like and pick one accordingly. Don't use letters you think are meaningless that sound like, or look like, undesirable things. I saw one username, *msfsto,* and immediately misread it as "Miss Fatso." The brain plays tricks on us, so if the letters in your username have any negative connotation when its read quickly, or when you reposition the letters, stay away.

Don't sound desperate. *Lonely67* tells me you are old and lonely, which is not very appealing, even if you just happen to live at 67 Lonely Lane. Either move, or change that silly username. If you are not very creative, you can always use your ZIP code. At least no one will think you are that old: for instance, *carla95102* won't be confused with Methuselah.

Try manly or sexy names. Just make sure you pick the right one for your gender. Don't come right out and say *sex4sally*. That's too direct. You need to consider subtler names like *kissmenow28*. I know you have this temptation to add the number 69 to that one, but don't.

Some good names for girls include variations of *briteyes1, blueeyes1, blondie1, happygirl1,* and *sunshine.* A good guy name is *mrgoodbar26.* Aren't all women looking for him? Mentioning your town is always a good choice if it is sexy: *californiagirl6, californiaguy9, indianajones34* (that one may be taken), and *nevadagirl1* work, too. *Kalamazoocalvin4* isn't one you want to use, nor is *picadil-*

lipatti2. I think you are getting the point to picking your username aliases.

You can use a variation of your real name in the username and that actually helps to avoid confusion. I was tracking several women who I was interested in, and the usernames were so odd and had nothing to do with anything that I had trouble making an association with their names and their pictures. If you are *bev36*, and your name is Bev, I can now associate the name and the picture. I'll be more likely to remember you and give you a call. *Bndnga60* means absolutely nothing to me and it's really hard to make a mental and visual association, so I'm not calling this one ... unless she's hot, in which case all of the rules go right out the window. Of course, if your name happens to be Bndnga, I'm terribly sorry that I offended you, and I have to figure you live in a foreign country, so what's the chance I'll meet you anyway?

Activity Suggestions – Write five of your best characteristics (e.g., beautiful eyes, smart, great body, kind heart, great dancer). Try to condense them into a username. Rank your choices 1 to 5, 1 being the best. That's your new name. Don't use all five characteristics in your username: *smartygreateyeskindheartdancerbody*. It's just too much. *Kindhearteddancer* does the trick.

14

POSTING YOUR PHOTO

YOU REALLY NEED to have a photograph posted on your dating profile. Every company tells you that you'll get more dates if you have a picture than if you don't. However, once you get online, you might think that there are some people who would be better off not posting a picture if they ever plan to get any dates.

Of course, there is a guy for every gal and a gal for every guy. It doesn't matter what you look like; if you plan on finding a mate, you have to be honest in the long run. The last thing you want is to have some gal shut the door in your face or to have some guy take one look and walk away before you can take off your coat.

So now that we have established that you need a picture posted, you have to figure out how to do it. Get a digital camera, or use your phone camera, and get with it. For crying out loud, it's the 21st century, and you need to be digital. For those of you who feel the world has passed you by, ask a kid around 12 years old to show you how to get your picture posted online. There are also services that will take a professional photo to make you look your best. This isn't a bad idea if you want to have an edge on the competition, but you can do it yourself and still be okay.

Next, you have to decide what picture to use. Just follow a few simple rules: guys should post a picture of Brad Pitt, and make it a little hazy so users just think you look like him, and not that this is *his* picture you scanned from *People* magazine. The gals should post a picture of Angelina Jolie, and use the same haziness technique as noted with the Brad photo.

Actually, if you wish to maintain credibility in the honesty and truthfulness department, you should use a recent photo – no photos more than a few years old at most. Try to post two or three pictures, as this gives a better representation for that potential mate to evaluate. You really don't want to waste anyone's time, and if you don't think there's chemistry based on someone's photos, move on as fast as you can, or you will go on lots of very unproductive dates.

Make sure at least one picture is close-up enough to allow others to see what you look like. Emphasize your best features. If you have none, use a picture that is tiny and hazy.

Don't post photos that show too much attitude. It seems odd that some folks post pictures that look like they are trying to appear glamorous or tough or bold. Don't go for the Marilyn Monroe look or the Bogart look. Try to look *normal*. Yes, that's rather direct, yet many people don't seem to realize this.

Get goofy smirks off your face. Don't look grumpy, for that matter; you don't want to look like any of the seven dwarfs or other Disney characters. Don't post photos with your best friend, ex-spouse, the guys or girls you bowl with every Wednesday night, your therapist, or your mom or dad. If you post a picture standing next to your mom or dad, you are telling your potential date just what you will look like 30 years from now – not a smart idea in most instances.

Don't post a cropped photo with your ex's arm on your shoulder. It looks like you had just one photo that made you look good when you went to Aunt Gilda's wedding 10 years ago while you were still married to that creep.

At most, you can post one picture with your dog or cat, but make sure you aren't posting the one with you humping Fido's leg. Above all else, if you post a picture with your dog, make sure the person calling you has no trouble telling which one is the dog.

Don't post photos with your friends in the frame, especially if your friends are all hotter than you. You don't want someone contacting you on the dating site and asking for your friend's phone number.

"A picture is worth a thousand words" is very true when it comes to online dating photos. With a little help utilizing advanced detective skills, you can easily learn just what to look for. For example, most people ignore the background in photos. You can find some interesting information by looking beyond the person in the picture. Often you can see a glimpse of how this person lives. Notice the trailer park with all the neighbors sitting outside playing banjos. Without even looking further down the page, you can tell this person makes less than $10,000 a year.

On the other end of the spectrum, I looked at the picture of one woman who was rather attractive, and I noticed she was posing with her hunting dog on an estate. This led me to believe she owned horses and stables. I knew without looking that this woman listed "will tell you later" under the section about her income. You see, wealthy people don't like to broadcast that they have lots of money, but if you are astute, you can figure it out. You'll also find that these people live in exclusive neighborhoods and have hobbies that include attending charity balls, polo, and cricket. *Investing* or *volunteer work* is listed under their employment. That means that, just like poor people, rich people don't work at real jobs.

Besides those two extremes, you still may be able to get a real insight into a potential date's life by looking at the background. The usual case reveals some of this person's tastes. You can see if this person has modern or classic furniture, cheap or expensive accessories, too many pets to allow you to live with him or her due to your allergies, and other assorted information not usually stated in profiles.

The hands and neck reveal a lot about the person, as they usually age much worse than the rest of the package. And while you may want a handsome or pretty face because it's a nice thing, just remember that once you get your clothes off, the neck is very often attached to the chest and stomach. So, by observing someone's neck and hands in the online picture, you get a glimpse of what you may find when you are engaged in acts of love and affection or when your new mate takes a shower in front of you.

By using some simple logic, you can make sure your pictures don't reveal too much about your life of poverty. This way, others who know these secrets won't ignore your listing. Post a picture of yourself while at the ski slope, wearing a bulky down coat, heavy gloves, a hulking crocheted scarf, and a wind mask. That's perfect! While this is meant to be a joke, you won't believe that some people actually post pictures like this.

It's almost embarrassing that I have to tell you to comb your hair. I'm not your mother. You would not believe how many photos are posted by the most unkempt-looking people. You could at least try to look good for the onetime effort of attracting a mate. However, once you meet someone, if you want to keep him or her, you may have to comb your hair every day for the rest of your life. In retrospect, for those of you who can't look good for your picture, it may be best to remain lonely and forget about finding a mate.

There are some pretty clever people out there who are even a step ahead of the best of us. It took me awhile to figure out what this one woman was doing by posting a picture of herself leaning over picking up an item on the ground. I know what you're thinking: that makes absolutely no sense, and it makes the person look like they're nuts. Who would ever post a picture in such an odd pose? As it turns out, I was drawn to this attractive woman in that exact pose and couldn't figure out why. After looking at her picture several times over the week, I realized as she was bent over, I could look down her blouse. Now that's a smart cookie. Using my brilliant deductive reasoning, I would have to guess that she was a waitress. Yes, waitresses have a secret. The ones who get the best tips from men are the ones who leave the top two buttons of their blouses unbuttoned. As previously mentioned, the pose putting on a shoe is another way these vixens attract us guys.

Avoid the *too formal* pose; the ones some photographers offer don't fit on these sites. A photographer can make you look great if he or she understands this isn't supposed to be a wedding picture. You want a natural pose, a good smile (unless you're missing front teeth), and a neutral background (not the formal ones used in studio photos). You can get this background at a park, by the sea, on the beach, or in your own backyard, assuming it's not cluttered with old tires, a mattress, and a dismantled car engine. Also try to avoid a background that shows that you live in a hut or a mansion. You don't want to broadcast your wealth or poverty level.

If you have a terrible smile, use a photo without the smile, but try to look happy. If you feel you have a fake or goofy-looking smile, have someone make you actually laugh, and have the picture taken just as you're coming off of the full laugh. That makes for the most natural, good-looking smile.

Avoid pictures that don't flatter you. Avoid exposing your worst features. If you have a large nose, avoid profiles and go for the frontal shot. If your ears are really big, use duct tape to hold them back for the photo. If you are heavy, try for the above-the-lips shot. While I am exaggerating here, you should get the point. You don't want to emphasize faults, but you don't want to be fake about it either. People don't like surprises. Don't figure that once they meet you, they'll like your perfume, fall in love, and overlook that you have a hairy wart on your nose and that there is no physical chemistry.

Play up your good features. Please, guys, that doesn't mean you use the picture with your butt crack showing or any picture that involves having your zipper down. If you are buff, post at least one picture with your arms exposed. But don't go overboard, or you'll be perceived as a narcissist.

You ladies should be proud of that cleavage and don't be afraid to show some. Again, don't overdo it, or you'll look like a hussy. If you have great calves, figure out a way to show them. Yes, you may want a picture of yourself bent over, putting on a shoe. Sound familiar?

If you want to avoid wasting time, include the following in your profile: *I do not respond to those who don't post their pictures.* I noticed this on some women's sites and it is rather smart to consider. There may be exceptions. One woman told me she didn't post her photo, even though she described herself as attractive, because she didn't want her picture all over the Internet. I can understand the need for privacy, but you have to take reasonable chances. In that case, she did send her photo to me by private email. Remember, not posting a photo is a good way to miss out on many potential mates who never respond to no-photo listings. Of course, posting a naked picture of yourself in the act of some sexual perversion *would* probably end up all over the Internet. Just be discrete, and don't be afraid to post your picture.

An interesting ploy I noticed being used by women involves pictures of themselves (often selfies) in the bedroom or bathroom wearing a slip or some scanty item of clothing. They say, "sex sells," and it does. You will probably get many more hits if you look seductive. You should, of course, decide if that's what you want to be selling, as it attracts a certain kind of guy who looks and acts very much like ... a pig.

Activity Suggestions – List your worst features you would like to avoid showing in a photo. List you best photogenic qualities. Locate areas around you to use as a background for your outdoor photos. Then take your picture, and post it on a dating website.

15

WINKS AND FLIRTS

THE FIRST WEEK ON TRULOVE.COM, I got a few *winks*. On JDate they call them *flirts*. The names explain what they are. These are easy ways to see if someone is interested in you. Along with the wink or flirt comes a *one-liner*, like, "Your profile looks interesting," or, "Your profile made me laugh."

These little catchy phrases are rather cute, and at first, I thought the other member made them up. I was immediately attracted to such a witty woman who recognized my comic genius. After all, if she could identify the qualities of a perfect catch, it showed me that she was pretty sharp. However, after getting a few of the same phrases attached to these flirts I realized it wasn't their creation. It was the choice offered by these savvy services that are trying to hook up couples. As it turns out, the more creative and interesting members, or at least the better-educated ones, actually email you their original thoughts, which may give you a better glimpse into them as people.

On the first week exploring TruLove.com, not much happened until I got a wink followed by an email from someone who signed her name *Angel Baby* (all names have been changed to protect the innocent and *me*). That username and her picture excited me.

It was mostly her picture – yes, push-up bras and cleavage excite me, and most other men, too, much like professional degrees with the possibility of a comfortable life filled with jewelry, vacations, and leisure that visit upon the imaginations of ladies looking for a new guy excite them. They learned better after spending a life scrimping with a man who struggled to make ends meet.

Getting back to real love, I contacted Angel Baby using TruLove's email service and told her I was interested in meeting. When using an online dating service, you do your initial contacting by emailing your prospective mate using the email from the dating service. This keeps the other person from knowing your real email and having the means to stalk you. Once you are sure this person is legit, you can always send him or her your real email address and continue your relationship without constantly logging on to the dating service.

Angle Baby gave me her phone number and immediately volunteered too much information, like that she had a second home in New York and all this stuff about her inheritance. Like I said, way too much information. That kind of information invites the predator, gigolo, and kept-man types to your door. If you have nothing else going for you, so be it, tell them about your money, as long as you can handle the phony bullshit these types offer.

Rather than call her, I continued correspondence via email, as this was my first Internet dating experience, and I was kind of afraid to talk to her. She invited me to meet her at the Wawa, a local convenience store in Podunksville, a small town in the sticks. *Oh, right*, I thought. *I'm going to meet you in a place that sounds like the location they filmed* Deliverance.

I told her I'd like to meet her at one of the local casinos. She preferred the Wawa. Now this made no sense to me. After all, meeting at a casino is rather public, and I assumed there is no worry in a place like that. Besides, what could we possibly do at a convenience store on a first date? I told her to bring a friend if it would make her feel safer. No such luck. She insisted on meeting at the

Wawa. I had this weird premonition that I would end up in a dumpster behind the Wawa with my wallet missing.

By that point, I figured there are a lot of other people who I will want to meet, so I decided against going to Podunksville. I never did meet Angel Baby, and who knows, maybe it was a mistake, but better safe than sorry.

If you see users you would like to meet, you can merely look at their profiles and they may take the hint, since often the settings on dating sites can let other users know you looked at them, and they'll contact you. If you don't hear from them in short order (that means 24 hours if you are desperate to meet someone) then send the wink or flirt or whatever your e-dating service calls it. If you want to add one of the witty one-liners offered by the Internet dating service ("Your profile looks interesting," or "I liked your profile."), you can, but just remember, other users have probably gotten a dozen of those same comments.

It is much smarter to create an original note of your own to send to other users. It doesn't have to be long and bard-like. It can be simple, short, and sweet: you mention something you read in his or her profile and note you'd like to meet. It should go something like this: "Hi Angel Baby, I liked your profile, especially your interest in walking on the beach. Let's meet so we can see if we would like to take that walk together."

Now that's cool! Notice I didn't mention the great looking cleavage. I just picked one of her interests and played upon how we could do it together. That's all there is to it.

Don't screw this up, or other users will never want to meet you. Don't try, "I noticed your nice cleavage and thought I could see it better if we walked on the beach." Notice the subtle differences between the two approaches. Never look desperate.

Activity Suggestions – Create two unique one-liners or notes you could use if you like someone's profile. Ask friends for help or to review your creations. For example, "I really like your _____ and hope to meet soon." Then fill in the blank with something from the user's profile or hobbies, such as his or her love of theater or interest in bird watching.

16

HOW COME THEY LOOK SO OLD?

QUITE OFTEN, when perusing the little photos of prospective mates on Internet dating sites, I think the dating service must have sent me choices from the wrong group of women. These women are much older than me. Annoyed, I would then look at the person's age, and I'm really shocked! These old-looking women are often 10 or more years younger than me. How is this possible?

Actually, there is a simple answer – I look just as old to all the women looking at my photo. Yes, you get old and don't see it. Many years ago, at 75 years of age, my father told me he couldn't believe that he was 75. Inside, he said, he felt like he was 21. At that time, I didn't fully understand what he was talking about. Now, I do. As we age, we don't see the cumulative effect. After all, we look in the mirror every day, and it's difficult to see much change from day to day. If you didn't see yourself for many years, you would be shocked at the way time takes a toll, just like when you see an old friend from years ago and you can't believe it's the same person.

There is a *set point* at which people actually look young to you. For each of us, this set point may differ a bit, and I think it changes as we get older. For example, I noticed that forty-something women looked young to me when I was fifty-something. Yet, when I was twenty, forty-something women looked old. I suppose when I'm eighty, the sixty-something women will look young.

Do people 10 and 20 years younger than you have any interest in becoming your soul mate? Good question. I would suspect that they are experiencing the same dilemma and looking at people 10 and 20 years younger than themselves. I always laugh when I see a woman, 56, online, saying that she is looking for a mate between 40 and 52. Does she think men in their forties are looking for her? Is her perception of "self" a tad bit warped?

It's a little-understood, but real, phenomenon – we don't realize how much we have aged, and we seem to be attracted to people who look like we *think* we do. Boy, are we deceived! Fortunately, there are some people who have aged very well. You'll know them when you see their photos, feel an attraction, and then become very surprised when you see their age.

17

CHOOSING THE PERFECT INTERNET DATE

ONCE YOU ARE SITUATED, having registered with an online dating service, provided a nice profile describing how wonderful you are, chosen a cool Internet dating name, uploaded your photo, and written some witty one-liners, you are now ready to search for a mate.

Keep in mind, if you are drop-dead gorgeous (a.k.a. hot, hot, hot), there will be so many daters emailing you at your dating site address that you won't have time to search for anyone yourself. So, let's assume you are just "hot," or reasonably gorgeous, or maybe even average. You folks will want to begin your search for Prince Charming or Princess Amazing, and there are some rules to follow.

You begin by doing a search to eliminate the thousands of potential mates who really don't fit with your tastes. For example, if you are looking for someone who is fat, or thin, or of average build, you can put those descriptors into the screening search and find a bunch of people who fit your desires. You can't find every characteristic with this search, but it helps a great deal. No one wants to read through thousands of profiles when you can cut that number down by eliminating things you don't want, or selecting things you do.

Depending on the dating site you join, you can usually search for smokers or nonsmokers; social drinkers or nondrinkers; various heights, body shapes, or weight descriptions; various races, religions, and locations (do they live nearby?); hair and eye colors; marital status; whether they have or want children; and a host of other variables. You should spend much time in your search at this point so you don't end up dating someone who is religious if you're not, likes the great outdoors if you don't, and so on.

The next step is to look at the little photos posted next to each profile. This is the chemistry part of the adventure. You will look at hundreds of thumbnail photos that offer a glimpse as to what each person looks like. Keep in mind these photos may be deceptive; however, this usually offers an awesome advantage in finding someone to love. You can often tell in a flash if someone is appealing to you based on a picture, so there's no need to read more or make a date with someone if you have no chemistry.

Many of you may declare that it is shallow, immoral, and inaccurate to base your search for a mate on a mere thumbnail photo. But let's face it: we do this in all dating venues. If you are at a bar and someone approaches, in one second you can tell if you have any interest in most cases. Sometimes, it may take two seconds if you've had too much to drink.

Obviously, once you find a photo you like, you should read the profile with a fine-tooth comb. It's not complicated; just look for people who do things you like to do and who have similar wants, needs, and desires. If you are looking for a meaningful long-term relationship, you should have noted that on your profile. Now find those who want the same long-term relationship. If you are looking for raw sex, mention it in your profile ... actually, that isn't one of the characteristics usually found in these profiles. However, if you are interested in a relationship devoid of sex, use the code words "looking for marriage." Just kidding! Remember, why waste everyone's time contacting those looking for a pen pal if you want more? Why date a person not interested in marriage if that's what you want?

Now that you've found your perfect match, or at least a few

prospective mates, it's time to be bold and take action. Yes, it's time to contact them.

Activity Suggestions – List the top five features you are looking for in a mate. List the worst five characteristics you cannot stand in a mate. Be honest. No one is evaluating your choices.

18

INSTANT KARMA: INSTANT MESSAGING

WE LIVE in a fast-paced world where we want instant gratification and instant everything. While this section has nothing to do with karma, it sounds a lot cooler than calling it "Instant Messaging (a.k.a. IM)," the actual topic at hand.

One embarrassing moment occurred when I was online, and an instant message came through. First of all, I heard some kind of outer-space noise, as if an alien had zapped me with a ray gun. I was all alone, and I had no clue what was happening. Finally, I realized the noise came from my computer, and it was some lady who was trying to IM me. And I didn't understand IM at the time. I wasn't yet "with it."

For those who have no idea what IM is, it is instant messaging. While you may be familiar with it on your phone as text messaging, it's much more invasive when it comes from a dating app or website. A strange noise precedes a window appearing on your computer screen, phone, or tablet with a message from someone who would like to communicate with you. In this case, it said, "Hi, I see you're online rather late [it was 1 a.m.] and I thought we could chat."

The last thing I wanted to do was to start a conversation that required me to type at the speed of an amphetamine addict and try to predict what to say next so that I can catch up with the other person, as they, too, type like a demon. IM was not for me.

The first problem was I didn't realize other members of Internet dating services can tell when I was online, and second, I didn't know technically how to respond to this IM, and third, I didn't realize I could just ignore this person trying to IM me from the other end of cyberspace.

After a minute, I figured out how to respond and I wrote, "Sorry, I don't respond to IMs." This denizen of the night didn't write again, as I am sure she found some other insomniac to correspond with somewhere.

There is no rule that says you have to respond to any of the IMs, emails, flirts, winks, or contacts of any sort if you choose not to. And for all of you who don't get a response, remember that *no response is a response*. It either means that person is not interested, has never looked at his or her messages, or is are no longer active on that site. For your ego's sake, just assume he or she is no longer on the site.

You can actually hide the fact that you are online in the settings of each e-dating site. If you look around the website, you'll find an explanation of how to hide yourself in a section called FAQs (frequently asked questions). You can even block others from seeing that you looked at their profile. Yes, each time you look at other users' profiles, they know that you were there looking at them unless you turn off that setting. You can forget about privacy when you really want to find a new mate. And it goes without saying, there is something almost erotic about being invisible and looking at people. I think psychiatrists call it *voyeurism*. Most of us know it by the common term: pervert.

But remember, if you do make yourself invisible, you may not get much action, online or off. The object of looking at other profiles and having users know that you are looking – or better yet, putting people on your *Hot List* (another dating site tool) – is so others can see that you are interested. They can respond accordingly. Each Internet dating service has a Hot List equivalent that allows you to save profiles of others for you to eventually decide if you want to contact them.

Once you learn all of the neat features of Internet dating, you can customize your approach for the hunt: be visible sometimes and invisible other times. For example, you may want to remain anonymous when you spend a lot of time looking around, and then make yourself visible again for those you finally decide to go after. Hopefully, you'll find someone to date before you become the world's authority on all of the features of your Internet dating service.

I have heard several people say that they feel an obligation to respond to anyone who contacts them. You don't have to and probably shouldn't. You may attract a cyberstalker. I, too, feel that it's the polite thing to respond to everyone, but even I've stopped. Everyone kind of knows that many of their requests go unanswered.

Don't let your ego become fractured by people ignoring your attempts to connect. While it feels like rejection, it's just the nature of the beast. Of course, if no one ever responds to any of your queries, use the Brad Pitt and Angelina Jolie pictures in place of your own as mentioned in the section on photographs and usernames.

Activity Suggestions – By now you have found a few websites that appeal to you. Find the FAQs on these sites and familiarize yourself with the features. Decide if you wish to be anonymous or invisible to others while you do your search for the perfect mate.

19

DATING ON TINDER

PAY ATTENTION because *Tinder dating* may be just what you are looking for, especially if you have ADHD, limited time, or the ability to multitask while dating. For you see, Tinder moves at a stepped-up pace and can get you going rather quickly at finding a mate, date, or companion. Tinder is one of the "lite," easier Internet dating sites that have become popular with the younger set. However, now, even older folks are getting in on the act.

First, you should understand that early on, Tinder was thought of as a "hookup" site. For you older daters, *hookup* means casual sex. People would go to this site expecting to find someone for a quickie. Now that's a term the older set should understand. Essentially, Tinder was a way to find a "one-night stand." Yes, that's another oldie term. There were even some professionals (women prostitutes) on this type of site that were trolling for guys looking to hook up. These guys didn't realize they would have to *pay* for the date.

However, it now appears that these "lite" sites have gone more legitimate. There are some users still looking for that quickie, but many are looking for true love. A more recent phenomenon sees many older (fifty- and sixty-something) daters posting to these sites. So what is Tinder all about?

Here's how it works. You join the dating site and initially pay nothing. Post your photo (preferably several with good shots of your face and body). The same photo rules apply as with any Internet dating site. You need not post 12 photos of your dog and scenery from places you visited. You set the parameters as to what you are seeking: tall, short, fat, thin, and all those things you want in a mate. You then set your *location*, the *maximum distance* you are willing to travel to meet someone, and the *gender* and *age range* for which you are searching. Finally, write a profile that is short and sweet, and you are ready to go.

Now comes the fun part. Once you are on the site, it searches your neighborhood based on how far you said you are willing to travel. You only see photos of people near you, based on your distance parameter. You can see when they were last on the site, which means you will see some that are on site as you "swipe."

You'll see a photo and short description of the potential date. You swipe the photo *left* if you are not interested, and you won't see that one again. If you like the photo, you have the option to see more photos, if the user has posted more. When you like what you see, you swipe the photo to the *right*, and you have now sent a notice that you are "interested" to Tinder, *not* to the dater. The dater never knows what you did, unless they, too, swiped you to the right when they looked at your posting. If the two of you both seem interested in one another (you've both swiped right), you both receive a notice and can begin a conversation on the app, as in messaging one another. This leads to a call, a meeting, sex, a pregnancy, a forced marriage, and a child. Actually, cut the pregnancy, child, and forced marriage, as those are optional. Well, not the forced marriage.

Tinder is rather fast-paced, fun, practical, and all wrapped into a nice package. Since you make no direct contacts initially, you don't get direct rejections. Of course, if you never get any matches, you are probably being rejected a bunch. In that case, maybe go back and set your standards a bit more realistically. If you are a grizzly mammoth, with missing front teeth, maybe start swiping left (reject) on all those beauties and swipe right (show interest) on sea hags and Medusa-like mates.

Now you can go through a hundred potential dates rather fast. You discard all those who don't turn you on by swiping left, and you send out word to Tinder about all those you'd consider by swiping right. You probably notice a lot of redundancy here explaining the swipe left, swipe right feature. That's because you are going to get confused and swipe some hot prospect left (rejecting him or her) and realize that you just passed on a cutie or a stud who you will never see again (yes, it's worse than that last scene in *Titanic*).

In time you'll get it right, but this is where Tinder makes money. While this site is free, if you want to be able to bring back someone you inadvertently rejected, this will cost you the monthly fee. They must have known everyone was going to screw up, as that became their revenue stream.

Once you've done some swiping, now you wait to see if there are any mutual matches. When you see a notice that there's a mutual match, you are now permitted to contact your future bride, groom, sex kitten, stud muffin, or whatever label you wish to ascribe to your new find. But be careful, Tinder is actually kind of addictive (no intravenous version yet), so don't get carried away. Limit yourself to no more than 16 hours each day to do your searches.

If you live in Los Angeles, New York City, or any other large metropolitan area, there will be tons of potential mates. However, if you live in a small rural town, you may not find too many daters online. Don't get flustered when all you find is your old girlfriend or boyfriend, or your divorced parent comes up as a potential mate. You may have to set your distance to search out farther. In Los Angeles, you can search two miles and find lots of people all around you (even in the same bar or club you're sitting in while searching). In Bird-in-Hand, Pennsylvania (this is a real town), you may need to set your distance to several hundred miles to find someone.

It's all fun. It's easy once you get the hang of it and figure out which is your right and left hand. Go forth and multiply, or at least practice the act of multiplying. Have a great time, and be kind to all you meet.

Activity Suggestion – Now you see that all the information you have been collecting has a purpose. No homework this time, except to try Tinder. No, we don't get a commission.

20

WHY NO CALLBACK?

THERE MAY COME a time that you wait for a call that never comes. Someone contacts you by email or phone and says he or she will give you a call, and then doesn't. This can mess with your head as you try to think of the 754 reasons why the person didn't call, when in reality it may be something innocuous.

First, let's examine the reasons you think your dates didn't respond to your emails. These reasons depend on your ego. If you are the confident type, you will immediately figure that they never emailed back because they realized by the initial contact that you were far superior to their simplistic intellect and would never appreciate the mundane lives they lead. You assume they realized they could never fit in with your jet-set lifestyle, let alone have a conversation with someone like you.

At the other end of the spectrum is the not-so-confident Jims and Janes of the world. They might think the reason for their dates not emailing back is related to tragic consequence, such as their prospective dates realizing that they had spinach caught between their front teeth. Maybe that's a rare example, but perhaps Jim figured that the person could tell he's a dullard by the font he chose for his emails.

In the case of phone contact, both of you have had the chance to learn more about each other than could be gleaned by mere email. You had the chance to hear each other's voices, as well as any associated tones that might be garnered in such a conversation, and you also had the chance to analyze the content of such a conversation. Now, if the person doesn't call you back, or doesn't pick up your calls, you want to know why. The confident people fault the other person, and those lacking confidence blame themselves, while, in fact, it often has nothing to with you personally. So let's explore the reasons people don't get back to you besides you being a loser.

The most likely non-personal reason (if your phone conversations and emails don't reveal you to be a total loser) usually relates to situations going on in the other person's life. Quite often, the other person has *found another person* while shopping around. That's right; if you are looking for a nice outfit, and have traveled to many stores, once you find what you want, you're not running back to the other stores. The same goes for Internet dating. That nice person you spoke with or emailed a few times has found someone else. Now, do realize the courtesy of an explanation is in order, but so many people are either aloof, too busy, inconsiderate, or generally ignorant to the fact that the proper courtesy is a simple explanation: "After receiving your email, I just knew you had spinach between your front teeth – central incisors – and that's a turnoff to me, so I won't be communicating with you any longer."

There are other explanations for why dates don't respond. They may have *gone back with a previous lover*. That is quite common. They may have *given up on dating* after having many unsuccessful encounters. And don't forget, they may have *died*. I know that's a morbid thought, but it can't be left out of consideration when trying to rationalize why you didn't get a callback. And let's not forget the possibility that they *may have moved* out of the geographical locale.

Now for some *personal reasons* that they may have avoided your calls and emails. One obvious reason is that you are, in fact, a drip. You folks usually know who you are. Perhaps you are a know-it-all and it showed in conversation, but the one thing you don't know is that you are a know-it-all. There is the possibility that you were not the other person's type, either from an educational view, a looks view, or a compatible-interests view, like one of you likes to ski, hike, and ride dirt bikes, while the other is a nester. There are tons of reasons why you may not be that person's choice for a date. You get the point.

Don't get hung up on searching for reasons why that one fish got away. Remember, there are many fish in the sea, or however that saying goes.

Activity Suggestions – List five reasons a person may not get back to you. Put them aside. Read them 24 hours later. Do they seem realistic?

21

WHAT'S GU MEAN?

"WHAT, PRAY TELL, IS GU?" That's the question I asked an e-dater who contacted me. She lived in New York, at least a hundred miles away. When she first indicated interest, I wrote back mentioning that I was looking for someone closer. I left out the part about how I am looking for someone who lives around five or six blocks away. That's right, you can't have everything, so I never expect to find someone one to four blocks away. I'm willing to go that extra two blocks, but not all the way to New York City!

She was kind in her response and noted that she understands how *GU relationships* can be difficult. So what the hell is GU? After much pondering, I wrote back to this woman who already knew I'm lazy and not willing to drive a hundred miles each way to see her. I started with, "I'm sorry to bother you, but I was wondering what GU means?"

She wrote back and told me that GU is *geographically undesirable*. I should have been able to figure this one out, if I, like most men, didn't have sex on my mind incessantly. I thought it must mean "genitally unique." After all, having unique genitalia sounds much more intriguing than being geographically undesirable.

By the way, I ran this question by women, too, and they had no clue what it meant either. Maybe it's a common dating abbreviation, or maybe it was just this particular woman's way of abbreviating words. Whatever (WE).

The next question is, "Can a relationship that is geographically undesirable flourish?" Being lazy, I don't think so. But even for those of you who have stamina and drive, do you really want to drive hundreds of miles? I don't think so. This type of relationship could cause one to enter into a commitment prematurely just to stop all the driving, as you throw up your hands and say, "Please marry me and move in, because I can't take driving this much every weekend."

The distance can also work against a relationship causing many to flee because they just can't do all the "road work." I suppose that if you meet the love of your life and he or she is far away, you can make it work. Yes, the *sex drive* is often stronger than the *long drive*.

However, there are many things going against this type of arrangement. Absence makes the heart wander! That's one problem. There are too many opportunities to be tempted to meet others who are closer. Each of you has to decide if the GU date makes any sense.

For the life of me, I can't understand why I am getting so many requests to meet women who live many hundreds of miles away. Have they run out of eligible *candeDATES* in their region of the country? Does everyone in their hometown know they're losers, or are they so picky that they have to search far and wide to find the right one? Who knows?

There is a phenomenon I have noticed on Internet dating: some very hot, young women contact me as soon as I join a site. It's almost like "new meat" is shouted around the dating site, and these women are ready to pounce. The trouble is that they may be hookers. They seem to be way too young for me, and they are wearing seductive clothing with cleavage showing way more than expected on a family-safe dating site. These women mention how they "like older men." They leave out the part about older men with money or older men near death who are willing to leave them money.

It's a tough world out there. Be careful!

Activity Suggestions – What is the farthest distance you are willing to travel for a date? This would be your GU threshold. What is the most desirable distance for you personally?

22

THE CANDY STORE

INTERNET DATING TAKES you on a nostalgic trip back to your youth when you stood in front of the counter at the corner candy store. There were so many things to choose from. You felt excited, happy, a little confused, but generally wonderful because you were about to pick out something that appealed to your sense of sight.

While you may think it was about flavor and taste, all of this junk is made of sugar, and as a kid, your tastes weren't that sophisticated. Let's face it: you really were attracted to the colors and shapes that the manufacturers used to draw you to their sweet products.

Suddenly, as an adult, you find yourself gazing upon that candy store counter and see hundreds of pieces of candy (that will be our metaphor for your prospective mate) from which to choose. And as shallow as I thought of myself, using nothing more than visual cues to decide who I might like to date, it dawned on me that the very essence of being drawn to that which we find pleasing is very normal and human. It really is all about the *chemistry of attraction*.

What I've learned by meeting a number of women from the Internet is that if I wasn't really attracted to them immediately upon seeing their photos, I wasn't going to be drawn to them in person either. Do understand that looks are not everything. It was only when you got older that you realized some candy was better than others, and that the color and shape – that is, the looks – weren't everything. Certain candies had better texture and flavor that could only be described with subtleties unknown to you as a child.

Your understanding of people works the same way. As you get older, you learn more. You realize the qualities that are important must be balanced along with looks to find true happiness. I can assure you that if the most drop-dead gorgeous prospective mate is not kind-hearted, soulful, intelligent, truthful, and loyal, and he or she turns out to be generally a nutcase, you will lead a miserable life if you were to partner with him or her solely based on looks.

The other day I met a very attractive woman who gave me the visual impression of being high maintenance. You know the type. Highlighted parlor-pampered hair, long painted nails with embedded rhinestones, Jimmy Choo high heels ... and a whip. Upon speaking with her, my impression seemed well founded. This doesn't mean people who spend lots of time making themselves look nice and who are interested in the finer things in life aren't good people. They may, in fact, be wonderful. It just means that, if you are smart, you have to look at all the attributes one has when picking a mate.

But remember, you are allowed to want someone who makes you feel good when you look at him or her. Yes, along with all those other important things, you must have *chemistry* for a relationship to work out.

Activity Suggestion – Make a list of the physical qualities of your total fantasy date (with hair or bald, hair color, weight, height, body type, looks). You need to define what it is that catches your eye on dating site photos. You may be overlooking some great potential partners if you don't actually know what you are looking for.

23

I'D NEVER DO INTERNET DATING

I MET A WOMAN FROM FRANCE, of all places. I have never been to France, so as you can imagine, I met her locally. It was a treat because she had a different set of values and philosophies that were refreshing, aside from the fact that she was pretty and sexy.

When I told her I was writing about e-dating, she told me that she "would never do that" to meet a man. I was rather surprised that anyone would cast aside a means of meeting others without knowing what it's all about, so I explained. I am sure she is not the only one who shuns this dating medium. Perhaps, once you read this entire guide to online dating, you may embrace it. We do fear what we do not understand, so fear may be your reason, too. You can overcome your fears with guidance.

When you think about it, there are only so many ways to meet your prospective special person. Let us count the ways: *the matchmaker* (a remnant from the past, though still practiced in more primitive cultures and by your busybody friends who mean well). Some rely on *personal introductions*, including *dating introduction services* (more specialized recommendations based on personal interviews followed by matching traits). *The workplace* was a great venue to meet dates, until all the bullshit legal ramifications of sexual harassment. Now it is difficult to flirt or date coworkers without fear of losing your job, imprisonment, and castration, figuratively speaking. *The club scene* is something better suited for the young, but it's still a place to meet others. *Fate* is the long-desired way to find love for the romantically inclined, and fate seems to play a role in all meetings. (The French woman told me that you meet that special one when it is meant to be. I don't know; I guess I do believe in fate to an extent, but I also believe you have to take charge of your life and pick one of these other ways to meet so that fate can do her thing.) *Organizational meetings* are another, like those at your house of worship or other organizations that may sponsor social events for singles, or you may just meet a mate at general interest functions. *The grocery store* is a great place to meet women. *Home Depot* is a great place to meet men. *Museums* and *e-dating* appear to round out the list of ways to find your mate. There may be other ways to meet your love interest, and you can list them in the activities at the end of this section.

Every medium has its pros and cons. You have to weigh the benefits of each and decide for yourself how to approach meeting your special person. Some folks rely on fate and only fate. You decide if you want to stay at home and wait, or if you want to take the bull by the horns and help fate bring that special someone to your door.

E-dating allows you to take charge. Even if you don't find a date, a least you are actively seeking Susan or Sam or whoever. The cool thing about e-dating, over many other methods, is that you get an instant chemistry test by virtue of the fact that there are little pictures of the people you are considering.

As shallow as you might think I am for bringing up chemistry, you are probably just as shallow. Sure, you can fall in love with someone that isn't beautiful in your view. After all, haven't we drummed that into our kids from childhood with stories like *Beauty and the Beast*? Well, I can only speak for myself, but I can tell you, I prefer the beauty. And so do you!

It is so very much a part of human nature to be attracted to certain things based on what they look like. You do this all the time when you choose furniture and décor and buy clothing, flowers, fruit, and just about everything. Ugly clothing will cover your private parts – it gets the job done – but that doesn't mean you buy it. It's the same with *girl watching* and *guy ogling*. I created the latter expression. The term *girl watching* was invented years ago, as the title of a popular song, before I became so clever and inventive. I think I may just write a song for a female singer and call it *I'm a Guy Ogler*.

You stare at people that appeal to you. What you feel when you do this is called chemistry, and it is a necessary component of choosing a mate. What makes you shallow, however, is when chemistry is all you base your choice upon, and that would be downright stupid, like marrying for money ... wait, what's wrong with that? You know I'm kidding. You need all the good human components, like kindness, a good heart, compassion, caring, honesty, morality, and mental stability – I could go on and on, but you know what I am talking about.

So e-dating provides you with an opportunity to rule out those with whom you have no chemistry, and as a bonus, you get to read all the things they say about themselves to woo you. And let me tell you right now, the visual chemistry thing may not be everything, but it sure as hell doesn't lie like some of the entries you will read on e-dating sites. For a fact, I know of a predator who takes cheating to new levels, and who had the audacity to write on his profile that *honesty* was an important virtue to him.

Nothing is foolproof, but at least you can see what you get – well, not always. (Make sure you read the earlier sections in this chapter on photographs and usernames.) Internet dating offers many, many choices. The medium has become so popular that if you pick the right site, you can find a date in just about any city in most countries. Sure, there are a whole lot of frogs out there, and you may have to have coffee or a meal (or some nice flies) with a few of them, but it sure beats a formal blind date that you know you have no interest in the minute the person comes to the door.

The monthly cost of a membership on an Internet dating site is less than you would pay for one date with that frog, and it will be well worth avoiding the lost time a bad date uses up. This doesn't mean you won't go on a bunch of bad e-dates. You probably will, because finding the right person for you is not an easy task, but you can have many choices of prescreened people to choose from, and that improves your odds of finding a good match. Just don't allow yourself to get too needy or too desperate; it will blind your soul and you may end up with a bad choice.

Activity Suggestions – What are some other ways can you meet dates other than those listed in this section? List all the reasons for not using Internet dating sites to find a mate. List the benefits of using Internet dating sites.

24

HOME ALONE

HOME ALONE WAS a movie about a little kid, left home alone, who had a great adventure and fun. This section is about an adult – that's you – spending the night, *home alone*, without any adventure and very little fun. If you consider sex fun, *home alone* is not anywhere near as much fun as marriage or living with someone. According to Tom W. Smith, a world authority on sex statistics at the University of Chicago, married people have more sex than single people.

I could not believe what I was reading when I saw the numbers concerning sexual frequency for married versus single people. What about those jokes telling us that once married, sex is over? You first have to realize that when they do these studies, the numbers are an *average*. Yes, on average married people may have more sex than singles – actually, I still don't believe it, but, I suppose, if married couples have more sex, it's because there is, after all, a partner around much of the time with whom a person could have sex if both partners wanted to engage. *They can't be including the escapades of the Casanovas and the nymphomaniacs among us*, you might say to yourself when looking at averages regarding sexual frequency. Yes, there are some singles out there having a whole lot of sex, but not nearly as many as you may think.

All you have to do is think back to the days when you and your friends were single, unattached, and hung out together. Back then, you wished you had a girlfriend or a boyfriend. Why? Because you often went home alone, even when you were at the height of dating and should have been having lots of sex. Madison Avenue and shows like *Sex in the City* portray having lots of sex as the norm, but it is not necessarily the case for everyone.

Now that we established that being home alone may not be as much fun as a good date, or a good marriage, or a good live-in partner, we should look at the other side of the story. Being home alone may not be all that bad either. Let's see what we do when we are home alone. We watch television, we read, we watch television, and we read. There you go, at least four things I could think of that stimulate and offer solace at the end of a hard day. There are other things to do if you have varied interests, like playing your guitar, piano, or flute; collecting things; cooking; and going online. We can even have virtual sex by utilizing Internet porn, so there, we can have fun alone, too.

The odd thing about single life, especially after a bad marriage, is that you may actually appreciate *solitude*. Unless you are the type that needs someone around every minute, it can be nice to relax and watch television without someone interrupting you to do this and do that. And what about the inane conversation you had to listen to when your mate had little of value to say? If you find that you enjoy the solitude, you may decide that you don't need anyone in your life. Couple the joy of solitude with age associated diminished libido allowing one to just take or leave sex, and some individuals can become reclusive and grow their fingernails and hair just as long as Howard Hughes did when he had some socializing issues. You should make it a point to connect with others, even if they are friends of the same sex to hang out with, or you may find yourself getting too comfortable with solitude.

Then there is the dating option. Do you go on dates with toads for the sake of having company? I think that, in the quest for a mate, there is nothing wrong with going on many dates as long as you screen them, preferably with a couple of emails and calls. But don't waste a bunch of time on a multitude of emails and calls if there is no chemistry. You can meet and decide how much you need to know about your date, and your date about you, within the first 10 minutes of the meeting. Be willing to go on *not-so-great* dates for the expediency of getting the first meeting out of the way.

Think about it, you can spend hours on the phone telling your life story and hearing the other person's, versus meeting him or her for an hour at the most and then move on if there is nothing there. Even if it costs you a coffee or a dinner, *time is money*, so why waste hours on the phone when you can see if there is chemistry in a few minutes? Plus, you learn from every experience, including your failures. Yes, a short date may be better than investing lots of time talking only to find yourself on a no-chemistry date.

If the person you are interested in needs some familiarity before you meet, try to oblige him or her. You can tell after a few conversations whether you want to meet. And you will find that sometimes, the sad issue arises when you enjoy this person on the phone and really communicate well only to find that there is no chemistry when you finally meet. It's enough to make you give up on phone sex.

Let's say you find the perfect mate and he or she is not ready to commit. Is it better to give this person an ultimatum or is it better to enjoy your date's company and see if it moves further along? That is a very personal question you have to answer for yourself. You even have to decide how much is enough time. Do you date this person for a few months or years, or do you cut and run after a short period of time? Certainly, if you love someone, and purportedly the feeling is mutual, there should be some level of commitment. It doesn't have to be marriage – a committed relationship is not always asking that much. Commitments and ultimatums are discussed in more detail, in Chapter 9.

There are those who have been so scarred in a past relationship they can't make a commitment, and that is sad, but sometimes a reality. There are also those who can best be described as *serial daters* who have no plans for commitment. If you have a great time but don't like that arrangement, give the ultimatum. Just recognize that you may end up sitting *home alone*, a lot, not having any fun. Also recognize that your relationship may be magical for a longer time because you don't see this person all the time. Honeymoons don't last forever, especially when your bride or groom is around constantly. Familiarity can breed contempt. And even more likely and more common, familiarity tends to breed complacency that then breeds contempt.

Here is a short love story floating around online. It sums up the marriage thing from a negative point of view.

A Short Love Story

A man and a woman who had never met before, but who were both *married to other people*, found themselves assigned to the same sleeping room on a transcontinental train.

Though initially embarrassed and uneasy over sharing a room, they were both very tired and fell asleep quickly, he in the upper berth and she in the lower.

At 1:00 a.m., the man leaned down and gently woke the woman, saying, "Ma'am, I'm sorry to bother you, but would you be willing to reach into the closet to get me a second blanket? I'm awfully cold."

"I have a better idea," she replied. "Just for tonight, let's pretend that we're married."

"Wow! That's a great idea!" he exclaimed.

"Good,' she replied. "Get your own f---king blanket."

After a moment of silence ... he farted.

The End

If that story sounds familiar, you may be better off *home alone*.

Activity Suggestions – List five things you don't like about being home alone. List five benefits of solitude. If you have trouble listing five from either category, that may say a lot about your potential for dating versus joining a monastery.

25

THE COMMUNITY

ONCE YOU GET on Internet dating sites, you have, in essence, joined a new community. And like the dynamics of real communities, there are some that come into play here, too, in your virtual community. One of the more interesting things I noticed about the online dating community was the fact that I was getting to know some people rather well, even though I never contacted them and probably never will. While that statement makes no sense to you, let me explain. All of the e-dating sites send you photos of many people who they think will click with you based on your profile and those of the people they pick.

What happens, however, is that after a few months you keep getting the same photos of the same people week after week. While you are looking for someone new, who you find appealing, you see the same old faces with the same old dating names. Pretty soon, you say, "Oh, there's *lovinlife49* again. I guess she still hasn't found Mr. Right, or they would have stopped sending me her photos."

If the person is appealing, you may click on the link and read his or her profile and usually get to see more photos of this person. Pretty soon, you get to know who changes their photos, updates their profile, and puts on clean underwear. Okay, the last one was just to add levity to this odd subject.

If you are astute, you may even be able to tell something about the psyche of this person. You can notice insecurities, timidity, frustration, and anger if you look closely at the things they say on an ongoing basis. All of this observation over time may even help you to pick the right person to date.

Do keep in mind that this is a process and takes some months before you can figure it all out. By the time you do, it may be too late for some prospective mates. You may find out that person you've had your eye on for months is no longer on the dating site and will never get to know you.

You can even become friends with others on these dating sites if you so choose. I know a woman who used to contact other women telling them she was looking for single women in her neighborhood to become friends with so as to socialize and go places ... to meet men. This is a great idea for any men or women who want to meet new people with whom they can go and do things.

Just like in any community, you should follow certain dictates of etiquette. You should remain civil and tactful to all you come in contact with because rumors can spread in the online singles community. You don't want to be known as the lecher from Maple Avenue or the slut from North Glendale. When you contact others, be respectful and courteous.

III

WHO'S LEFT FOR YOU TO DATE?

26

THE SEVEN CATEGORIES OF PEOPLE YOU WILL MEET ON THE INTERNET

THERE ARE seven main categories of people on dating sites: the single, the separated, the divorced, the widowed, the lecher, the crazy person, and the predator. Each one comes with a higher probability of certain risks and rewards depending on the category.

When you first start dating, you may be a bit excited about meeting someone, and this may translate into not using your head when it comes to choosing from all those choices. It is like a kid in a candy shop not knowing what to pick, and very likely getting something less than the best due to impatience.

You can find some great mates in any of the categories of marital status: single, divorced, widowed, or separated. Just be aware of the various problems you may be confronted with, more or less depending on their circumstances. When you list your profile choices, don't hesitate to request the ones you wish to consider (e.g., divorced and widowed) and leave out the others. While you will never likely see a profile choice for requesting the lecher, predator, or crazy person, if you do, pass! It isn't as easy as checking a box, so how can you avoid them?

27

THE LECHER

LET'S begin with *the lecher*. At first thought, isn't everyone on this Internet site single? Of course, they are supposed to be. Sadly, there are men and women (though mostly men, based on tales of woe) who fraudulently portray themselves as single, when they are actually married and looking for conquests or testing the waters before they jump ship.

Some may consider a serial dater a lecher, but that is really a preference that must be respected. You may not want to date serial daters, but as long as they let you know they aren't interested in a monogamous relationship, you have the choice to avoid them, and thus they aren't lechers.

The lecher is dangerous and should be avoided at all costs. At worst, he or she could be a psychopath, though more than likely the lecher is just looking to score with an unsuspecting man or woman.

It's difficult to defend against this type if you are kind and too trusting. Little things should give these frauds away, like they can only meet you on Tuesday nights. They will have a story: "That's the only day I don't have to take care of my kids," or "That's the only day I have off from my 100-hour-a-week workload." The truth is that

Tuesday is the only day his wife knows he will be out late because he tells her it's bowling night or card night with the guys. Yes, there are jerks out there. Just look for things that do not make sense.

A characteristic of lechers (and predators) that could help give them away is that they are usually very comfortable with the dating scene. They are cool and sexually aggressive. Of course, don't confuse the lecher with someone who is just cool and sexually aggressive. That didn't help you one bit. The point here is that we would all like to be with someone who is cool and comfortable with sexuality, especially if we are shy. This type of person easily breaks the ice. He or she could be that great love of your life. Just be aware that the lecher is usually good at this kind of thing, too, so give it some thought if this person is too good to be true.

It is sad that we have to be cynical about true love, which should, most certainly, feel like it is *too good to be true*. Romantics just have to be cautious! If you really like the person and are willing to make a little investment, stalk them. Well, not really, but find out where they live, park outside, and see what goes on at a few different times of the day. If you see his or her mate is living there, and that's not part of the story you were given, stay away.

Of course, don't jump to conclusions. They may be seeing someone besides you, or it could be a sister or office manager that stops by. If you don't have the nerve to stalk, then hire an investigator if you are really that worried and like the person that much.

In the next few sections, we'll discuss the other types of people out there in the dating game.

Activity Suggestions – With regard to profile categories (single, divorced, widowed, and separated), which to do prefer most and least? What do you think are the benefits and risks of each category?

28

THE WIDOW AND WIDOWER

IN YOUR ONLINE quest to find the perfect mate, a widow/widower may be the perfect candidate, assuming that he or she didn't murder their previous spouse, or drive the person to a slow death by subtle means, such as nagging, or other stresses related to money or sex. Then there is the possibility that a widow/widower just lost his or her spouse through natural circumstances, like lightning strikes, heart attack, or other assorted things that make life so unpredictable.

Widows/widowers may come with some money if they planned their lives with insurance, or if they accumulated a good-size estate. Of course, they may have had no insurance and have lived from paycheck to paycheck when the breadwinner (the one who brought home that paycheck) died. In that case, they may be in dire straits and looking to find a new breadwinner. This could make for an unstable relationship if it is solely grounded in breadwinning. You have to do your homework to figure out the situation.

Little hints may guide you, like when on the first date, the guy tells you he's taking you for Dunkin' Doughnuts coffee because he can't afford Starbucks. It's things like that you have to be aware of.

Since the widow/widower may have still been in love before the death of his or her partner, unlike the separated and divorced group, this person may have other issues that make dating difficult. There are those who were so in love that they may never get over their grief. That type of person is usually not on a dating site, but if he or she got there by the coercion of a friend or loved one, you may find yourself forever compared to the lost love.

Just because someone lost a spouse doesn't mean he or she had a good relationship prior to the death. You still have to do your due diligence to see what type of person this potential mate will be.

Widow/widowers do have the potential for being great mates. They are neither discarded nor obviously tainted. If they had good marriages, they will want to repeat the experience. Just make sure they don't keep you hanging on, telling you they haven't gotten over their grief. While grief is personal, waiting too long to be able to enter into a relationship may indicate deeper problems.

Dating death. Life is filled with joys and sorrows. You can't have one without the other. While we try to fill our life experiences with more joys than sorrows, the fact remains that we cannot escape the inevitable grief of death. And what does death have to do with dating? For some, it has everything to do with whether to date or not to date.

The mourning of lost love is a monumental sorrow. The more you loved that person, the greater the sadness. Healing feels insurmountable, and the depths of despair are cold and dark. For many people, the healthy period of mourning turns into a different kind of love and an appreciation for what they've lost. They heal and move on.

For some, moving on doesn't include finding another life partner, while others welcome the chance to love again. For some, finding another love feels like a betrayal. Others accept that finding another love is appropriate and even a blessing that helps recovery.

After losing a loved one, the choice to date is a very personal one. It is also not likely to be considered right away. You need time to heal. Just how much time to heal is again a personal matter. If it may help, the more you loved and were loved, the more likely it may be that your lost partner would want you to find happiness. Since companionship is so very important to human joy, that person would likely have wanted you to date and have a fulfilled life once again.

Activity Suggestions – Do you feel dating again after the death of a loved one is a betrayal? If you are widowed, how long do you expect to wait before dating? Would you consider talking to a therapist about grief issues? If you are not widowed, would you consider dating someone who has lost his or her love?

29

SINGLE PEOPLE ARE NOT ALL CREATED EQUAL

WHEN SPEAKING OF SINGLE, many are actually single in the truest sense of the word (never before married). The younger the dating site, the more single folks. By the time daters get into their forties, most of them have been married for the first time. You have to ask yourself, why are these people single (never before married) at forty- or fifty-something? The answer may well be that they are still single because they are smarter than the rest of us, or they may be fussy bachelors and bachelorettes who have not yet found their princesses and princes.

Just because someone isn't married by 40 doesn't necessarily mean he or she isn't a great person, but there could be issues. "Issues" is a nice way of saying the person is nuts. The next time you are at a bar, ask the bartender if you could have a bowl of *mixed issues* to snack on, and see what he brings you.

A downside of the older single person is that he or she may have gotten comfortable with living alone. This could make the adjustment to sharing a life unnatural for one who has developed certain habits not conducive to cohabitation. On the other side, this person could be a fabulous catch in that he or she hasn't been burned out by a shallow or toxic relationship – that is, he or she may be ripe for, and appreciative of, a meaningful marriage. But remember, many single people are not willing to settle for a mediocre existence just to say they were married. That is much smarter than someone having children with some nitwit and making that person's life and that of their children screwed up.

While you should aware that there *could* be issues with older single people, in recent times, however, marriage is no longer the institution it used to be. Never being married no longer has the stigma it used to. The *old maid* is a relic from yesteryear. There are many more people choosing to remain single and loving every minute of it, reaping the dual benefits of dating (and sex) and solitude on an as-needed basis.

If you are looking for a meaningful relationship that culminates in marriage, the single person who prefers being *single* may leave you disappointed. If you have no interest in a relationship with this type of person, you should have a discussion early on to determine if this person is right for you.

There are divorced and widowed folks who feel the same about not wanting to get hitched again. It just is that the odds of a single person staying single may be stronger than with those others who have experienced marriage and would consider it again.

Activity Suggestions – Would you consider dating a person who has been single all his or her life? Do you want to remain single and have no interest in marriage? How long would you wait before bringing up the subject of settling down with your new date?

30

THE SEPARATED DATER: GOOD OR BAD?

OF ALL THOSE available online daters, the *separated* individual could be a big risk and not a good choice in some respects. These are individuals who may or may not go on to become truly available for a meaningful relationship. Since they have not yet finalized their marriages through divorce, they may be inclined to go back to their spouses and cause you to experience a deep hurt if you fall in love with them.

It is important to understand the dynamics of a separated person's marriage. For example, if the wife left the guy, and he is heartbroken, but she realizes that she should have never left, he may be happy to take her back. That means your future with this guy is predicated on the whim of someone who decides to return to the nest. You don't want that. You don't need to be pulled into the gutter with dysfunctional people.

This means you are entitled to ask this prospective date about his or her backstory. Of course, not the second you make contact with him or her, but in the course of your first conversation (on the phone or in person) you have a right to know where your date is coming from. Separated sometimes means "not sure yet."

I know a woman whose husband left her out of the blue. One day, he just told her he was no longer in love and wanted a divorce. She insisted they had a great marriage, great sex, and that she had no idea why this happened. I personally think he was cheating on her and found the *perfect* new woman. She thinks that is not the case. And while she is mad as hell at him, if he decided to come back, I do believe she'd jump at the chance, because at that time she was just mad at him and in denial, and hadn't had enough time to realize he was a prick.

It doesn't mean you should completely discount the separated Internet dating candidates, because they are truly fresh meat, and one could turn out to be a winner. If you are willing to take the risk, you may be getting a first chance at snagging a good catch, assuming that this person hasn't been separated for the past five years. For one reason or another, some people let their separation drag on, and you could have potential problems getting them to make a commitment, or they may have great difficulty in finally obtaining a divorce once they fall for you.

You need to do your homework to find the prime, *recently* separated candidate. Actually, any newcomer (separated, divorced, or widowed) could be the one looking for a committed relationship. So if you are astute and online 24/7, you have a fleeting opportunity to find the person who may be eager to enter a committed relationship. These new candidates are snapped up rather fast if commitment is in their nature – that is, they are not interested in dating lots of people and will settle down with the first person they find appealing.

You do need to be careful, as all new entrants into the dating world could also be those who were spurned and have no intention of future commitment early on. You have to be discerning to know the difference, or you may wind up with a lovely person who will never consider marriage. If marriage is your goal, you should try to figure this out before you waste too much time or fall too deeply in love.

The way to know a potential mate's intentions is by asking the right questions. Once you find out his or her spouse left and he or she is feeling blue, you know this person may be flighty. If your date has anger issues over the lost spouse, he or she may have commitment issues. If your date is happy to be away from a difficult spouse, that has potential. And finally, if your date is very solicitous and kind, he or she may be the right one. Keep listening, and you learn a lot.

Activity Suggestions – If you were separated, would you take back your spouse if he or she left you for another? Rate what level of separated individual you would be comfortable dating: a person just separated, separated for 6 to 12 months, separated for one or more years. Do you understand that some people never get over a lost love?

31

THE DIVORCED

THE *DIVORCED* CANDIDATES have pros and cons that need to be considered. Since they are no longer married, you don't have to worry very much about them going back to their previous spouses; however, you always have to ask yourself, *why did their marriage fail?* Yes, you have to ask yourself. If you ask them, they will give you their version of the divorce, and that will invariably be one-sided. Not that you can't listen to their stories, because their sides may be very real and convincing. For example, if your potential date's ex was bipolar and ran off to live in the Arctic with an Eskimo, you have a good chance that this candidate may have been a victim rather than an abuser. Their stories will often contain many clues into their psyche, behavior, and personality. Look for red flags.

Another good question to ask the divorced candidate: *is this your only divorce?* Everyone knows you should try to avoid the three-time loser. Any relationship with a divorced individual has the potential to go either way: you may be getting involved with someone wonderful or with someone that has issues, especially if the person has been married several times. Remember, when someone has *issues*, it's a nice way of saying he or she could be nuts, in case you forgot.

Never discount the fact that many divorced individuals are great people. At the same time, never discount that they may be divorced because of problems that they, not the other party, have. Yes, it takes two to tango, but some people just don't know how to dance at all.

After a few dates, you should be able to see various traits that may not be conducive to a good relationship. See if this person is nice, caring, thoughtful, empathetic, and down to earth. If you notice little things about your dates, like they make unreasonable demands, expect you to cater to their every need, or they happen to be the type who screams, "I am the god of hellfire," when things aren't going their way, they are not keepers.

I noticed one date treated her relatives and friends with disdain and curtness in situations that were mildly stressful while she was fun loving and kind to me. It's always good to see how people treat those with whom they are most comfortable because that's just how they are going to treat you once they've got you.

Divorced people usually have scars whether they are a victim, an abuser, or a little bit of both. People with scars may be more defensive and have difficulty entering into a committed relationship for fear of repeating their previous experiences with marriage. On the other hand, they may be more desirous and dependent on getting into what they perceive as a good relationship. You should try to figure out what they want and need before you invest too much time if you are looking for a committed relationship from your online dating experience.

Activity Suggestions – Do you think divorced people are riskier to date? If a person has been divorced several times, is this a red flag for you? If you are divorced, do you want to tell your side of the story to all of your dates?

Dating a divorced person. Years ago, few people got divorced. That has changed radically over the years, and now there are tons of divorced people looking for dates on Internet sites. The question arises: is it okay, or perhaps even better, to date the divorced person versus the single or widowed person? This leads to other questions: how is it possible that so many amazing divorced people exist in this world? Who would ever let these wonderful people get away?

When you read the profiles on dating sites, everyone seems, oh, so nice. Actually, they seem incredible. Go ahead and read the profiles of all those divorced people, and you will find a world of saints. However, you can be assured that there is at least one group of people who would have a negative opinion of all these saints. Yes, the people from whom they are divorced!

One would have to guess that when two people can't get along in marriage, at least one of them is either unreasonable, difficult to live with, or outright *nuts*. Your job is to figure out if this person is the *shell* or the *nut*. It's always nice to believe that those who divorce were just not compatible and went their separate ways; however, they loved each other at one time, and something happened. Did they grow apart, lose interest, or age at different incompatible rates? Or was there an organic deficiency, a disease state, that resulted in the incompatibility that broke them apart?

Often you will find that one or possibly both of the parties are depressed and that could have led to the breakup. If you married a relatively normal person and he or she became depressed, he or she is no longer the same person. Living with a depressed person who doesn't get treatment for a number of years can result in irreparable consequences to a relationship. Your job when Internet dating is to check your date's medicine cabinet to see if it was your date, or the ex, who was on the psych medications.

Besides depression, bipolar disorder, if not controlled, goes far and beyond in making life miserable. If the medicine cabinet reveals meds for bipolar disorder, you may want to rethink this person as a mate. Uncontrolled bipolar disorder is a roller coaster you don't want to ride.

How about alcoholism? This disorder is one bane of society in which up to 30% of the population has or had a serious problem with alcohol or drug abuse. Living with an alcoholic or a drug addict is not a fun thing either. These people can be as nice as anyone yet change into Mr. or Ms. Hydes when under the influence. They will often lose their jobs and become angry and abusive.

Your detective work in finding the right mate for you is to figure out why this wonderful person (in their profile description) was divorced. Besides the potential mates with mental conditions or alcohol/drug problems, there are those with anger management problems, individuals with a low tolerance for stress who make a commotion about everything, wallflowers who have no interest in leaving the house, cheaters who never want to stay home, cheap people who won't spend a dime, poor people who don't have a dime, and sexless mates who will eventually withhold sex. The list goes on. Think about all of the people you know who've gotten divorced, and add those reasons to your list of things to avoid.

On the bright side, there are likely many wonderful divorced people. Sometimes there were incompatibilities that allowed them to divorce their former spouses, and they are still both wonderful people. Sometimes you will find the one who was really stuck in a bad deal while he or she was truly a great person.

An advantage of dating a divorced person is that he or she has a better understanding of marriage since this person has been there. The downside is that he or she could be jaded and never wish to marry again. This can be a concern if you are looking for marriage.

Don't be afraid to test the waters. Give a date a chance. Don't get too invested in anyone until you have had a chance to understand them and get to know them for a while. What's "a while"? It could take several months, even a year, before bad traits show up because most people are on their best behavior in the early stages of any relationship. As soon as you see grossly negative traits coming out, head for the door.

You are not going to rescue anyone. You are not going to cure this person's depression, anger issues, personality disorder, or drinking problem. Remember, there are a large number of divorced people who are not anything like their profiles. Don't be duped into a bad relationship. It might be better for you to find a single person or a widow to date.

Activity Suggestions – Talk to your divorced friends and colleagues and ask what happened to their marriage. Ask for suggestions to keep a marriage hot and strong.

32

THE PREDATOR

THERE ARE PREDATORS OUT THERE. You must be very careful in your Internet dating quest. You don't have to get paranoid about everyone you meet, but common sense should prevail. Having your guard up is helpful. Most people are very naive to predatory behavior because most people are trusting, and predators are very good at what they do. With a little caution, you can avoid being a victim. There are two main types of predators: the sexual predator, and the money predator. They can come in both female and the male versions, though generally speaking men are more often predators, in both the sexual and money types.

Women predators are usually known by another name: *gold diggers*. This is the woman looking for a guy with a lot of money and little confidence. A shrewd woman can take a rich guy with low confidence by the nose and get him to do most anything, like buy her lots of stuff. Most women predators are not sexual predators. As a matter of record, if you know any, I'd appreciate your sending them my way for scientific study.

The sexual predator is very much like the lecher, so go to that section to review this type of individual. Here we are concerned with the money predator. For you guys, don't flaunt your wealth if you have any. Driving up in the fancy car or taking a woman to your luxury Manhattan condo sends the right message if you want to hop into bed, but the wrong message if you want to avoid the gold digger.

Since you made a lot of money, assuming you didn't inherit it, you have to have something upstairs. Don't be tempted to think with your alter ego – Mr. Penis, also sometimes known as Mini-Me. If you do want to flaunt your wealth to attract hot women, go for it, but don't fool yourself. They are not in love with you as much as they are in love with your money.

Since men are the predominant predators, you ladies have to pay attention. There are guys you may meet on Internet dating sites who want nothing more than to live off of your wealth. They want your money. They are looking to hitch a ride to easy street.

You don't have to be a millionaire to be used for your money. A steady job with a decent income (and a decent income is a relative thing) can allow the predator to meander around doing a menial job while he lives in your house while you have you pay all the expenses. Of course, he'll love you forever and ever, and these people are usually pretty good at this kind of bullshit. If all you're looking for is to have a *kept man*, this may work for you, but if you want a meaningful relationship, then you have to figure this out and move on once you realize you are being played.

Women have to avoid flaunting their money, too, however you came into it. In addition to keeping your income private, try not to mention things like your inheritance, trust fund, or anything that may indicate you have a lot of money. There are times you just can't hide it. If you were divorced from a professional person or a successful business person, the predator can figure this out relatively easily. For example, you live in a big home and your ex-husband, either from death or divorce, was a professional man. You drive a Mercedes and dress classy. These are signs that you may have some money, and they are difficult to hide.

You may want to drive up to the first date on a bike, wearing sweats, and discuss how interesting it is cleaning homes to pay for your old college loans. Even better, it may also be wise to avoid discussing financial matters, and if you do, play down your money. You may even be wise to mention things like you may have to sell your home due to the big mortgage that keeps you struggling. Stories like that will discourage the predator.

If a date is too interested in your financial affairs, beware. If he or she asks you how much you make, how much you pay in real estate taxes, or how much you pay for various items, these are all bad signs – unless your date wants to pay the bills for you. When you are in a relationship, the basic rule is that if it is *too good to be true*, you might be in a relationship with a predator. Unrealistically, we are all looking for that too-good-to-be-true relationship. The tricky part is that great relationships start in the honeymoon phase, and the honeymoon is supposed to be too good to be true.

The reason your parents, friends, and loved ones have told you, and will continue to tell you, not to rush into a relationship when you tell them you are in love after two months is that you need to give the honeymoon phase a chance to end. That way you can see the true form the relationship will take. The longer you wait to make a commitment, the greater chance you have to find out if this guy or gal is a fraud.

Ladies, know that the money predator may cheat on you while professing his love. You may notice little inconsistencies in his stories. A predator can maintain multiple relationships while pledging his love in each one. If you are observant you will catch him in little lies that indicate he is cheating on you, his "one and only true love."

Really good predators will wine you and dine you if that's what you want. They are good at reading your wants, needs, and desires. They will tell you how beautiful you are and how smart you are. Yes, they will drown you with compliments. They know how to play the dating game with little gifts, like tickets to shows, and taking you to do everything that your spouse never liked. A predator will play upon your past negative experiences. If your ex-husband badgered you about keeping the house clean, this guy will be sure to tell you that doesn't matter to him. If your husband complained about your weight, this guy will tell you it's more for him to love. He will play upon your emotions and weaknesses. The predator is the ultimate controller, but he does it in a smart fashion. It can sneak up on you. Suddenly you have no friends, and you are kept away from family until the control is complete.

The predator will eventually want to discuss things like moving in or buying property with you (using your money), and he may also appreciate your help with little things like his rent. He may hint at gifts he could use, like a new car if you have a lot of money, or some clothing if you don't have the big bucks. When you are in love, it is easy to want to shower gifts on your lover. Please beware the predator. The relationship will end in ruin if you fall for this type of person, and you will be heartbroken.

Activity Suggestions – Review this section and list five warning signs of the predator. Recognize that a person may have one or two warning signs and still be okay, but too many warning signs are a major red flag.

33

DATING THE DYSFUNCTIONAL

NO ONE WANTS to date people who are dysfunctional, other than, perhaps, others who are dysfunctional and don't know better. Actually they, too, don't want to go through that hell. The sad thing about the world today is that there are a whole lot of dysfunctional people out there, and it doesn't often show on their faces. It doesn't even initially show in their behavior in many instances. However, over time, the dysfunction will begin to surface. Whether it is as simple as obsessive-compulsive behaviors or as severe as hostile abuse, over time you will see mental dysfunction manifest itself as the relationship moves forward.

Warning signs abound when it comes to detecting dysfunction. It is, however, difficult to distinguish *bad behaviors* from mentally dysfunctional ones, and we all tend to discount bad behaviors, regarding them as just a "bad hair day." In reality, most people who have had to live with dysfunctional people admit that there were many signs that they frequently ignored.

Some of the things to look for include moodiness, intolerance toward stressful situations, anger, withdrawn behaviors, sleeping too much, and argumentative natures. The problem is that all of these warning signs can be seen in all of us at some time or another. That is why they are so often not recognized as dysfunctional or they are just plain ignored. But unless a person is really demented, you will not see bad behaviors early on in a relationship. There are a few more common dysfunctions that warrant discussion in order for you to identify and then avoid them.

People with *personality disorders*, like borderline, narcissistic, paranoid, schizoid and antisocial to name just a few, are usually very aware that poor behavior will keep anyone from bonding with them, but once bonded they are able to do their thing. Those afflicted by some of the personality disorders will try to take control of your life. If successful – that is, if you let them – they will pull you away from the sanity in your life to keep you under their control. While looking at this kind of scenario from the outside, you may think that could never happen to you, but once you are under their spell, via the bond of love, you may do many stupid things.

If you find that the person you date tries to control you, get away. It is not often easy, since these individuals are clever and know they need to charm you in order for you to relinquish control. Certainly, if there is any physical abuse, you should head for the hills. It is sad how many people, mostly women, will tolerate any kind of physical abuse. They often rationalize that their mates have anger issues, they drink too much, or they had a rough day at the office, and that makes it acceptable. It is never acceptable! Very needy and lonely people are more likely to put up with such behavior. Hopefully, that is not you.

People who are *depressed* may exhibit many types of behaviors that should give you a clue that you may be entering into a bad relationship. Untreated depressed people will often have a low tolerance to stresses, exhibit moodiness, sleep a lot, and be inclined to avoid social discourse. The good thing about dating is that you will not likely meet *severely* depressed people since they usually are not looking for relationships. More likely they are curled up in a fetal position at home. There are, however, many mildly depressed people who eagerly seek out relationships and then let their negative behaviors surface. If you are dating someone who seems relatively normal, but who over time exhibits moodiness, appears easily frustrated, or seems inclined to be withdrawn, you may be in a relationship with a depressed person.

Bipolar individuals exhibit a range of behaviors, from completely normal, to incredibly exciting, to dangerously adventurous, to severely depressed. Depending on the stage at which you meet this person, you could easily fall in love, only to be thrown for a loop by their aberrant behavior. Once again, you have to be able to discern the dysfunction and escape from the bonds of the relationship before you get too deeply attached. Be aware that bipolar individuals can be in a good phase for months. On medication, they may be good for years. If your "perfect lover" becomes a person you don't recognize many months into the relationship, you may be dating a bipolar individual.

Normal people don't abuse or, in extreme cases, kill their lovers. People with major mental derangements do. Discussing mental illness is never easy. No one likes to think that he or she has this type of affliction. The number of mentally ill people is astounding if you include all of the people on antidepressants. While most of them like to think that their affliction is not really mental illness, just ask their partners what it is like living with them.

To help you figure out if a prospective partner has mental problems without going through the time required to make such judgments and risk falling in love, you can be proactive. When the opportunity arises, look in the medicine cabinet of your new date. If you see prescription pill bottles, jot down the names of the drugs and then look them up to see what possible problems are lurking in the minds of your prospective lovers. Is this moral? You have to decide if detective work can be forgiven if it keeps you safe.

Many people with mental conditions are well controlled by medications and therapy. They may make great lovers. But there are many people with mental conditions who are not being treated, and they pose the biggest danger.

Activity Suggestions – Research personality disorders and learn about five. Describe the major elements of these dysfunctions.

Are you meeting a nut? Only the Shadow knows. Who knows what lurks in the hearts of others? This is a great philosophical question when you think about the concept of meeting strangers in any venue, but especially when engaged in e-dating.

Here you are, trying to meet the person you want to spend the rest of your life with, and you might even want to trust him or her with all sorts of personal things, even your money. So, you would like someone who is *sane*. Ironically, in all the people's profiles I have read on Internet dating services, I have never seen anyone actually write, "Looking for a sane individual." Sure, they all want *honest*, *good-looking*, and *funny*, as these are commendable assets. Some even have the temerity to ask for *wealthy*. With a wish list like that, and the mere fact that they are looking for new mates, quite often because they already had experience with people with *issues* (a.k.a. *nuts*), you'd think they'd be more careful in constructing their shopping list and ask the dating gods for sanity in their next mates.

A great-looking lady (assuming that she posted her real photo) contacted me with the usual *flirt*, or some such device used on dating sites to let me know she was interested. I responded and got a message from this woman indicating she'd like to meet. I was very much impressed with her profile, which seemed to be either copied from others or written by a public relations firm. It was that good. Her response to my email was rather good, too, indicating to me she was very witty and on the ball and may have actually written the profile herself.

After setting up a time and location online for a lunch date, I had to call her the day before the meeting. The usual small talk started, and pretty soon we began to discuss the kind of things you talk about on the actual date. In this short introduction, she told me she was a teacher. Interestingly, she knew my best friend. This would surely offer a unique insight into this potential date/mate if I were to call him for the inside scoop.

Just as I was thinking about making that call to my best friend, she read my mind. She asked me to judge her when I met her, rather than listening to others. Was this a red flag? Well, yes. So immediately after hanging up from our conversation, I gave my best friend a call. When I mentioned to him that I was going to meet a woman he taught with, I was surprised at his response.

"She's – expletive deleted – crazy!"

Whoa, this certainly didn't fit into the *Bambi Rule* – "if you can't say something nice, don't say anything at all" – taught to us by our parents. He repeated his response three times at correspondingly higher decibel ratings before he heard me yell, "I haven't told you her name yet!"

How odd; he knew who I was talking about without me mentioning her name. Could he have taught with only one woman all these years, or is he prescient? Sure enough, he knew exactly to whom I was referring. He went on to tell me that she was not the one I wanted to meet. I told him, "I get it. I'll just go to the lunch date for the sake of learning all about Internet dating."

He didn't want me to meet this woman to the point of obsession, so much so that I finally agreed I would cancel the date. I never saw my best friend so adamant about someone, and I figured, the way he described her, I could end my lunch date with a butter knife in my ear if she was as nuts as he told me. "Okay, okay. I'll cancel the date." He wished me luck and told me to pray for his soul and mine a well. I didn't know what he meant by this last admonition, but it sure seemed like it was something said in *The Exorcist*.

I called her the next day and canceled using the *little-white-lie* technique. I told her that I went back with my girlfriend last night and had to give that relationship a try. She wasn't happy and insisted that I spoke with my friend. I told her that she was wrong, but there was something in her tone that told me canceling the date was the right thing to do.

I thought that was the end of it; however, a few days later I got a nasty email on my dating service where she mentioned that she sees I am still active on the site and correctly assumed I listened to my best friend.

What did I learn? I learned that it might be better to avoid a white lie in some circumstances. While you don't want to hurt someone's feelings, you may be better off saying it like it is. "Yes, I spoke with my best friend, and he told me we wouldn't be compatible." You can leave out the "because you are freaking nuts" part. Remember, other users can see you online unless you turn off your visibility in the dating site's settings. If you do that, then other users won't know you have been interested in looking at them, and you may miss out on meeting your perfect match.

So what else have we learned by this unusual coincidence? There are nuts, lunatics, weirdos, and miscreants online. No matter how much you might request a *sane mate*, the very nature of nuts is that they don't generally tell you they're nuts. While they may be nuts, they know that no one would want to meet them if they announced such a trait in their profile. You have to understand that the risk of meeting a nut exists, and you have to know what to look for.

You may find out early (within the first few dates) that they need therapy, Thorazine, or a thrashing; otherwise, you may actually find out when it's too late, like a month or so before you file for divorce, or while they are in the process of killing you. Lunacy comes in many degrees. This means that the subtler one's nuttiness is, the more difficult it is to detect in a short period of time. This is especially true when most of us, even the nuts, are on our best behavior in the early stages of dating. It can even take years to figure out you hooked up with a nutcase. In some situations, the lunacy is latent or needs a catalyst to show through, such as stress or depression.

Just keep your eyes open for aberrant behaviors, including but not limited to aggression, anger, hostility, extreme sarcasm, negativity, belligerence, a short temper, egotism, narcissism, petulance ... ah, the list goes on and on. Also, it is important to note, like beauty, nuttiness is in the eyes of the beholder. Perhaps you would not see the nuttiness that others see. However, there are certain universal truths.

There are cashews, almonds and pistachios, whatever the name, they are all nuts.

Be ready to move on if you see signs of insanity. And consider putting in your profile that you are *looking for someone who is not insane!* Maybe potential nutty dates will take the hint and go after someone else who is unsuspecting once they know that you are on guard.

That's about it for the 7 common dates. Next let's talk about some of the less well-known types of dates

Activity Suggestion – List all the people you know, or have had contact with, that seemed to be irrational and basically nuts. Now take the 50 pages containing all of their names and throw them in the trash to symbolically remove them from your life.

34

DATING A TRANNY

SEVENTY YEARS AGO, one would think the title of this section contained a typo. Yes, one would think this section is all about dating a *granny*. Today, no one is confused about the title containing a typo, though there is still much confusion. It appears that the entire new world order is filled with sexual confusion. There are those confused about their sexuality, having a condition called gender dysphoria. There are those confused about the many *trans* titles being used. And there are those dating who are confused about who they are about to meet on that first date.

Some definitions are in order. A *transgender* person is someone who identifies with the sex that is opposite his or her assigned gender (birth gender is an unacceptable term). This would be a guy who identifies as a woman, or a woman who identifies as a man. A *transsexual* is one who wants to take this identity concern to the next level by getting medical assistance to actually change his or her sex through hormone therapy and sex-reassignment surgery. And a *transvestite* is one who dresses in clothing that is the opposite of his or her biological sex. This term is no longer acceptable and has been replaced with the term *cross-dresser*.

DATING AGAIN

Please note that while some transgender people may use "tranny" to describe themselves, and you may be familiar with the term, others find it extremely offensive. However, in the title of this section, no offense intended, but it rhymed with "granny." If you want to learn the rules of what is correct in naming transgender people here's a link: https://www.glaad.org/reference/transgender

Yes, we live in a new world order, and it can be very confusing for older folks looking to date. Unlike the young children today who are taught all about various gender dysphorias, the old school often just knows "male" and "female." They may also be familiar with "gay" and "lesbian," but using common sense, older folks wouldn't expect a gay man or lesbian to be searching for straight people to date.

Do these definitions help? Not completely. After reading this section, I decided that I'm actually no longer a straight male. I think I now identify as a lesbian because I want to have sex with women. Oh, the confusion is boundless. The reality in today's dating world is that you could very possibly go on a date with a trans person. Taken to the highest level, you could fall in love with a transsexual person, get married, and never know it because the surgeries are rather sophisticated today.

For many older daters, this may not be palatable. For them, it's not a homophobic thing, it's just a matter of taste, tradition, and ... okay, for some it's a homophobic thing. Actually, are there really any sex phobias, like phobias to snakes and spiders? Is there such a thing as a heterophobe? Are all gay people heterophobes? Perhaps it is simply a preference. Just because you don't like something doesn't mean you are phobic. For example, some people don't like hotdogs. This doesn't make them hotdogophobic. They just likely prefer hamburgers.

Getting to the essence of a dating world with way more choices than we had years ago, one has to be aware that some surprises may pop up, as in you're making out with someone you thought was a woman only to find something... pop up.

The best way to avoid gender surprises in dating would be to make your preferences known. On your dating profile, you might want to add that "trans dating is okay." Notice that covers all trans people. Others might add "not interested in trans dating."

If you meet someone at a bar, a club, a dance, or any other venue, it's rather weird to ask the person you are interested in if he or she is "trans" anything. However, if you are averse to trans dating, you should broach the subject in a subtle manner. Perhaps a question about this person's genitals would serve you well. "So, how's your vagina feeling today?" Followed that up with "Was it ever a penis?" We all know those questions are not going to go over well. A better approach might be to ask to see some of his or her childhood photos. Oh, that's right, people probably don't carry these in their wallets.

The best way to find out if there is any gender dysphoria going on or the person is transgender is a frank discussion either on the first call, the first meeting, or the first date. This shouldn't be your first question, but somewhere during the conversation, you might bring up the subject of gender dysphoria. If they say, "What's that?" you are with a heterosexual who never reads the newspaper. By discussing gender dysphoria, it allows you to have a frank conversation that would likely reveal all you need to know about your new date.

While much of this matter has been discussed, tongue in cheek, gender dysphoria is a very serious issue. Many people struggle with their sexuality, and it can affect them in many serious ways. They need to be respected. Everyone needs to be respected, including heterosexuals.

Activity Suggestion – Describe how would you handle a surprise trans date. Would you be polite or hostile, respectful or indignant if you decided this wasn't for you?

35

HOW TO TELL IF YOUR DATE IS A SHREW OR A WIFE-BEATER

IT IS REALLY difficult to tell if a man or a woman you meet on an Internet dating site is *good*. "Good" here is meant to be all encompassing: honest, kind, thoughtful, conscientious, responsible, and you can include any other traits you can think of that mean "good." If you think a thumbnail-size photo and a self-description are indicators that you are finding someone who is good, you are being rather naive. It is your job to figure out *good* in your emails, texts, phone conversations, and finally on dates.

You must be rather discerning and make sure you don't let the fact that your date is cool, handsome/pretty, rich, employed, or any such traits that have nothing to do with *good* influence your decision to remain in the relationship. There are all sorts of telltale signs that we call red flags, which you often only see after the fact, once you are hurt by this person. As such, it is important to see these red flags early on and understand what they mean.

Some examples of red flags may be noted in how this person treats family. It is not uncommon for all of us to treat family members differently than *other* people. We often take family for granted and may even snap at family members in a way that we would never treat friends or strangers. People who are not good notoriously treat family members with disdain, contempt, and a lack of respect.

Now, you have to remember, sometimes family members deserve disdain, contempt, and no respect, but often the more negativity you find expressed by your date toward family members, the more likely you will be treated the same way once you become family (marry). You don't want to be in this kind of relationship with a *bad person*.

Another red flag is how often you argue with this person. If you argue a lot in the early stages of the relationship, you will very likely argue more as it moves forward. This, as you can imagine, is not a good thing.

Flirtatiousness is not usually a trait of a good person, unless his or her flirtatiousness is directed at getting a mate (you) and not for searching for the next mate while standing next to you. Those who are too flirty will very likely get responses that may easily lead to infidelity. Wouldn't you rather be with someone exhibiting some modesty rather than be married to the guy or gal who's always hanging all over everyone of the opposite sex?

Is frugality or cheapness a red flag? That could be a hard one to evaluate. If you are frugal, you will want to be with one who shares this trait. Even if you are not frugal, sometimes your date will be more likely to provide for your well-being in the long term. However, there are those who are not actually frugal but rather *cheap*, and that can be a bad trait, especially when they are also people who are not good. This type of person will often be rather controlling about all matters concerning money – and not a fun person to be with.

Take off your rose-colored glasses, and look for red flags. In most every retrospective of your failed relationships, there are many red flags that were ignored. If you catch them early, you may just save yourself from much aggravation and grief. The most important trait in anyone you have in your life is that of a *good heart*!

36

DO YOU WANT TO DATE A GUN-CARRYING GUY?

GUNS ARE VERY CONTROVERSIAL. Crime is rampant. But to condemn or fear someone who has a permit to carry a firearm is not warranted. If you find out that your date carries a gun, man or woman, don't freak out, unless you found out while exploring his or her underwear. Discuss the matter. If your date is a cop, no problem. You will be safer on this date than most others. If your date is a concerned citizen with a permit to carry a concealed weapon, and is trained in its use, and is not crazy, you should feel safe and appreciate that there are those out there willing to protect us all.

Some gun-carrying people have personality issues. They may have a complex about their ability to defend themselves. Others may have a fast temper or exhibit poor judgment. These people may not be the best to date. An easy test regarding temper and tolerance involves taking a ride with them and seeing how often they use their horn and curse at other drivers.

If your date carries a gun, don't be shy about discussing the matter. Often, you will find that your gun-toting date is a good person with a desire to protect family and friends. Go with it. You might even find that this person will pique your interest in understanding and knowing how to use various guns for self-protection. Just beware of bizarre people who carry a gun, exhibit odd behaviors, honk and curse relentlessly while driving places, or have a criminal record.

37

DO YOU INVESTIGATE BEFORE YOU MEET?

ACCORDING to Match.com Presents Singles in America, 48% of single women research a date on Facebook before the first date versus 38% of men. Many of these sleuths would cancel a date due to something found while researching their date. The idea of most commentary regarding searching dates is that it is sad and shallow. However, it is both fun and smart.

This is actually a serious subject. To best answer the question, "Do you research a prospective date?" think about this: would you like to know if this person is an ax murderer? We all know the answer to that question. Certainly! While you are not likely to meet ax murderers on Internet dating sites because there aren't enough to go around, you could meet other unsavory characters. If you have the heads-up, you can avoid much grief.

What types of things do you want to know about your date that you may be able to find online? An easy one is a criminal record. You don't want to date a host of ex-cons, like bank robbers, sex offenders, and that ilk. There are those who have served time for assault, embezzlement, tax evasion, and a multitude of crimes. Don't you think a guy who beats up people may have anger management issues that could affect your relationship? A tax cheat may also cheat on you. How about someone convicted of multiple DUIs? He or she is likely an alcoholic.

It's not snooping for snoop's sake. It's all about *protecting* yourself. If you wish to go through life believing in the good of humanity, go for it. But if you want a little help in spotting Mr. or Ms. Wrong, you should consider a background check, especially since it is so much easier to do with the Internet at your disposal.

We are no longer in Kansas, Toto. There are too many unsavory characters out there, and you most certainly deserve better than to be in danger when there are simple ways to know a little about your date *before* the first date.

Activity Suggestion – Google yourself. See what others may see. There are companies that specialize in "fixing" your online reputation, if necessary. Make sure there's not another person with your same name. If there is, make sure you mention it to clarify who you are.

38

AVOIDING THE GOLD-DIGGING DATE

WHILE MANY DATERS look for financial security (women more than men), or for domestic security (men more than women), they usually are willing to make a commitment once they find the security. The gold digger is looking for security in the most exaggerated manner.

The gold digger is an opportunist who is looking for the best deal at the moment. A dedicated gold digger will drop you if a better deal shows up. A gold digger is by definition the term associated with women, while men looking for financial security are more often described as kept men, dirt bags, or opportunists. Gold diggers come in all shapes and looks; however, to be a successful gold digger, the more beautiful, the better. Guys with a lot of money and little in the brain department are often looking for trophy girls to hang on their arms. The prettier the woman, the more money she will be able to attract and *extract*. The more money he has, the prettier the girl he will be able to attract and *shack*.

If you really don't care and are willing to pay for this type of woman, go for it. However, remember, everyone is thinking, "What is she doing with that nerd?" Recognize that if you aren't vigilant, and if she is really slick, you could lose a great deal of your money. Some gold diggers actually have an agenda and timetable: meet, marry, divorce, and move on with half of his money. This should be a warning to you that gold diggers are dangerous and need to be either avoided or limit their control over you. You decide what works for you depending on your bank accounts, abilities, wants, needs, and desires. Many guys fall for the charm and beauty and actually fall in love to the point that they meet all the demands of the gold digger. These guys get them jewels, vacations, clothing, and some even get expense accounts.

Identifying the gold diggers is not all that difficult once they attempt to convince you that there is absolutely no need for a prenuptial agreement when you start talking about marriage. The argument goes like this: "What, don't you trust me?" Ask Paul McCartney about how this works out.

The gold digger is very impressed with the kind of car you drive, your home, how you vacation, and how you dress and dine. After all, she plans on being with you on all of those vacations and she is certain you will want to have her dressing in the same manner as you. Realize that most women will be impressed with wealth, but the gold digger obsesses over it.

When gold diggers troll Internet dating sites, they look for men who post their earnings above the highest category ($150,000 plus on many sites). They are not looking for a fellow making $35,000 to provide them with security, even if your photos indicate that you own your own mobile home in a nice trailer park. While you could post that you make $35,000 to make sure you won't attract gold diggers, you may meet nobody unless a date wants to live in abject poverty.

Gold diggers don't just look at your salary posting. They look at your occupation. If you are a professional – that is, lawyer, doctor, or architect – there is a much better chance you will be contacted by a gold digger than if you are a teacher or a sales clerk. There are certain rules of life, fair or not, and one seems to state that pretty women do get the wealthy men. They often know they are beautiful, and they use that asset to get what they want. As cruel as that may sound, think about the reverse. A guy is very bright. He starts up an Internet company and makes a fortune. Yes, he, too, used his assets (brain) to get money and sex from a pretty woman just like she uses her looks to get his money.

You have to avoid becoming tainted by the fear of being used. There are really nice people out there who are not interested in your money, but be cautious. Try to find the good heart over the good looks or good net worth.

Activity Suggestion – Review your profile, and make sure you aren't flashing your wealth if you have wealth. (This assumes you don't want to use your wealth to attract really hot men and women.)

39

THE MEDICINE CABINET AND DATING

AND NOW FOR some more unusual dating advice that you won't find anywhere else. While mentioned before, this is a difficult topic and needs more discussion. Do you really want to know what health concerns your date has? Is it even ethical to snoop around and try to learn of potential problems? Can playing detective be a way to protect yourself from some serious illness? Would you want a serious relationship with someone who will be forever troubled by medical conditions? All of these questions are important for you to consider before you make a commitment.

The morality of snooping in your date's medicine cabinet to see if you can learn about his or her health condition is not defensible, nor is most snooping in general. However, what if you are dating someone who is putting you in jeopardy by not disclosing a contagious condition? Obviously, this person is not thinking about your safety, and that is a terrible moral lapse, too.

These are serious considerations, and only you can decide how you want to handle the matter. You also have to realize you may jump to conclusions that are entirely false. For example, you see a herpes medicine in your date's medicine cabinet and never realize it belongs to his or her roommate, cousin, or someone else. Maybe your date is doing clinical research on preventing herpes in the white-rat population. There may be a simple explanation that would still let you kiss without risk.

If you do wish to venture into this detective-like sleuthing, make sure you don't get caught. It will not bode well for the blossoming relationship. If you do find a trove of pill bottles, jot down the names (or take photos if you are tech savvy), and then when you are home, google each medicine to find out what may be going on. Some of the medications that could be of concern include antiviral medications (for herpes or AIDS), drugs for mental illness, and medications for chronic illnesses, like multiple sclerosis, arthritis, skin disorders, and cancer. Do you really want to live with someone with HIV, a serious mental illness, or chronic diarrhea? I think not.

As morally questionable as it is to snoop in this fashion, do note that we usually do more investigating on the cars, shampoos, and stereos that we buy than we do about the people with whom we are potentially going to spend the rest of our lives.

Now a bit of advice for all of you with medical infirmities that you do not wish to become known. Keep your medications in a safe place – not in your medicine cabinet.

40

BEWARE THE FRAUDULENT DATER

THERE ARE numerous articles written about fraudulent daters who post phony pictures that they stole on the Internet and then use to create a fictitious character. These jerks then contact as many women as they can over time and dupe them into giving them sex or money for one scheme or another. Notice that I said, "These jerks ... contact ... women." For some reason, most of these articles tell stories about men who take advantage of women, almost as if it never works the other way. Well, it does. There are women who do the very same thing. They get men to send them money, never to be heard from again. And sometimes you will never know the sex of the other person because they can pretend to be anyone necessary to scam you.

To understand the prevalence of such fraud, I quote an article in the October 2012 edition of *Glamour* that states in the title, "One in 10 Guys Dating Online Is a Fake." Wow! That's 10% if I did my math right – which I did. So, it's not such a remote possibility that you could be contacted by a fraud.

How about the women? This particular article didn't address that problem, probably because *Glamour* is a women's magazine and doesn't care about us guys. However, if you search for Internet sites promising to find you a wife, you will get a good idea about how incredibly prevalent that is as well.

You must be diligent, wise, and strong to resist these schemes because they are well thought out and can victimize even the savviest Internet dater. The forlorn and lonely are much more vulnerable to these schemes because they let their emotions override common sense. However, there are some signs to look for, and some rules to follow, to avoid becoming a victim of dating fraud.

First, let's look at the signs that may indicate your dream date is nothing more than a bad dream. These people usually live far away, even overseas in many cases. At least that's what they say; they may actually live nearby. The guys often claim to be in the military and tell you they are stationed somewhere around the world. This plays on your sense of patriotism and the possibility that you may admire a guy in uniform.

Frauds who claim to be living far away have a built-in excuse for not being able to meet you. There will come a time in this email/text/phone relationship that they will have a problem getting home – to see you – and they just need some money to buy a ticket. They were usually robbed or some such calamity befell them, and that's why they have no money to buy that ticket. "Why not use your credit card?" you ask. Nope, that was stolen during the robbery or break-in. They have the best excuses. Others include they need an operation, they have an amazing investment opportunity for you, or they inherited a large sum of money and need to hire a lawyer to get it out of probate. The stories are clever and varied.

So, what are the rules? It's not very complicated. There is really only one rule to avoid getting ripped off: never, ever send money to anyone you met on the Internet and have never met in person.

We all know there are frauds out there who do come to your home or who you do meet in everyday settings. If they scam you, at least you met them. If you were jilted by a phantom person, you'll feel rather terrible telling your story to a friend. "I trusted him because he said he loved me in a text message." Yes, that looks pretty stupid. It just goes to show how desperate we can get for a relationship.

There are websites you can go to if you suspect a fraud. Wait a moment! If you suspect a fraud, just get away. Stop communicating with this person. I know. You can't. You're in love! Okay, if you have to, check out this person at http://www.romancescams.com, or if they claim to be in the military, go to http://www.militarygear.com/asp to see if this guy scammed other women. You can also report the scammer to these sites and, even better, send a report to the FBI's website for Internet fraud at http://www.ic3.gov.

Here's a neat little trick that may help you in your Internet dating. There is a number embedded in every email that reveals where the sender's computer is located. It is called the IP address, and it may help you figure out that you are dealing with a predator or scammer. Information on how to find the country of origin of the computer you are communicating with can be found at http://www.iptrackeronline.com/header.php, including how to extract IP address information from someone's email. If someone tells you they are in Ohio, and yet his or her computer is in Nigeria, you've got a problem. For some odd reason (probably poverty and cunning), many of the scammers seem to emanate from Africa. You know, it's the same as the Nigerian prince who needs your bank account number to deposit his fortune that he will gladly share with you once he comes to America. Don't fall for it.

Try to avoid being stupid. If it's too good to be true ... it is! People that tell you they love you in a matter of weeks while never having met you are either scammers or losers. Stay away! Never share your social security number or bank account numbers with anyone online. Don't ever send nude photos to your new Internet lover. They can then blackmail you by threatening to post them all over the Internet unless you send them money. Just think before you do things that may get you into trouble.

For all you bad boys and girls who do this fraud, there are FBI agents and other agencies out to get you. If you're caught, you may be dating your cell mate for merely a sexual relationship that is not very meaningful. You know ... karma!

Activity Suggestion – Visit some websites that talk about romance scams to familiarize yourself with some real stories.

IV
ALL THE FISH IN THE SEA

41

WHAT ARE YOU LOOKING FOR?

THIS MAY JUST BE the most important question you have to ask yourself when embarking on the quest to find a date or mate. This question may be on par with "What is the meaning of life?" After all, you may find out you don't even want to date. Perhaps you feel pressured by friends and family to find a companion or lover. You may be eager to date, but you haven't yet decided what you are looking for. Pause for a moment to think about your own desires and needs. In finding a mate to live with *forever*, what does a prudent person want?

Companionship, which includes the broad umbrella of *communication and conversation* to allow for discourse, seems to be very important. But do you really need a companion? Many people get used to living alone and only want discourse on a limited basis. Men and women are from different planets, as we have been told, so their companionship needs differ greatly.

Some guys may find happiness being alone, and only put up with social discourse to get sexual intercourse at the end of the night. Yes, that's shallow, but you have to remember guys are wired differently.

Please, let's not discount that there are women out there who also prefer to be alone, and may only want to put up with us trolls, for a bit, just to get their sexual desires met.

You have to decide whether or not you are mate material. If all you want is sex, this will not likely lead you to a meaningful relationship, and that's okay as long as you are up-front with your dates. If all you want is a friend to talk to, make sure you state that up front, too. You have to decide if you prefer to be alone or in a relationship for companionship.

Sex is another desire, often important for relationships to be whole. In the physical world, there is a big overlap between *sexual fulfillment* and *physical contact*. We separate sex as an individual want, need, and desire because it is so very important for some, but it is best described within the broad category of physical contact.

Physical contact is a basic human need; this includes everything from the simple handshake to the highest form of physical relationship, which, as we all know, is the proctologic exam. Oops, I mean sexual intercourse.

Since physical contact is such an important need for many, yet a nonissue for others, it is imperative to make sure you are compatible with your new mate regarding frequency of physical contact. How often will you have sex? How long will you spend cuddling after sex? How often will you cuddle without sex? How often and how long will you hug? As odd as it seems to quantify such activities, if you and your mate are on different pages, there will be tension, frustration, and conflict because you may not be *compatible*.

It has become rather common in modern America for men to be able to find sex for sex's sake. While women don't generally use the services of male prostitutes, they, too, can get into plenty of physical relationships because there are lots of horny guys out there. However, for anyone who desires regular sex and physical contact that is more than just the physical, it will be necessary to have a *real relationship* with someone who has similar desires. Yes, you should thrive on conversation with this mate before *and* after sex.

All the great conversation in the world won't help if you expect to have a great physical relationship and later find out your mate has very little libido and only used sex to catch you. You could get frustrated by this new relationship as it turns stale (a.k.a. sexless).

Just as important is the disappointment you will have in a relationship born of lust that soon turns pale in the light of having nothing to say to one another after the act.

The importance of finding a compatible mate with regard to physical and social desires can't be overemphasized. Hopefully, during the dating process you will learn more about your new mate and figure out what works and what doesn't.

Cooking is a skill that is the basis for the saying, "The way to a man's heart is through his stomach." Hopefully your cardiac surgeon didn't say this. Keep in mind, people also said, "A diamond is a girl's best friend," and "A dog is man's best friend." What the hell do they know?

While cooking is an important skill, it's much less important than in generations past. Today we get the finest foods prepared for us with a trip to a store or a restaurant. Generally speaking, having a mate who's a good cook is a *guy thing*, unless you ladies are looking to snag an Iron Chef of some sort.

Security has a lot more to do with the *diamond* quote above and is a good attribute in a mate. Security can be broken down into physical security, as in wealth to provide for necessities, and psychological security, as in being there to deal with difficult times.

Commitment is a much-desired quality to find in a mate — unless that's not what you're looking for. With true love, can you expect your mate to stand by your side? You might want to ask yourself a companion question: For how long?

Will I ever find anyone who would be there for me if I had a sudden illness requiring a caregiver relationship? At first glance, you may not realize the importance of this concern. How would you like to be with your new mate for a year or so, get married, and become ill? How many dates, and how deep does the relationship have to be, before you can expect this significant other to stay by your side?

We all know that if you go on just one date with someone and then have a stroke, they are not likely to take care of you for the rest of your life. More likely, they'd be out the door in a hurry.

What is realistic to expect of a mate? Let's face it: there are some people who abandon their marriage oath of many years and jump ship at the slightest provocation. Others recognize the commitment to their significant others and stand by their sides through thick and thin.

I think it is reasonable for a mate to jump ship if the other party has a catastrophic event while they are still in the discovery phase of the relationship – like after around 700 dates. Actually, until one makes a verbal and written commitment, as in the formal marriage vow, it should not be unexpected that some will leave when adversity strikes. After all, while it would be nice to have that level of devotion, most people will choose to move on to find what they are looking for, and let you go your way.

Loyalty, trust, honesty, and integrity fill out the list of needs. So it seems that there are just 10 needs in a mate. Oh, I almost forgot. You want someone who is *sane*, as noted in an earlier chapter. Yes, sanity should be a very important item on your list. Now that you know what you're looking for, don't you feel relieved? Oh, by the way, if you are lonely, but really don't want or don't belong in a real relationship, consider getting a dog.

Activity Suggestion – List all of your wants, needs, and desires in a relationship in order of importance. Are there any you couldn't do without?

42

LOVE AT FIRST SIGHT

LOVE at first sight is a romantic notion, and one that some are fortunate to find. You may feel good about someone from the moment you meet, but unless it's a chemical *explosion*, it's not going to be at the same level as love at first sight.

I posit that love at first sight and chemistry are in general made up of both lust and the heart – both sex and emotion – with sex being the stronger component of the thing we call chemistry for men, while emotion is the stronger component for women.

Many relationships are lopsided, where one experiences love at first sight, while the other sees nothing and would never pursue the relationship. When love at first sight isn't mutual, a relationship could be clouded with subtle cracks that allow it to fall apart for no apparent reason. And when things that made for the initial chemistry fade, it is not likely that your lover is going to tell you he or she is not really that into you out of either a wish to be kind to you or a lack of understanding about how the relationship went sour.

The lucky ones are those who truly experience love at first sight and the feeling is mutual. They are using two extreme forces to bind them together – the *emotion*/heart and the *sex*/lust – which makes up the very strong glue of relationships.

The third component that makes up relationships has to do with *reason*. What are some of the reasons people get into relationships? Oh, there are so many reasons, but the big ones are for money, prestige, dependency, sex, companionship, security, leaving a bad situation, and the list goes on.

For those who enter into relationships using nothing more than reason (the brain), they are often doomed to frustration and break up over time if the reason for being in the relationship disappears. Everyone knows that if you marry only for money (a good reason if you want to live a rich life) and the money is gone, your relationship falls apart.

It's all about balance. You need sound reasons, combined with emotion and sex – that is, chemistry – and a whole lot of "other things" for relationships to work out. You may even want to include luck.

43

DATING THE CREAM OF THE CROP

THIS SECTION IS NOT a treatise on dating farmers or the farmer's daughter. Here, *cream of the crop* refers to the best dates in terms of various important traits.

Most everyone would like to date the best people out there, especially if they have the intention of moving the dating relationship toward something more involved, like living together or getting married. So how does one find, and then attract, the cream of the crop?

There is an old saying, "You've got to be a friend to have a friend." And the same holds true with most things in life. If you want to date the cream of the crop, you have *to be* the cream of the crop, or at least you have to have a whole lot of money to find the *materialistic* "cream" looking for the *wealthy* "crop."

When on Internet dating sites, you get to see many, many photos of potential dates. If you look closely with an analytical mind, you will notice that there are many great disparities between the ages of some of these people and the way they look in their photos. Let's, for a moment, assume that all of these men and women on dating sites are being honest about their ages (though they are often not). You have to realize that there may be a host of folks who look anywhere from their stated age to many years older or younger. Why is this so?

It's all about *genes* and *lifestyle* and plain old *style*. If you look at those who look many years younger than their stated age, you will notice that they have great skin (few wrinkles) normal body weight (not overweight, fat, obese, or morbidly obese), and great style, the one factor that can be relatively easily controlled compared to all the others.

Let's face it: it's not always easy to control our weight, especially if we came from an obese family where we learned terrible eating habits and have a genetic tendency toward being heavy. Sure, there are those who have fought and won the battle of the bulge, but it is not easy and may always be a challenge. If you want to date the cream of the crop, you must get control of your weight with a combination of proper eating (most important) and exercise (yeah, go on a treadmill for an hour and burn enough calories to eat 1.275 Oreo cookies).

With regard to your skin, if you spent your youth sunning to the point that you looked great every summer with that bronze tan, by the time you get into your forties and above, your skin is mostly shot, unless your genetics are sun-damage resistant. By now, you can consider various skin remedies to make yourself more marketable. These include skin resurfacing with various peels (medical peels being the most effective, costly, and uncomfortable). More radical considerations include laser treatment (with a real laser, not the light-pulsed kind that does next to nothing), and a full facelift if you really want to take your appearance to a new level. But be careful. You could turn yourself into a freaky Michael Jackson or Joan Rivers look-alike if you try too hard to look young.

The most universal and easiest way to make yourself a cream-of-the-crop dating candidate is to engage in some style changes. Go back and look at the photos of all the frumpy, old-looking folks trying to find a mate on dating sites, and you will notice that they are mostly out of touch with style. They have hairdos from the fifties, clothing from the same era, and a face graced with eyeglasses that look like they were stolen from the Smithsonian.

How hard is it to get a style makeover? It's really not that hard. You find people with great style and ask for help. This can often be done by asking the salespeople in the many department stores you visit to buy clothing and makeup.

Hairdos are probably the most obvious flaw and the easiest to remedy if you are willing to make the commitment. You may have to learn, and practice, how to make your hair look great, but it is doable, and this is where you should begin. If you are a woman and your hair is falling out, you may want to consider hormone therapy, a weave, or a wig.

Hair issues are a concern for guys just as much as ladies. The men with hair half gone might do better with a hairpiece, a weave, transplants, or just going bald for that special look. You know, the macho, penis-head look that seems to attract women much more than the comb-over of years past.

Once you make yourself look nicer and younger and more like the *cream* you are seeking, the better your chance of attaining your goal – dating the cream of the crop. Of course, if you are lactose intolerant, cream may be a poor idea.

Remember, dating is not all about looks – far from it. The most important attribute in a loving and successful relationship is a good heart. However, before you will have any chance of winning over your next true love with all of your fine qualities, the first thing he or she sees is that little thumbnail photo that allows us to say yes, no, or maybe. Make sure you stay in the game with a nice appearance.

Activity Suggestions – Look in the mirror and take an appearance inventory. When was the last time you changed your hairstyle? When was the last time you got new glasses? How modern is your clothing? Could your teeth use a cosmetic makeover? Is your hair color fading and making you look old?

44

COGNITIVE DISSONANCE

COGNITIVE DISSONANCE CAN BE SIMPLY DEFINED as a state in which the mind is in conflict. It actually goes deeper than that, but at this stage in your life, you need to keep things *simple*, because your mind is ... in conflict. So let *conflict* define it for now. It's time to explore things that may induce cognitive dissonance as life happens.

While on a coffee date, I realized that my eyes drifted toward every attractive woman who happened along. Knowing this is rude behavior, I made a concerted effort to stop the gazing and completely avoid gawking over these unusually attractive women who were probably sent as a test of my integrity.

There seems to be a rule of dating, the *universal law of negativism*, that states *there are no attractive people around when you are alone and looking for one, and conversely, when you are on a date, there are many beautiful people who gravitate to where you happen to be, no matter where you are in the universe.* Furthermore, *the number and beauty of these godly creatures are inversely proportional to the looks of the person you are with at that moment.* That means the more ordinary the person you are sitting with, the more incredible looking those strolling by.

This doesn't always happen, but I believe many of you know there is some truth to this observation. The last time it happened to me, I was with an attractive woman in her late fifties. She was very young looking, and only my keen observational skills led me to see through the Gestalt of her youthful appearance. I had just turned 60 and was lucky that I had such a hot date in such good shape. Why, then, was I staring at, and longing for, those women walking by who were entirely too young for me?

While this may sound trite and egotistical, it is something many of you will experience. It is simple to explain. It doesn't matter how old you are; your taste for fine things doesn't decline as you age. I don't know of many elderly people who suddenly develop a taste for Thunderbird wine, cheap costume jewelry, and black-velvet pictures to hang in the living room.

This doesn't make you a *bad* person. It means you are a *real* person. And when it comes to admiring the aesthetics of the opposite sex, you will be no different.

Wanting and getting is where the problem arises. You can want that young gorgeous thing, but the reality of you getting him or her, and having a good life, is rather slight. No young gorgeous gal or guy wants an old worn-out mate.

You can have an intimate sexual encounter with a Victoria Secret-like model anytime you want, as long as you are willing to pay for it. Women, too, can find gigolos to service them if they so desire. But buying sex isn't a relationship of substance.

Why would you want a wild time in bed with no attachment, no obligation, and limited financial risk with a man or woman whose job it is to tell you how great you are, when you can have the intimacy of a partner willing to have sex with you on an infrequent schedule when it won't interfere with his or her physical or mental state, which could be strained by a bad day at the office, headache, hormonal imbalance, a day at the spa, or the possibility of messing up hair and makeup? Even if all the planets are aligned, and you do have sex, you may wonder if it was worth the hassle after your orgasm is over.

Now I think you have a clearer understanding of cognitive dissonance, and it is real. If you just came off a bad marriage or romance – no matter how you lost your mate, whether to death, divorce, or adultery – your state of mind is not good. You have many questions about whether or not you ever want to get married again.

Do you really want *commitment* when that term sounds very much like you are getting *committed*, and we all know what that means? Is solitude all that bad? Does the essence of relationships predict a natural decline?

You see so many miserable couples out there in restaurants, at the mall, everywhere. The ones in love are usually the younger set who have not had the time to see their relationships fester, or the newly formed relationships when everyone is on their best behavior. You will see it with dating. When the relationship is new, there is an exceptional desire to be together and treat each other with love and passion.

Can passion last? Thinkers from every field of study know what the *honeymoon phase* is all about. It is real, and it doesn't last. Should you just date many people and thereby have little chance to burn out each relationship?

Many of those in romantic relationships that don't get to see each other every day, state that the lovemaking is grand, and the respect and treatment of each other border on wonderful. Just talking on the phone can be a turn-on during the romantic phase of a relationship.

When you see your love interest every day, do you take each other for granted? I think the answer is, too often, yes. Sure, there are those whose relationships remain romantic forever, but sadly, I really don't think that's the norm.

As you date, be practical about who you can get, and how the relationship should realistically mature. If you have a lot of money, you may easily get a person out of your league of cool. As soon as the money is gone, or your partner decides to move on for more money, you get dumped. That really isn't a great relationship for most, but if it makes you happy, go for it.

A good long-lasting relationship takes a great deal of work, grounded in communication, understanding, compassion, and compromise. Getting counseling in these areas may be something you should consider.

Do you settle? Good question. You'll be in a state of greater cognitive dissonance if you do. However, while waiting for Mr. or Miss Right, the one who fulfills your every want and need, you may find yourself waiting forever. You may pass up some very good mates for the one that is elusive. On the other hand, if you are fussy and lucky, you may get that almost-perfect person to spend the rest of your life with until death, demonic possession, or divorce do you part.

Most will notice that when looking at the photos on Internet dating sites, chemistry is a very real phenomenon. Most people can look at a little picture and immediately know if there is an attraction.

I'm not suggesting that looks are the only important thing about dating, because they are most certainly not. However, why waste your time on calls and dates with people you don't feel that chemistry with when you look at their pictures?

Recognize that if you are really fussy, you may never find the right person, especially if you look like a toad and are requesting dates from the best of the best. But go for it, and try to get the best you can.

I felt sorry for one woman who emailed me on a dating site and asked rhetorically why no one responds to her letters. She was a doctor and had great credentials, but she wasn't terribly attractive – yet nothing a makeover couldn't fix. I could see why she may not be getting a ton of hits. Then there are those who are so hot that they get hit on all the time.

It is best to try to maintain some level of realism when seeking connection with those on dating sites. Know your league and stick to it. If you want to reach for brass rings, expect disappointment and realize you may never find anyone. But, who knows? You may just get lucky!

Activity Suggestions – What things in your dating life cause cognitive dissonance? How would you rate your attractiveness from 1 to 10? What are you looking for in a partner from 1 to 10? If these numbers are too far off, you may not be successful in dating and be suffering from cognitive dissonance.

45

THE OBLIVIOUS NATURE OF SOME PEOPLE

I'M NOT sure if it is obliviousness, deceit, or poor judgment, but I had a woman send me a flirt and when I looked at her profile, she indicated that she is "stunning."

You have to remember, on some dating sites, they give you a *checklist* of choices to describe yourself. It goes something like this: under "Looks" you have choices – average, good-looking, very good-looking, stunning. Now with this particular woman, I guess she wasn't sure what to write, since they didn't have a closer match for her, like a zombie, a weirdo, or someone just plain vanilla ugly.

It is disconcerting to see how many people misrepresent themselves when it comes to their own description. What was she thinking? That prospective dates are never going to notice her picture clearly doesn't define one who is stunning? Does she not know what stunning means? Is she oblivious to reality? Is she flat-out lying? Does she hope we won't notice that she is far from stunning? And finally, does she think she'll catch a blind guy by using this ruse?

I don't have an answer, though I wish I did. I wish I knew how to tell these people what they are doing wrong before they brood over having no one contact them month after month. They should be told that they are not representing themselves realistically.

With a picture, it's easy to tell those who are living in a peculiar reality, but what about the ones who say they are *caring* yet they set cats on fire?

I don't have an answer to any of these questions. I guess we have to test the waters and abandon ship when we realize we picked an oddball.

Here's a suggestion that may help all of us e-daters. Try to be honest, and when you have to make a description, maybe even reverse exaggerate. Yes, if you are stunning, say you are good-looking and surprise all of us out there with a refreshing dose of humility.

46

POOR GIRL, RICH GIRL

DATING a poor girl can be a double-edged sword. Generally speaking, the poor gal will appreciate everything you do for her. She will be happy on *any* vacation because she is not used to ... *any* vacation. A night on the town to a fancy dinner will just about guarantee great sex that evening and forever more. A poor gal will likely put you on a pedestal and think you are very special for treating her so nicely. Things like bringing her flowers and candy she considers heartfelt, even if the flowers are daisies and the candy is half of a 3 Musketeers bar. Do know that if you are just as poor as her, none of this applies.

The double-edged sword comes to play when this gal smiles. You notice she's missing a few teeth, and those that remain are green and yellow. Conversations may be somewhat shallow when she wants to tell you all about the latest episodes of daytime television.

Contrast this poor gal with the prima donna rich gal. Interestingly the prima donna doesn't even have to be rich. She just needs to have rich tastes and be on a mission to get those tastes satisfied. The vacation you have in mind for her better be top-notch. The gifts have to be worthy of her station in life. If she is really rich, and not just wannabe rich, you may have trouble finding gifts that she likes because she has so much already. Basically, it is very difficult to make this woman excited about anything material because she already enjoys the finest things in life. She will be the one on that pedestal, and it will be hard to meet her there unless you can shower her with stuff.

There are wonderful poor girls out there that could make you happier than any rich gal. There are rich girls out there who are anything but material and would make wonderful wives. The problem is, that in a very material-oriented society, both of these wonderful types are not readily found. They are gems that need to be mined in the world of dating.

47

ARE ALL SINGLE WOMEN HORNY?

WHEN MEN, who still have intact libidos, enter the dating game after a long marriage, they may be in for a pleasant surprise. Many of the women they meet actually want to have a lot of sex. This is a foreign concept for some previously married men. You see, if they had such women in their lives when they were married, there's a good chance they wouldn't have gotten divorced and be forced to experience this kind of unexpected bliss. There are very few couples who have mutually great sex that then get divorced.

Remember, this appetite for sex found in single women is not universal, but Darwin's theories are definitely in play. Women who have no interest in sex are not likely to be found in this pool of Internet-dating candidates. Women who were in marriages where sex issues were the reason their marriages failed – and if they are smart, or shall we say cunning – know that sex is an important part of snagging a new guy.

This interest in sex doesn't mean these women are going to jump your bones on the first date. To the contrary, many will hold off for a few dates before committing to a physical relationship. This is probably very smart on their part. It eliminates the juvenile guy who is trying to bed as many women as he can, as if he were a sophomore in college. It also allows a chance for both of you to decide if you have any feelings for each other.

Usually, a guy isn't going to go back for more dates if he doesn't feel chemistry, even though he may sleep with the woman if she is willing to participate early on. On the other hand, most women need to have some feelings for the guys they date before sleeping with them.

How many dates should you need before you enter into the physical realm of the dating process? This is a very personal question that each individual has to answer for him or herself. There are those who have old-fashioned values who hold off on sex until they enter into marriage. The other extreme is those who have sex on the first date.

If you are modern in your values, you can expect to have a *sexual encounter of the first kind* in two to five dates. This question is explored much more thoroughly in Chapter 5 in the section on "First Sex," so go there if you haven't already read it.

I have heard about women who hold off for four or five dates before offering a kiss. That kind of behavior could define someone who is just friends, cautious, smart, or *frigid*. These slow-starter women can be fun, attractive, and nice (a really good combination of characteristics). You can take your chance with this type of woman and hope she turns out to be very experienced, great in bed, and horny all the time. You just never know.

That brings us to the title of this section, "Are All Single Women Horny?" Is being horny only used to catch us guys, followed by the eventual abduction of our being into the throes of holy matrimony? Or are these women going to be *horny in marriage*, something that I actually think of as an oxymoron? Other women have sex early on in the relationship and then hold off once they are married. Yeah, just what the typical guy is looking for.

There are women out there that are really interested in *casual sex*. I shall term this a *sexual encounter of the second kind*. If you've been paying attention, a few paragraphs back I mentioned sexual encounters of the first kind. The sexual encounter of the first kind is what most would describe as a *normal sexual relationship*.

Casual-sex women are a bit wild. They are usually very experienced and uninhibited. This type of woman, who I shall term a *man-eater*, is great in bed and will wear out all but the most robust of men. Unless you are Hercules (or a porn star), you may not actually be able to see this type of woman too many days in a row, or you'll literally run out of juice. Early on, you may think you've died and gone to heaven, but if you are an older divorcee or widower, and you try to keep up with this type of woman, you may actually die and go to heaven (a nice way to go if you have to go).

While all single women in the dating game seem to be horny to some extent, and even discounting their use of sex as a means to marriage, there is the forbidden-fruit or honeymoon effect at play in the dating scene that may account for much of this horniness.

Often the older dating woman isn't jumping into bed with every guy to come down the pike, so when she finds one she likes, it is a treat. And with all the societal taboos baby boomers experienced, sex with this new guy can be very exciting. Add to this excitement the fact that dating is for fun, and you have a nice atmosphere for sex. It's not like your marriage where you have taken each other for granted and sex is relegated to special occasions. After all, in too many marriages, doing the wash and dishes and fixing things around the house take precedence over passion, sex, and relaxation.

48

RICH GUY, POOR GUY

JUST LIKE THE RICH GIRL, poor girl issues, guys have the same baggage. With rich guys, many are womanizers. They have everything, and they are often egotistical and narcissistic. Men like this look at dating as a conquest and are often interested in one thing ... and it ain't you, and it ain't even just sex. They are often rich because they run successful businesses and remain married to their work. If you do marry one of them, he will usually not be present much of the time, other than while in bed, sleeping, or making love. That doesn't make for a good marriage.

Do great rich guys exist? Certainly. It is just hard to find them. Look for the red flags. Does he engage with you when you are together, or is he always doing other things? Does he show appreciation for you and all that you bring to the table, or is he looking for a reliable sex partner?

How about the poor guys? Like the poor gals, they will generally appreciate much more that life has to offer outside the material world. They will usually spend more time with you and prop you up on that pedestal. The downside is that they may not be able to buy you that pedestal. They may not be compatible in so many other ways, including their lack of teeth as well as a host of social graces.

Great rich guys and poor guys do exist. However, they are hard to find. The consequences of picking someone out of your class – and, yes, we do have various classes – may be disastrous. Keep your eyes open and try to find the perfect match that you can stay with, till death do you part.

Activity Suggestions – Hey, rich guy, what are your motives for dating? Do you do you state your intentions up front? Hey, poor guy, are you ready for dating? Do you have responsibilities in your life you need to address before adding someone else to the mix?

49

ARE ALL SINGLE MEN HORNY (A.K.A. LECHERS)?

YES! Some topics in the greatest pieces of world literature are meant to be short and to the point. However, I realize you need more elaboration on this topic than a simple yes, so let's explore the nature of the beast/lecher.

Ninety-nine percent of all pornography is bought by men. Ninety-nine percent of all prostitution is men procuring women. That should tell you something about the lecherous nature of men. However, those stats are exaggerations to get across the point that men are more into all things sexual. Women watch porn, too, especially today as they try to be more like men in the bedroom.

There are several types of men, and it is important for you women to determine which one you are dealing with at any particular moment if you want to be successful in your quest for a mate. The faster you determine your date is a lecher, the sooner you can move on to a better catch.

Depending on what you are looking for, you need to know if there is any compatibility with this potential mate. It's not always easy, since some of the traits of each type can be intertwined and hidden under the surface of the actions you see.

If you are looking for a friend or companion and have no interest in sex, you need the same type of guy. This means you should limit your search to men who are over 90 or dead. There are men who are not interested in sex, but they are hard (strike *hard*) ... difficult to find in younger age groups. Men who have no interest in sex are usually impotent and fearful of sexual relations. As such, they are not usually looking for dates that might lead to the bedroom. That doesn't mean they are not out there. They are, but more likely they are found in the older set looking for companionship.

The fear of sex may be related to health issues for some men, who have had bouts of heart disease, prostate problems, or other health concerns that make them fearful of performing or fearful of dying while trying to perform. This thought should be a wake-up call for guys to take better care of themselves when they are young. Pass this information on to your children.

One woman related to me how many of the men where she lives are retired, lustful, and on Viagra. This is a dangerous combination, resulting in obnoxious men who suddenly feel like Zeus and want to go around and bonk every woman they can.

One rather wealthy guy was so bold that upon first meeting this woman, he told her, "I want women to fuck and suck me." Nice way to start a relationship! That type of guy is fine if all you want is sex. Guys like this may even take you out on a really nice date if they have money and aren't cheap. I don't want to be judgmental (actually, I do), but in that type of relationship, you will not likely be the one-and-only unless you are really hot and offer this narcissist something he can't get from others.

There are some guys out there that are very dependent on a marriage relationship. They can be caught relatively quickly if you hit it off. This type of guy is usually more traditionally value oriented and is not looking to date 50 women. Once he realizes you're the one, he'll pop the question. He will like sex to whatever degree he did before, and you can expect a relatively stable relationship with little likelihood of him straying if you play your cards right. (Double down on two aces, where aces represent his erections; actually, *going down* is a better term in this poker metaphor.)

Then there's the guy who's not ready to settle down because of any number of reasons. If he was jilted in his previous marriage, he may be gun-shy – from shooting his ex. This guy may be afraid to make a commitment. Or, he may have financial issues that make him shy away from another commitment.

Sex could be normal with this guy, or it may be difficult for him to perform if his previous marriage had issues that related to badgering, dominance, or cheating on the part of his spouse. This guy could be vulnerable, and if you are nurturing, you may help him get back to normalcy, as well as into commitment.

Performance issues, as noted, keep some men out of the game, while others will do the best they can. If you really like a guy, you should be supportive and understand that it is difficult for some men to perform when they just went through such a difficult time. These guys are not lechers; to the contrary, they are extremely vulnerable. This proves not all men are lechers after all. If you can help give a man in this situation confidence, he could be very loyal to you.

There are those who don't want to commit because they are having too much fun dating. Years ago, dating wasn't as much fun as it is today. Back then, to have sex you may have had to get married. That's right, in the Dark Ages, sex was taboo and reserved for those who were married. And, boy, was that a strong incentive to get married.

Today, so many women are giving away the milk (that is an old-fashioned metaphorical reference to women being cows for sale): "Why buy the cow when you can get the milk for free?" I don't think those who dreamed up this saying were carnivores because they totally disregarded the steaks and chops – that is, they didn't seem interested in the meat.

In summary, when you ask if all men are lechers, the answer is not a simple yes, but rather just most of them, with active sex drives and no erectile issues.

Activity Suggestions – How much time in a given week do you devote to watching pornography? Do you think you have a problem? If your gal is turned off by pornography, will that bother you? How often would you like to engage in sex? If sex is withheld, would you seek a new partner?

50

COMPROMISE AND COMPATIBILITY: THE CONTROLLER

PEOPLE in the dating stage don't usually think much about control issues with their new mates, because they are in heat, having great sex, and are more concerned with making their new partners happy so they won't leave.

For many married people, years go by without any issues about being controlled, until the impending divorce. Then, the therapist or the close friend decides for one of the partners that he or she was controlled, and he or she embraces this reason as the cause of all the tumult in the marriage. I suppose it also helps in getting a better divorce settlement if a spouse can convince some family court judge that he or she was a *victim* who had been *controlled* throughout the marriage, causing him or her to be unfaithful and become a drug-using alcoholic.

Since you are now dating and should plan ahead as to whether or not this mate is a controller, we will explore some of the issues that will not come up until you are married ... again, when you realize this person wasn't the perfect match you thought he or she was while you were in heat.

Let's look at the couple that is not in heat but is, rather, on the threshold of divorce and trying to reconcile with the help of a therapist. Most therapists tell couples in treatment that *compromise* is needed for any relationship to work. This subject tends to come up in therapy when one partner complains that the other is a controller.

When people date, they seem to think of all the shallow things first, like chemistry and material things, like the cars they drive and the houses where they live, instead of issues like personality traits and the character of the individuals they're dating. It's not that shallow interests have no place in relationships. You most certainly do need chemistry, and if you ignore the material stuff, you could end up having a blissful relationship in a trailer park that airs on a reality show. Not what you're looking for? I didn't think so.

This stuff is important to understand, so pay close attention. The concepts noted below are going to provide you with the basis for happiness, but they are the most often ignored, neglected, or misunderstood aspects of relationships.

What is a controller? It's the person who wins most arguments in a relationship and makes the most decisions. For you see, all people want to do things their way. Most people think they are right and want to do what they want to do. That's only normal. After all, who thinks what they want to do is stupid or bad? Only a schizophrenic with dual personalities has a fight with himself over what to do each day.

While everyone has needs, wants, and, desires, if your needs, wants, and desires are not the same as your mate's, there is conflict, resulting in the controller winning and getting his or her way. If the controller tends to get his or her way all or most of the time, the other person, the controllee (not a real word) feels discounted and without a *voice* (another term you will hear when you are in therapy).

The therapist remedies this imbalance of differences by suggesting compromise like this: "Try for 50-50, where each of you wins half of the time." While this is, by definition, the ultimate nice way to compromise, it inherently means that both people in this relationship will be frustrated and do things they don't want to do any of the time they disagree with their partner.

What does this tell you? It says life in a relationship can really suck if you have to compromise and thereby be frustrated doing things you don't want to do for *half of your life*. That alone can make staying single pretty inviting.

You don't have to have a life filled with compromise and frustration if you do just two things. The first thing is pretty simple. Find yourself someone with whom you are very compatible. This means if you are not a dog person, don't hitch up to a dog person. If you are a night owl, find a night owl. You get the point, so I don't have to go through a hundred of these little examples. If you are sure of what you want in life, this should not be a problem for you. This way, you live with someone with whom you are highly compatible, and there is less chance either of you will have to compromise. If you pick right, you should have a much better than 50-50 chance of enjoying your life.

The other thing is not so simple. Try to find someone who not only wants but also *needs* to be controlled. What could make for a happier life than to live with someone who loves to do everything you want to do? What, that doesn't sound good to you? You may think this is absurd, but it is not. Just ask a few people you know who live with control issues.

I know what you're thinking: *opposites attract*. And, yes, they do. Are they happy? I don't really know, but whoever gave us that quotation had an obligation to let us know the statistics for divorce of all those opposites compared to those who pick compatible mates.

Compatibility is the real secret to successful relationships! Meet someone who likes everything you like, and you have a fighting – or, shall we say, peaceful – chance at a good relationship. Because finding Mr. or Ms. Compatico is very difficult, and because you may never agree on everything, you still do need to learn compromising skills as part of having a great relationship. It is not compromise that makes a great relationship as much as it is finding your compatible soul mate!

Activity Suggestions – Do you like to take control, or do you appreciate someone else making all the decisions? Ask the same question about each of the following situations: money issues, sex, house decorating, housekeeping, grooming, social events, and vacations choices. List five things that must be a part of your life or you would be miserable. How many of these things would you be able to compromise to keep a relationship going?

51

DESIRABLE TRAITS: PICKING THE PERFECT MATE

WITH ALL THE talk about first kisses and first sex, we may have overlooked the need to find the right person to kiss and have sex with. You need to find the person with all the desirable traits you want in a mate.

Desirable traits are a personal thing. However, there are some universal traits you may want to consider in your new mate. If you have trouble relating to many of these good traits, you may just be a poor candidate for a relationship.

When you read a well-written profile, you will find all the desirable traits that are supposed to help you find eternal bliss. Since it is my job to guide you, I already went through those good profiles, read all the traits, did a complete analysis, and now offer them to you at no additional charge.

Keep in mind that people exhibit good traits most often when they are on good behavior during the courting process. Even the not-so-bright Internet daters know that they have to be on their best behavior in order to make a catch. It's up to you to see through the phony people out there and look into the heart of the one you want to spend the rest of your life within a sound, grounded relationship.

The typical application forms you have to fill out from the various e-dating companies have check boxes for you to enter your traits, which are then posted under your profile. This helps you, and others, find the perfect mate, who may exhibit certain traits that you and they find desirable.

The following are many of the traits that good candidates list on their profile pages, along with my interpretation of the possible underlying truths, noted in parentheses: *adventurous* (irresponsible), *artistic* (starving artist), *conservative* (dull and uninteresting), *clean cut* (not very stylish), *earthy* (hippie who forgets to bathe), *easygoing* (semicomatose), *flexible* (practices yoga and is good in bed), *open-minded* (willing to try anything; i.e., irresponsible, but possibly great in bed), *eccentric* (belong in an inpatient facility, but due to modern laws we let them wander the streets talking to themselves), *flamboyant* (show-off exhibitionist), *flirtatious* (slut), *playful* (slut), *friendly* (lonely), *kind* (sucker), *high energy* (has ADHD or possibly is a methamphetamine addict), *humorous* (village idiot), *intellectual* (dull know-it-all), *low maintenance* (liar), *sensitive* (complainer), *nurturing* (like to have their breasts suckled; however, more likely by an infant than you), *loving* (slut), *outgoing* (hooker), *practical* (cheapskate), *quiet* (a bore), *shy* (a bore), *romantic* (predator), *self-confident* (narcissistic sociopath), *serious* (no fun), *responsible* (no fun), *simple* (think Simon), *sophisticated* (braggart), *worldly* (prostitute), *spiritual* (atheist in denial), *talkative* (has ADHD or possibly is a lunatic), *unconventional/free-spirited* (ex-convict).

I hope you are getting the idea. You see, if you look at the italicized traits noted above and don't recognize that there is the possibility of underlying meanings, you may get burned.

While this list of traits is actually what you will find on Internet dating sites, and the parentheses are in jest, there is often truth in humor. Some of these hidden meanings are not so far from the truth when it comes to some individuals. Keep this in mind when searching and choosing those you wish to meet. Remember, people sometimes check off what they think others want, and they themselves may be nothing like what they indicate on their profiles.

Besides the personality traits noted above, there are some undesirable traits the dating sites throw into the mix. I find it hard to believe that anyone would actually include these traits offered online in their profiles. Maybe it's really a test or a secret code for those "in the know."

Whenever people include negative traits in their profiles, you know they must be deranged, and you should avoid them at all costs. Things like argumentative (nasty), compulsive (those who will never let you go even if you want them to), high maintenance (gold digger), procrastinating (i.e., he or she never calls, so forget this one), and stubborn (ornery) are just a few of the negative traits that some people actually put in their profiles. You may want to avoid these people like the plague.

If you don't see the negativity in those kinds of traits, then even you can find a match among the losers of the Internet-dating world. Again, please take note of the hidden meanings in parentheses.

Trolling through the profiles can be interesting. You are looking for someone who you think will think and act like you, or at least think and act like you would prefer. Remember, opposites attract, so you may need to look for the opposite of how you behave, though I don't subscribe to that theory. I think you should find someone who likes things you like and has the kinds of traits that you admire.

The most important trait you should all be looking for is honesty. All the others come into play, but if you are with someone who isn't honest, your chance for happiness is poor.

There are not too many stupid people on dating sites. (Actually, there are, but it's not nice to say so; you remember the Bambi Rule.) However, there are some dishonest – or, shall we say, fraudulent – people out there who, interestingly, put honesty at the top of *their* lists of traits they possess and desire in others. It is truly scary that some real jerks are out there looking for a mate. Be careful!

Activity Suggestion – By now you have contacted a few people and may have gone on a few dates. List some of the discrepancies between the profiles and the real-life people you have encountered.

52

LOOKS AND DATING

WHILE ON A CRUISE, one of the comedians told a joke that went like this: "They say two out of three people are ugly. Now look to your left and right, and if you see anyone that's decent looking ... You know what that means."

Yeah, we all laughed, and I suppose most people were too drunk to get the joke or make the realization that there is much truth to that statistic, unless, of course, they were from Lake Woebegone, where all the children are above-average looking.

So, what do looks have to do with dating? Very simply, a hell of a lot!

Did you ever wonder why you do (or don't) get many people flirting with you on your online dating service? It's not really a wondrous, inexplicable phenomenon. You're either hot or you're not.

I hate to be blunt – or, shall I say, politically incorrect – but people tend to want to date good-looking people who are pleasing to their tastes, and if that comedian's statistic is correct, then two thirds of you may not get lots of flirts, while those lucky "beautiful people" get tons of flirts, even more than they can handle.

If you think about what it's like being "good-looking," it really is a major life benefit. Great-looking people have an upper hand when it comes to most everything. They have a better chance (not a guarantee) of getting the job, getting on the good team, being picked for nice things, and being liked by others. It's almost built into our DNA, as exemplified in psychological studies of children, who always describe pictures of the "beautiful people" with all sorts of positive attributes, like *honest, kind, good, smart,* and so forth.

Success for beautiful people doesn't always work that way, because there are those who are not so attractive in positions of power, to offer jobs and other good things in life, who are jealous of all the beautiful people. They may just slight you if you are beautiful, but most times beauty tied to success is the way life operates.

Even those who are in the two-thirds group – you remember, the "not so hot looking" group – once they have something desirable (like money), they, too, may want to "buy" those beautiful people. Just look at all the examples of not-so-great-looking people holding trophy mates on their arms.

Let's face it. Everyone likes pretty things: beautiful artwork, good movies, good food, great vacations, beautiful houses with fabulous furnishings, clothing, and jewelry. It's just the way it is, unless you are a monk, Goth, or some other type dedicated to the higher values in life. So that's why most people work hard to get all that great stuff.

Fortunately, there are things that can attract the beautiful people to you besides money. Yes, things like expensive cars and drugs. Just kidding. There are many virtues besides looks and money. Personality, kindness, intelligence, wit, and a sense of humor are a few great qualities that attract the beautiful people.

If you desire beauty over substance, there is a good chance you may get less than you expected. All too often, the people who know they are "hot" come with an attitude and expectations, are high maintenance, or have the curse of always being hit on. That curse is yours, not theirs.

When people are constantly staring and flirting with you, it can give you a false sense of worth. As such, very attractive people may have affected egos, leading them down paths that can cause much grief. They often attract the shallowest people, and their relationships can be fragile. If temptation plays into their egos, they could end up in disastrous affairs that also prove to be rather shallow and even dangerous at times. And once the looks go, their relationships may crumble. Even their self-worth may suffer as they age.

Does all this mean you should follow the dictates of that old song that says to "make an ugly woman your wife"? You ladies can substitute "man" in the lyrics because all of this stuff applies to you, too.

I don't think it's necessary to only mate with those who are specifically not good-looking; however, the point is, you want to use discretion and find a mate not solely based on looks.

Be alert to the person who is stuck on themselves, overly materialistic, and overly flirtatious or puts too much emphasis on looks and wealth. This is all commonsense stuff, but common sense seems to go right out the window when we let shallow desires lead us into bad relationships.

Here is an interesting test to see how money and looks and dating are closely tied together. Take a look at who's driving the next 10 high-end cars you see on the road. In almost 45% of the cars in my recent test, these were the "beautiful people." That's a very large number. I think you won't find that large of a percentage of really hot men and women driving Honda Civics.

The people in these high-end cars are often hot, hot, hot. This tells me that they did something special to get these cars. And while I know I am generalizing, I suspect either they worked very hard at "catching" a big moneymaker or they worked very hard in their chosen professions.

You have to remember that many of the big moneymakers are very smart, and to overly generalize once again, when growing up, the very smart kids were not always the "beautiful people." Was it just in my school that this happened? Didn't you have a "Mary Smart" in your class who excelled in every academic endeavor? Yeah, now you remember. She was the one that all the guys picked on, allowing her to hone her academic skills at home all weekend because she never had a date. How about Goofy Gottfried, the teacher's pet, who went on to Princeton and became a rich, geeky computer entrepreneur?

So it is my theory that many hot women go after the wealthy guys even if these guys aren't "beautiful." A guy like this is so happy to get a hot woman because she would never look at him if he didn't have money. Yes, life is cruel and it's certainly not fair.

Same with the really hot guys in those fancy cars (still talking about the 45% of beautiful people). Yes, they are gay and have hooked up with really rich, old, ugly gay guys who "keep them" and let them drive their cars.

Much of this material is mocking, but there is some truth to all these comments. I know there are many attractive people who make it on their own. There are at least five of them.

The other day, when I was developing this theory and testing the hypothesis, I saw two hot women in front of me in a fancy and expensive Benz. I followed them so I could get a good look. Now here's what I saw when I pulled alongside: they were not very hot at all. As a matter of fact, they were old and haggard. They had way too much sun exposure over the years, causing all sorts of wrinkles, making me at first think a shar-pei was driving with a pug in the passenger seat.

These women were part of the other group. This is the "not so hot" 40% of people who have lots of money and can afford to spend thousands on a car, their hair, makeup, clothing, and jewelry. From the back, all I saw was beautiful, flowing, poker-straight blond hair that had to cost a ton to maintain. These women knew how to take care of themselves, and I suppose they love people staring at them, just like most narcissists. And while the women like this often do all they can to look hot, the men in this category are often hopeless. They are often not great looking and not cool. They don't know how to get a makeover, or they are not good specimens for such a makeover; however, they love to flaunt their money by driving those cool cars so they can attract beautiful women to date.

You've seen the ones I'm describing. Very likely you have even made a comment that goes something like this when he's sporting a hot woman next to him in his fancy car: "What does she see in that guy? I guess he has money." You notice how you never assume she is with him because of the size of his ... And I doubt that you ever said, "I guess she's with him because he has a great personality."

Now let's look at the last 15% driving those expensive cars: those who have money and are not from the "beautiful people" but don't really care. Those are the ones who are down to earth and usually very nice. They have no pretenses and do not need to look a certain way to feel good about themselves. These are the people who you should ideally try to find for life partners.

In summary, if you are very attractive, there are more people who will want to date you, but it doesn't mean you will be happy. To the contrary, it can sometimes make your life more difficult if your values are shallow.

For the rest of you, the other two thirds, you may have fewer choices that match what really appeals to your eye, but you, too, can end up with the wrong, high-maintenance person who will make your life miserable if your values are shallow.

So, the moral of the dating story is, don't be shallow. This advice works for all daters, no matter what they look like. Good luck in your search!

V

THERE'S A FIRST FOR EVERYTHING

53

THE FIRST PHONE CALL

WHEN DATING ONLINE, you may try to set up a date by email, though it's probably smart to speak by phone before you meet. But do you want to invest a lot of time talking with someone you may never want to be with once you meet? That, of course, is *my* take. You have to decide what works for you; but remember, there are pros and cons to phone relationships.

A big advantage of the phone call is that you may be able to feel out what this person is like, and that may prevent you from arranging a wasted date. At the same time, phone calls may allow you to get to know the person well and get to like him or her. That said, a preconceived expectation could mean major disappointment, and embarrassment, when you have to say there is nothing there physically. This could make you look shallow, even though chemistry is a fact of life. A good compromise would be to call, talk for a bit, then make the date and continue your conversation in person before you get too friendly.

When someone calls to set up a date, it's a good idea to answer the phone. Trust me when I tell you there are people who need this advice. One woman I contacted through the dating site email gave me her cell number. I didn't call right away, and after two months, she emailed again. I apologized for my delay and promised to call. The next day I called, and called ... and called. She never answered.

The *first rule* is, if you sound like a sea hag, witch, drunken sailor, or dullard, hire someone to record your answering-machine greeting. And when you pick up the phone, use your sexy voice filled with loving kindness if you are a woman, or your sexy deep baritone if you are a guy.

One woman's answering-machine voice sounded curt and asthmatic. Maybe I'm exaggerating, but you should try to sound, at a minimum, nice – preferably seductive. This applies to both men and women. This isn't to say a great voice is always a good indicator of what to expect in person. I have known unpleasant-looking people with voices that could get them hired at phone-sex companies in a minute. But remember, this is often the first and most influential contact. Don't blow it.

The second rule is, if you plan on having people call you, for a date in particular, it's a good idea to make sure your answering machine isn't full. I don't believe I have to tell you this either. It's annoying to learn that the mailbox is full or to hear a phone ring endlessly. For some people, getting up the nerve to call is traumatic. The last thing you want is for them to give up because you're hard to reach.

So, what do you talk about?

Space is limited, so how about some basics? Be yourself. It's classic advice for a reason. You can't be something you're not. If you're dull, you'll have to hope you called someone who is into dullness, because it will soon be discovered.

If you aren't a natural at conversing, write out a list of things to say and ask. You either say something or ask something. It's that simple. Oh, if the person asks a question, you do need to provide an answer.

Begin by saying something like, "Hi, I'm John from Dates Are Us. As I mentioned in my email, I was going to call you. Is this a good time to talk?" Notice you said something and then asked something. You're on a roll.

Now, you have your foot in the door ... figuratively speaking. They will usually reply yes, even if they are in the middle of something pressing, because as much as you want this date, so do they.

Stay away from dull, clichéd conversation such as, "Nice day, isn't it?" Go for something like, "This Internet dating thing is kind of awkward, but it seems to be a good way to meet interesting people."

Now you sound like a regular human. You just tossed the ball into her court, and she'll say something that keeps the conversation going. It's that easy.

For you ladies, I'd suggest you try to sound *agreeable* even if you don't agree. "Internet dating sucks. All the guys I meet are creeps," is not the way to toss the ball back into his court. Instead, answer, "Yes, it can be a really good way to meet." See how easy that was?

Don't be surprised if this person would like to talk for a while. Some people like to get to know the person on the phone before investing time to actually meet. This kind of person will usually ask all sorts of questions to keep the conversation going. Go with it. It may make sense to learn a little more about this potential date.

The other person might ask you about your situation: "How long have you been divorced?" This opens up a conversation that could last all night and will usually reveal something about this person. Other topics might have to do with your job, your kids, and things of common interest.

As noted, you may invest a lot of time and effort only to be disappointed when you meet, but it is for you to decide what approach you prefer. Even if you don't connect with this person, you get to brush up on your conversation skills.

I don't think you have to talk by phone more than once to set up the date, though some women want to get to know guys more before they put themselves in potential jeopardy. If they are fun to talk to, let them get to know you better.

This is just my opinion, of course, but I don't think it's a good idea to talk too much unless the other person insists. I prefer to set up a time to meet. As noted earlier, if you bond well over the phone, but don't like what you see in person, it can be awkward. Ask if he or she would like to get together for coffee (even if you don't drink coffee) or a drink (this is a good way to see if this person is an alcoholic like your last spouse).

That's all there is to it. You are now ready to meet this person who could turn out to be your soul mate ... figuratively speaking.

Activity Suggestions – Make a list of questions you would like to ask on the first phone call. List a few discussion starters. Be prepared for similar questions in return.

54

THE FIRST DATE

OKAY, you made the first contact by phone, email, carrier pigeon, or whatever. Now it's time to meet. For you neophytes, Starbucks seems to be the meeting place for the Internet first date. There's one on every corner, it's a public place, and it's safer than a Motel 6 or the parking lot of a convenience store in the woods. Of course, you can choose any public setting.

On my first formal date, the woman asked me to pick her up at her apartment. My son, who had, at the time, never tried this type of dating, immediately criticized me for two serious e-dating errors. "How can you go to her apartment? She could be an ax murderer!" And, "How could you possibly date anyone who hasn't posted a photo?"

While this level of suspicion may seem odd, I'm glad my children learned so well from their paranoid dad. His advice was good.

Why would you want to go on a blind date when today's photo-upload technology offers a way to see if there's a semblance of chemistry first. And going to her apartment did start to sound kind of scary, like something out of that James Caan–Kathy Bates movie, *Misery*.

After my son's warning, I gave this woman's address and phone number to my family members, who would be the most likely ones to arrange for my burial. They could give this information to the FBI or whoever would investigate my disappearance and retrieve my body for said burial. While I jest, these are two strict rules you must follow.

First, no picture, no date. Sure, a potential date could post someone else's picture, but no picture tells you this person has something to hide. If he or she did post a phony photo or an old one from his or her heyday, you have a perfect excuse to say, "That picture you posted looks nothing like you."

Wait for an answer and get ready to politely say, "I'm sorry, but trust and honesty are very important to me, as I noted in my profile, and there is something about that picture that seems less than honest."

Naturally, you don't get to use that line if you don't heed the second rule and end up at this date's apartment, duct-taped to a chair with a leather mask so tight you can't breathe through your nose. In that case, you say, "You look so good in that picture. I'd like to show it to my mother so she can see how cute you are. How about cutting me loose so I can do that?"

Second, don't meet or ask anyone to pick you up at your home. Yes, your date might be an ax murderer, as my son warned. In my case, the lady was very nice (not my type, but nice), and she didn't kill me, which is why I am able to offer this great advice.

You don't want a potentially dangerous stranger to know where you live. Plus, if you're not into them, the last thing you want is to have him or her take you home and try for that always-awkward first – and, in this case, last – kiss. Meeting at a public place usually prevents this disaster.

Assuming you trust my advice and don't need to live on the edge, you will now pull up to a Starbucks or whatever place you picked. You can place yourself strategically near the door, and you'll usually figure out which person entering the establishment is your date by using *the universal law of negativism*: the guy or gal that you have no interest in meeting based on how he or she looks is probably your date. If your date gave you a recent picture, you will be able to recognize him or her. Because you placed yourself strategically, you can probably escape without this person seeing you if your expectations aren't met.

I don't think it's very ethical to leave before meeting this person, however. What's the big deal in having a cup of coffee with a stranger, not counting the fact that he or she could slip a date-rape drug into your coffee when you go to the bathroom? Pee before your date gets there, and, yes, paranoia keeps you safe.

Now that you decided to stay for the coffee encounter, it's your chance to shine. If you like what you see, show this person all you got. No, don't pull down your zipper or lift up your blouse; that is just an expression. Have a conversation and find out all about this prospective mate. If there is real chemistry, you will surely be seeing this person again without all the nervousness related to the possibility of being rejected when you say, "Would you like to go out again?"

Activity Suggestions – Ladies, since you will likely be the one to pick the place, find a local Starbucks and scope out the layout. This way you can picture your first date and lose some of the nervousness. Find other locations that can work for you besides Starbucks. Guys, just go to your local Starbucks to get a feel for the kind of place you will be meeting.

55

WHAT TO TALK ABOUT

CONVERSATION SHOULDN'T BE such a difficult thing to do, but there are some rules you need to follow:
- Don't show yourself to be an idiot, a braggart, a pompous ass, a know-it-all, or a dolt.
- Try not to express your views on religion or politics, and never tell your date about the vast fortune he or she could share with you if you were to marry.
- If you're smart, let the other person begin the conversation. If they, too, read this book and took this advice, you'll have a nice time staring at each other. Now would be the perfect moment to practice the silent meditation you learned in your yoga class.
- You have to learn to be natural. If you are a talker, go for it, but *let the other person talk, too.* If you are quiet, don't expect to woo your date with your oratory, but be willing to answer a question or nod your head like you understand what he or she is talking about. If you are not too bright, you, too, should try to answer a question and nod your head when it seems appropriate.

Small talk doesn't cut it. You actually have just a few minutes to get this person to like you, so don't be afraid to ask all the usual questions. If you already did this on previous phone calls, you should know something about this person. And if you are smart, you would have done some research on their dating site profile and already know about mutual interests. "So, as an amateur entomologist, tell me something I don't know about the mating practices of the north woods cricket." Your date will love you!

While I jest, there's nothing wrong with doing a little research to allow you to engage in a conversation that interests this other person. If a woman is a retailer in the garment business, you can ask about the upcoming fashions. If a fellow is a trash hauler, you can ask where he thinks Jimmy Hoffa might be nowadays.

I may be a traditionalist, but I think you can expect the *guy* to fling for this high-ticket date. I don't think it is necessary for the lady to offer to pay. If the guy asks you for your share, don't make a scene, and take out your money. At this point, he better be pretty darn good to make up for all the credibility he lost by being a cheapskate.

Once you've found a table and settled in with your drinks, you can ask about what your date does if you don't know. "What's it like to be a dentist [goat herder, massage therapist, lightning expert, etc.]? How has your summer been?" (Winter works here, too, if it is the winter.)

The standard questions don't really show off your personality, so you may want to consider starting a conversation about the Internet-dating experience. Both of you should enjoy this topic, as you are living and breathing it as you speak.

An easy start might be, "How long have you been doing this Internet dating thing?" This opens the door to some good material. Many times, you can discuss your predicament – that is, how you got here. Most everyone is a gossip. Your situation, especially if it's at the level of a *soap opera*, is great fodder for your conversation, and your date would likely love the chance to hear about it.

Just be sure to avoid portraying yourself as bitter, vindictive, hateful, or angry, even if you are. It's much better to come across as hurt, shocked, and victimized while avoiding the extreme in any of these areas of victimhood.

Most conversations tend to go well with reasonably normal people. If there is nothing going on, it means that one or both of you are dullards, one or both of you are not having a good time and don't want to give the impression that there will be a second date, or there are no common interests.

Don't force it. If nothing clicks after trying a few tries, mention that you have to get going. Get up, and get on with your life. If you are having a fabulous conversation and time flies, either you or the other person is a great conversationalist, you both have a lot in common, you or the other person is trying to be polite, or you have found your soul mate. Enjoy the time and recognize that there may be some future to this relationship. However, don't get too excited, because there are some genuinely nice people with great personalities who make the most of any meeting, and they may not be interested in getting together again.

Next, we will be addressing acceptance and rejection. I can't wait!

Activity Suggestion – Begin thinking about conversations starters. Be sure to include questions you most want to discuss. Write them down for study purposes only. Do not take out your list during the date.

56

REJECTION OF ACCEPTANCE

THERE COMES a time on every Internet date that you have to decide *yes* or *no* and how you are going to end the encounter. You should make every effort to be kind and compassionate if you want to reject a relationship with this person. Remember, there are some pretty lonely people out there, including you after a few months of not finding the right one. So be nice even if the picture your date posted was not anything like what he or she looks like in person. Remember, this is Internet dating and it's not always what you expect.

If your date was less than honest, you may be ready to jump ship the moment you first meet this person, and you have the right to walk away without comment. It may even be tempting to let your date know of your displeasure, but you have to figure he or she is pretty lonely and not likely to get many dates. Instead, you may want to give him or her a pass and keep your mouth shut.

The other option is that you can still be polite and say something like, "You can't be Mary. She looks a hundred pounds lighter, and she has front teeth." For you ladies, you may try, "You can't be John. The profile never mentioned that he had eaten a basketball that lodged in his stomach, and his head wasn't bald with little warts residing where hair once grew." Remember, be kind.

Then, of course, there is the option that you hang out for a short while, make some small talk, and politely say you have to be going. "Well, it was nice getting to know you, but I have to be going. You take good care now." You turn and walk away. You don't have to explain everything to everybody.

My feeling is if they lied, and posted a fake or an old picture, you say, "How come you don't look anything like the picture you posted?" They will then have to tell you that it was an old picture, to which you can reply, "I find that to be rather misleading. I couldn't have a relationship grounded in deceit." You then flip your scarf over your shoulder and walk off.

For the rest of your encounters, one of four things happens: (1) you like your date and your date doesn't like you; (2) your date likes you and you don't like him or her; (3) you like each other; or (4) you don't like each other.

Sadly, it isn't always clear which of the four scenarios is occurring at the moment. So you have a 25% chance of getting this right without any real analysis. I actually don't like those odds, nor do I accept rejection well, so there are ways to make this work.

You like your date. At the end of the encounter, you say, "I had a really great time and I would like to see you again." Pause just a bit in case your date wants to agree, and then you don't have to get fancy.

If he or she doesn't respond at the nanopause, you then add, "I never like to put anyone on the spot, so if you feel the same, I'd like *you* to give *me* a call and we'll go out again. This way the ball is in your court." This line works well to keep everyone comfortable. You let your date know how you feel, and he or she can take it from there. If your date isn't interested, you won't get a call. There is no embarrassing in-person rejection (or even over-the-phone rejection, if you call for a second date), and you just move on if you never get a callback.

There is the chance your date will tell you right then that he or she, too, would like to get together, in which case you shut up and say you'll call, or make another date before you leave. Refrain from jumping up and down while yelling, "Whoopee!"

There is the chance your date doesn't like to beat around the bush and will tell you he or she isn't interested. Since you gave this person an easy out, this is not likely to happen, but if you get a response like, "I don't want you to wait with bated breath, so just know that I won't be calling you," you very politely say, "I gave you an easy out. So, screw you," and walk away. No, you actually respond classy and say, "Thanks for being so honest ... bitch."

Sometimes you just know you have great chemistry, and at the end of the evening you make a date or say you'll call. That's not a very hard encounter, and there is no problem saying good night, except for the possible fact that you can't get your tongue out of your date's mouth long enough to say good night. Hey, don't count on this scenario.

You don't like your date. If you don't like the person, it can get tricky. Now you have to say good-bye *forever* and mean it.

Some take the indirect approach and just say, "Well, I had a nice evening, and I'll see you around." That's vague for those who can't take a hint, but you just never call so it works. The downside is that they may say, "When?"

Most people get the idea, so don't worry about what to say. For those of you who worry about everything, when your date asks, "When?" you say, "When the chickens come home to roost." At that point, he or she should realize you are nuts and drop it.

An easier way to reject is to be a tad more honest and say, "I had a nice time, *but* [the proverbial *but*] ever since I caught this leprosy, I realize I shouldn't be dating until they find a cure."

Even more honest would be to say, "You seem like a really nice person, *but* [here we go again] I'm not getting the kind of feeling I'm looking for. It's a chemistry thing. I do wish you luck in finding someone who works for you."

Now that's honest and to the point, and it isn't really putting the person down. It's still a rejection, but it is honest, and it works. If you're a wimp, use the leprosy line and there are no hurt feelings.

Your date doesn't like you. You shouldn't take rejection badly. It's just that most relationships need to start with some chemistry, and if it isn't there, it makes for a bad beginning. Recognize that not everyone is compatible, and you will find someone who likes you in time. And if *in time* seems to be a case of *never*, you can get an inflatable Bob or Sally doll with multiple functioning orifices. The other option is small farm animals – no, silly, not for that – for companionship.

Your date may be nice about rejecting you, or he or she may be outright rude. Don't take it personally. If your date's rude, you are lucky you don't match, or you would have a life of rudeness thrust upon you. You lucked out!

Your date likes you. As noted, if your date likes you, he or she will seize the opportunity when you say you had a great time. You may not even need to worry about rejection when the person exhibits a lot of body language that shows interest. You need to recognize the subtle signs of endearment so that you'll know your date will be receptive when you end the evening with the request for another date.

Some of the subtle signs that your date likes you include things like the woman pressing her breasts into your arm any chance she gets. And likewise, when the guy keeps pushing his arm into your breast, it usually means there is some chemistry, or he has a terrible spatial-relations problem.

While the breast thing may be too subtle to notice if you have low testosterone levels, you should be alert to the touchy-feely kind of encounter. Some people are great at giving a little touch or rub here and there, and it really does help let you know that they are interested. If you get some of that physical contact (they keep touching your hand, arm, thigh, or sex glands), it usually means there is some chemistry.

Positive chemistry is also conveyed through your conversation. If this person hangs on your every word, or if they look and sound passionate about what he or she has to tell you, it's a good sign. By the end of the date, you will be comfortable in asking him or her out again.

Well, the date is over, and one of the various things noted above has happened. What now? Do you shake hands or give a peck on the cheek or go for the lip lock? We will discuss this next.

Activity Suggestions – Imagine what you might say in each of the four scenarios. Remember to be compassionate.

57

THE FIRST GOOD-BYE: HUG, KISS, HANDSHAKE, OR WAVE?

AT THE END of a first date, there is always the dilemma of how to say good-bye. There are really only four choices: wave, shake hands, hug, or kiss. If you wish to get technical, the type of kiss can add additional choices, from kissing the hand or the cheek, to the lips and even the French kiss, which involves a conjoining of tongues. This, too, shall be addressed so you will be prepared.

Obviously, the decision as to how to say good-bye has much to do with how well you got along on your date. If the person appears to be repulsed by how you look, how you dress, and everything you say, the French kiss is out of the question, but most of you know that. In case you still need guidance, in that situation, just wave good-bye. Conversely, if everything went really well, you don't have to wave good-bye. You pick one of the other options.

The hard part of how to end a date comes when you don't know how well you hit it off. That's when you have to make a decision. After all, some people are just being polite and act like they are having a nice time. If you go in for the kiss, you may find rejection keeping you company on your ride home.

If you really, really hit it off, you may actually find yourself in bed with this person (keep in mind, this is after a Starbucks Frappuccino date, which should find you rather perky in the sack), so the French kiss is an obvious way to say good-bye in this case.

Again, it's those times when you just can't tell how well it went that you'll find yourself searching for the proper way to say good-bye. Here's the rule of thumb. You can never go wrong with *a handshake* – unless you've just had sex.

The handshake shows class while revealing nothing. It prevents that embarrassing moment when you go for a hug and the person jumps away with a look of unforgettable repulsion. When experienced repeatedly, it can result in PTSD (Pretty Terrible, Stressful Dates).

It can't hurt to shoot for a little more if you think things went well. Yes, you can try for the hug or the cute little kiss on the cheek. If things went *better* than well, you can always try for the kiss on the lips. It should be short and sweet. The first-date good-bye is not the time for passionate kisses unless this is a date with a hooker, former hooker, gigolo, or former gigolo.

Keep in mind that this moment of saying good-bye is a special chance to make a big statement about how you feel. It can make the difference between a callback and radio silence. If you have no interest in pursuing this person, the wave is all you need to do, unless your date puts out his or her hand, in which case you can't be rude. You shake and say, "It was nice getting to meet you," as you walk away. If you get a wave, you probably shouldn't call this person again. If your date comes in for a hug or a kiss, it means he or she wants to see you again, and you should go for it, if you, too, want to start a relationship.

If you already stated your desire to see this person again, and he or she agreed, go for the hug or cheek kiss, as it is the classy way to say good-bye. This doesn't preclude the option for a serious kiss if the chemistry is there. You will probably know if the chemistry was not there if they punch you at this stage of the date.

Remember, saying good-bye is the final chance you have to let this person know that you may wish to pursue the relationship. It's a two-way street. If you read people well, you'll know what to do.

58

NEVER TALK ABOUT MONEY

HOW MUCH MONEY you have should be a taboo subject. While everyone is curious about how much money everyone else has, and while many people count other people's money, revealing your net worth to a date is a poor idea. How much money you have is more of a gold digger's concern, though lots of guys want to date rich gals for obvious reasons – think *kept man.*

People tend to have expectations about how generous you should be based on how much money they believe you have. If you're a guy, and your date thinks you're rich, she certainly would expect you to take her to upscale places to eat. She would expect nice gifts, a big house, and a fancy car, assuming the relationship got that far – three months if she's on the fast track to marriage and separating you from your wealth.

If your date thought you were of modest means, she wouldn't expect such upper-crust treatment. A date night including dinner at Denny's, a round of bowling, and television at her place would be fine (since you don't have a television). Her vision of a future with you would be gifts that would include a shared case of beer on Friday nights, living in a nice Section 8 dwelling and driving around in your ten-year-old car when you weren't using it to look for that elusive job. Actually, she would probably not date you in the first place knowing you were poor as a church mouse. That's one reason some guys put on the Ritz, hoping that they will attract hot women.

While much of this tale of two cities is an exaggeration, the basic truth abounds. Think about how perceptions truly come into play. For example, your date knows that you are worth several million dollars. You decide to take her on a vacation and you spend $5,000 on a lovely cruise. You don't get the suite or even a room with a balcony, and the cruise line is good but not the high-end ones that cost at least double the price you paid. Let's face it: you're sensible ... frugal ... cheap. That might even be how you came to be worth so much money. Your woman may be rather ungrateful for the vacation you came up with because she knows that you can afford much more, and she expects more.

In another case, you are of modest means, worth on the order of ... well, you're living from paycheck to paycheck, but you've saved a little each month and decided to go on a cruise vacation. The cruise line is of the lower order, where you meet all kinds of nice people in your similar situation. The room you can afford is on the inside, which means you have no window to see the beauty of the sea. If your woman knows your financial circumstance, she is happy just to be with you, especially if she, too, is of modest means. She has no expectations, and you shall get along just fine.

While you may not come out and tell your mate what you are worth, you may be unaware that you send messages that can be even worse. You may be driving a car you can't afford. You may have fake jewelry that makes you look rich. You may dress to the hilt because you shop at a discount store.

A lady on a dating site mentioned that she had an inheritance. At first, I thought I found a financially independent woman who wouldn't likely be looking out for a sugar daddy. Upon further inquiry, I found out that the inheritance was a house, or perhaps better described as a shack, in some shanty town. It wasn't much of an inheritance, but she sends the wrong message to prospective dates.

The first thing that comes to mind for most people when they hear the term "inheritance" is that it involves a whole lot of money. That's not always true. My Uncle Eddie left me a blow dart from the Brazilian rain forest worth, oh, about three dollars. When you leave subtle clues about your wealth, you may send the wrong signals. It's just as bad as coming out and telling your date how rich you are (or aren't). It's actually even worse because your date will take your subtle hint and magnify it to signify great wealth when it may be next to nothing. And if you do have lots of money, you let the cat out of the bag (albeit a Persian pedigree with a diamond tiara).

When people know, or think they know, how much money you have, they may treat you accordingly, in a manner that is not in your best interest.

Activity Suggestions – What are your financial expectations of your prospective date? Do you consider yourself generous or stingy? If stingy, practice spending some money on other people.

59

THE FIRST KISS

HERE WE GO. A big and scary first. *The first kiss.* The first kiss has always been difficult for most people other than rapists, pillagers, and invading barbarians. For those of us who have been more or less civilized and socialized, there is a protocol to the first kiss that we know exists yet is not very well understood. Does that make any sense to you?

While your parents may have tried to teach you about the birds and the bees, they didn't likely go into the first kiss, as they probably didn't know what to tell you.

It is important to remember that we live in a world of double standards, and while the world is changing rapidly, it is the guy who usually, and traditionally, initiates the first kiss, unless he's dating a hooker, nymphomaniac, female rapist, or a very smart woman who wants to get her man. This task puts pressure on the guy, and if he has a fragile ego, the task is daunting.

Much of the difficulty lies in the *rejection factor*. One of the most humiliating experiences has to be going in for that kiss and having the other person turn away. And that is only if they are polite. Worse yet is if they are vocal about it, and shout out, "What do you think you're doing!" If they add "the hell" after the word "what" that stings even more. And worse yet is if they throw up on you.

To allay your fears, having your date throw up on you when you attempt the first kiss is very unlikely (maybe one in five – just kidding).

So, the first step in managing the first kiss is to get over the rejection factor. If you have any semblance of reality testing, and if you are a reasonable judge of character, you should be able to tell if this person is going to reject you before you go for the kiss.

Use common sense; if it isn't the first date, and your date liked you enough to go out with you a second time, you should not expect rejection for your kiss. However, even with all this logic in your corner, the first kiss is always awkward.

Will she like the way I kiss? Will she think I have bad breath? Will she expect the presentation of the tongue? (What a dignified way to say, "French kiss.") These are just some of the thoughts you may have.

Don't be afraid. What's the worst that could happen? Yeah, remember the throwing-up scenario just mentioned? Big deal. You'll never see this person again. You are a grown-up and you will get over it. Just consider carrying some antiseptic cleansers and deodorant products specifically made for cleaning up after such biohazard events.

It does make sense to attempt this task of giving the first kiss at an appropriate moment. The most obvious time is at the end of your date when you are about to say good night. This is most likely not the first date that we are currently speaking of (first-*date* kissing is discussed elsewhere). This is a second date, or even a third date, that you want to end with a kiss. When you are about to leave, you stand close, put your hands on her waist and hope she doesn't yell, "Rape!" This moment is her last chance to pull back before the kiss begins, and she knows it. So if she pulls back, just say good night and forget this chick.

Assuming you now have your hands on her waist, and she's not struggling to get away, say something clever, like, "I've been waiting all night for this." Lean in and kiss. If the chemistry is there, she should respond, and she may even invite you to stay a bit longer. Whoo ah! It worked.

If you aren't the verbal type, forget the line and just lean in and go for the kiss. In either case, if she responds well, the kiss should last 6.4 seconds – don't look at your watch, you can learn to judge this by purchasing an egg timer and practice kissing your hand, a firm grapefruit, a plump gourd, or a slender zucchini depending on your taste in women.

You go for this short-term kiss because this is the *test kiss*. This is the kiss to see where you stand. If it's really good (i.e., she seems responsive), and you are still holding her by her waist, say, "That was so nice," and immediately you go for number two. No, you moron, that doesn't mean you poop in your pants. You kiss her again, and this time it should last 12.8 seconds. You may even want to try the tongue thing; however, if the gate begins to close, get your tongue out of harm's way immediately. Don't forget the French also invented the guillotine.

Kissing and sex are very personal, so she may want more and ask you to stay, or she may want more and tell you good night so as to not appear "loose." Don't let this variety of responses throw you. You should be able to tell when someone likes you. They may have some moral reason to hold back a bit. Remember, this is the first kiss, and it should lead to more as you move forward in the relationship.

Because we aren't children, and most of us are no longer virgins, you can expect to get a kiss on the second date. If you don't get a kiss by the third date, cut your losses and move forward with your next dating exploration.

If the chemistry is amazing, and you are up for some adventure, you can try all of this first-kiss stuff on the first date. Realize that you may be reading your date all wrong, and the person is just polite and cordial on this first date. In that case, you may get rejected. That's why you are probably better off waiting for the second date to go for the first kiss.

Also, remember, the first date is often coffee at Starbucks. Kissing good-bye (or getting thrown up on) at the entrance to a coffee shop is not cool. If you're ever not sure what to do, just ask yourself, "Would James Bond do this?" For you women, just ask yourself, "What would Julie Andrews do?" (Or Beyoncé, for those younger women out there.)

Now some more thoughts for you ladies. If the guy doesn't kiss you on the second date, and asks you out again, he is probably shy and has great difficulty initiating that first kiss. This is where you can shine and easily snag the poor sucker. Shy guys generally love the girl who takes that first step because they are so inept at it. You don't want to come off as a floozy, but you most certainly can do what was described above for the guys to do. That's right; put your hands on his waist, lean in, and go for it.

Women don't realize it, but there are many men who are timid with the first kiss due to an overwhelming fear of rejection. Yes, it hurts our egos. So, if you want to score big, be the aggressor.

There are other men who either are very experienced, have strong egos, or are lechers, and all of them will be the aggressors.

The first kiss boils down to being savvy enough to sense the chemistry of the first date, while a first kiss on the second date is easier, because they already told you they were interested.

Presenting the tongue should be reserved for the second kiss of the second date or later. While it can go over great on a first kiss if you are good at it, and if your date likes you, holding back lends to anticipation and excitement.

Today, most people French kiss. If the first kiss is very sensual, it makes for a better crescendo to wait for the tongue to come alive on the second or third kiss. It's like building up to rapture. It's like oral foreplay, so to speak.

There are those who do not like French kissing, and you have to respect that preference. Notice that I didn't say you have to go out with them again, just respect the preference, and remember, if they don't French kiss, a blow job or cunnilingus is probably out of the question. You decide what you want and act accordingly.

If you really want to let a person know your feelings without being too forward on the first meeting, a little hug or even a kiss on the cheek is the way to go. People who are not interested do not generally show those little affections, so this is a simple, fast way to say, "I like you and would like to see you again."

Guys must keep in mind that *women are nuts*. They could accept a second date, and by the end of it realize that you are a dud. If that happens, you're going to notice a coldness as the evening wears on. If that's the case, don't even consider trying for the kiss.

Women must keep in mind that *guys are nuts*, and they really want that kiss, so don't lead them on if you aren't interested. Given that a guy doesn't need much to get physical, if you aren't interested, don't do those charming little hugs, cheek kisses, or touchy-feely moves and later reject the poor soul when he tries to kiss you passionately.

I do hope you realize that much of this treatise on the first kiss is tongue in cheek, not tongue in *mouth*!

Activity Suggestions – Decide if asking for that first kiss is something you might want to consider. Make sure you have chewing gum or mints when preparing for that first kiss.

60

THE FIRST NAKED

WHEN DATING ... again, there will come a time that you will be seen naked, not by your medical doctor, a nurse, or the barium enema assistant, but rather by your new date, lover, or mate. It may be by mistake, such as when he or she walks in on you while you're stepping out of the shower, or it may be when you make love and it's not pitch black in the room.

While some people are so modest that they will not let you see them naked, you usually will eventually. There is a variety of reasons why they won't let you see them naked. This includes original sin, which led to original modesty related to Adam and Eve being expelled from the garden. An easy remedy is to stop eating apples. Then there are those who have a poor self-image of their nakedness. If they doubled their normal weight over the years, they may be justified in remaining in the closet of nakedness. The remedy here is a bit harder. Don't eat that apple, the apple pie, the ice cream, the lasagna ... You get the idea.

If you are with someone who is very modest, don't push beyond his or her comfort level. Respect your lover's boundaries. Hopefully, this person's modesty isn't related to a recent sex-reassignment operation; even worse would be when you reach down there and find an organ you weren't expecting.

Generally, over time, modesty fades, and pretty soon you will find you and your mate prancing around naked. This extreme is also not necessarily a good thing. There is something special about modesty, forbidden fruit, and imagination that can be ruined when nakedness becomes the norm.

Perhaps, it's best to play a little bit coy at times. Make that naked body a special thing to gaze upon only on certain occasions – like during sex, but not during the Super Bowl, especially if you have friends over.

If your body is truly not good to look at, it may be best to remain covered until the opportunity to have sex in a darkened room. Stay hidden for most other occasions. Don't frolic about like a nudist colony adherent. Show your better qualities, like fixing things around the house, or cooking, or going to work and bringing home the bacon.

Activity Suggestion – Rate your comfort level with nakedness on a scale of 1 to 5, with 5 being a nudist.

61

FIRST SEX

I DON'T KNOW WHY, but the title of this section sounds like a Sylvester Stallone movie. If I was as smart as Stallone, I could get eight or nine books out of this one theme. I could call each book *Rocky Sex*, I through VIII. That's right, first sex can be rocky, and we shall get to that.

Anyway, as noted in the kissing section, we are all pretty much no longer virgins, so sex should not be quite as hard as it was when we were 16 in the days before free love.

Many people today are products of the free-love generation and have a healthy, modern attitude about sex. This allows them to hop into bed with you relatively soon and without all the hoopla that used to proceed sex in our prudish past.

Sex is no longer a taboo that results in condemnation to hell and an eternity of shoveling hot coals (snow in the Northeast) – unless, of course, you contract some sexually transmitted disease (STD) that causes your private parts to feel like they have been shoveling hot coals for an eternity.

There is really no schedule or rules about having sex for the first time with your new lover. Much of the decision is all about common sense. If you are the shy type, or if sex is painful, or if you are not looking for a sexual relationship, it may not happen so fast or at all. It is not proper to force sex on anyone unless you are an invader, a plunderer, or a rapist.

If sex is important to your relationship, and the feelings are mutual, it's going to happen. Here are some guidelines for those of you who need them:

- As a rule of thumb, or shall we say *a rule of penis*, after three to four dates, you can reasonably expect to have connected sexually assuming both parties desire sexual activity.
- If you engaged in sex on the first date, that may be considered inappropriate or whorish, even for an Internet date. It's just not classy, though it is fun.
- *First-date sex* is more common when you meet someone at a bar and get sloshed prior to the actual sex.
- *Second-date sex* on your e-date is not unheard of and is generally related to chemistry (a good thing), horniness (not always a good thing, since you are letting your hormones dictate your behavior), or desperation (a bad thing).
- Holding off sex for too long is a way to lose out on some people. We are grown-ups, and as such, it shouldn't take you 10 dates to figure out if you want to sleep with a person.

I can see holding off on sex for up to five dates, but after that, there may be something wrong, unless it is a morality question and you, or your date, don't believe in premarital sex. This, of course, tells you that you, or your date, want marriage as the outcome, and that's okay as long as both parties agree.

There are those women (I think you know this isn't generally a guy thing) who will not sleep with guys without a *commitment*, and that doesn't have to mean marriage. It could just mean a commitment to an exclusive dating arrangement (a.k.a. committed relationship, a.k.a. monogamous relationship). If you are really old and still have any memory left, it used to be called "going steady."

This "no sex without commitment" rule is more old school, often has religious overtones, and is actually very noble and probably safer both physically and emotionally. You have to respect that in a woman, and if you really like her, you will. If it's the guy who feels like this, wow, he's a keeper, or a nutcase, or has something wrong with his penis.

In most cases, there should come a time for the first sex. So how do you go about this oftentimes awkward act? It is best to set the stage. Rather than trying to do it at a movie theater or a restaurant, wait until you get back to your place. Try luring the person into your bedroom by suggesting that you watch a movie or cable special using the great line, "I only get cable on the TV in my bedroom." This offers the opportunity to lay in bed and watch the movie.

Now, if you are clever, this movie should be so bad that you start talking and pretty soon you lean in for the kiss. This should not be the first kiss as discussed in "The First Kiss" section of this chapter. By now you have kissed this person good night at least once or twice.

You take it from there. It's kind of natural, like riding a bike. No, it's more like climbing a tree. That doesn't explain it well either. It's more like doing the mambo in a horizontal position. Oh, just "do it."

Since you are over the first-kiss thing. It should be smooth sailing, unless there are issues to address, like, "Before we do this, I wanted to mention my penile implant," or "I think you should know about my colostomy bag," or the fact that you had sex-reassignment surgery. These are all issues that could hinder the normal progress of first sex.

Assuming everything is okay, you can expect either a very receptive partner or perhaps some coy, playing-hard-to-get protestations like, "What kind of a guy do you think I am?" Oops, it will more likely be, "What kind of a girl do you think I am?"

By the way, the answer to that question is, "The kind of girl I've always dreamed about."

Realize that first sex is not always ideal sex. You may be so excited by the *newness factor*, the *forbidden-fruit factor*, or the *performance-anxiety factor* that you guys may become impotent or ejaculate prematurely. The women, for the same reasons, may become frigid, dry, or emotional.

If you are a caring person, you have to show compassion and understanding. It is best to lightly joke about it, and try again later, now that the ice has been broken. Just a note of trivia: Alaskan ice fishermen never have these problems with breaking the ice.

Since first sex may not be ideal because of the essence of first sex, you have to be open to see the potential that it could get better, or you may miss something really good. It is very likely that if it's not great the first time, it will get much better as your comfort level matures.

There is also the possibility that it will be the best sex you've had in the past year, partly because you haven't had any sex in the past year, or because the chemistry is there, and there is nothing hotter than first sex with a new partner if you can get over your inhibitions.

Of course, it could also be terrible because you, or your partner, are just not very good at sex. The good thing about dating versus the old-time custom of arranged marriages is that if you are not compatible, you can move on.

Second and third sex should get better and better. It only starts going downhill after you've been together for a while, especially if you got married, and you've had time to take each other for granted. Don't let that happen, or you will be on Internet dating sites as a divorcee in no time at all!

Activity Suggestions – As you contemplate first sex, are there any issues, physically or emotionally, that you need to face first? It is mandatory these days for both men and women to have a condom handy and ready for use. Go now and look at that old condom that has been in your wallet or purse for the past 10 years and replace it with a new one. You don't want a partner for life with a name like STD.

VI
SEX AND DATING

62

SEX AND DATING IN AMERICA

TO HAVE a discussion about dating and not talk about sex means you are not having a serious discussion. Certainly, there are those who, for one reason or another, are asexual, experience sexual dysfunction, or have no libido, and as such have no interest in sex. For the other four billion folks, let's talk.

Dating and sex have a long history if you count Adam going out with Eve on their first date. To limit our discussion, let's go back a mere 70 to 80 years. Dating was much different then, especially with regard to sexual behaviors. You weren't likely having sex on dates. Most women were saving it for marriage. Most people adhered to this sexual morality. If a guy did want to have sex, he had four choices: get married, find a prostitute (they've been around forever), find a rare but willing partner, or do it himself. This may be why guys are so handy around the house with do-it-yourself projects.

In that era, many women were looking to get out of their parents' homes and create their own families. Sex was not the priority, other than as a means to escape and have children. If a woman wanted sex, she had four choices: she could get married, become a prostitute, or hop into bed with any willing guy against the morals of the day. She could also do it herself. But since it wasn't accepted societally, she usually didn't – thus the reason women are not as handy as men. When boys did it themselves, they were told they'd go blind. Who knows what they told little girls if they got caught, but it probably bordered on eternal damnation.

Sexual modesty and discreet behaviors remained in place until around the Woodstock era. You remember: free love, sex, drugs, and rock and roll. Suddenly, someone (most likely a guy) convinced women that sex was good and should be engaged in as often as possible (guys knew that). The culture took it way beyond "sex is good" and developed an ethos that considered sex with anyone, no matter how indiscreet, was just fine. San Francisco bathhouse activities, pre-HIV epidemic, was a testament to the idea that sex with anyone was okay.

The song "Love the One You're With" became the anthem of every guy, and the women went along to be cool and to remain popular. Virginity was no longer a virtue. No longer did horny guys need to get married to have sex. No longer did women need a guy to have children. And what did we get? Lots of unwed mothers to be celebrated, lots of single mothers living in poverty with children they couldn't afford to raise, government-subsidized everything, lots of drug abuse, violent gangs, plague-like diseases, and most important, lots of sex.

So, who really won the culture war? Obviously, the guys. They got all the sex they wanted with no commitment, no responsibility, no bills, and no worries. It's not really all that simple, but it helps to understand the historical perspective to comprehend sex and dating in the current age of enlightenment.

If you are older than 60, there are still those in your age group who revere sex and what it means to a serious relationship. These people recognize the spiritual importance of a sexual union. The herd is getting thinner, and you may have difficulty dating someone who feels this way.

Many folks, especially the young, hop into bed by the first or second date. The old-fashioned, wait-until-marriage group is the new dinosaur.

Those younger than 60 will find more partners willing to have sex without commitment. Each younger generation finds more and more dates conforming to the current values of free love. Even teens engage in sexual activities that were taboo not so long ago.

The question is, what are you looking for? Do you just want lots of sex, or do you want a serious, long-term relationship? It doesn't have to be marriage, but a complete relationship means you have someone to count on for companionship and sex. You have a partner to stand by you in times of tumult and in times of joy.

You have to feel sorry for some groups of people within the umbrella of American culture. They sleep around, live in poverty, contract an inordinate number of STDs, and change partners as often as they change their underwear. However, they are having lots of sex and often many, many children who don't actually know who fathered them and who you and I end up supporting without ever having had sex.

If you are looking for more than a hookup, you need to be explicit and up-front with your date. If you discuss sexual issues during your first phone conversation, you will save yourself much time. But this should not be your first order of business on the phone.

At some point during the conversation, whether your first phone call or first date, you can say, "I'm looking for a serious relationship. What are you looking for?" If you meet a person who just wants to hop into bed, you'll figure this out when he or she stops calling after that first conversation.

If your date asks stealth questions on a first date, this should offer a clue as to his or her intentions. "Are you cool with sex in a relationship?" They now wait to see if you offer clues like, "Sure, after the fifth date." Darn! Your date might never call back.

Inquiring about your sexual interests is not always done by stealth. Some dates will come right out and ask, "Are you cool with sex on a first date?" Your answer will determine where you spend the night.

Sex is ever important in many relationships. The lack of sexual engagement has caused many to be frustrated and has destroyed relationships, as well as marriages. Sexual tension can actually cause stress and anger, making people sick, as described in *The Sexless Marriage Fix*, by myself and Dr. Roberta Foss-Morgan.

If you are interested in a relationship that has no sex, be up-front about that, too. There's a lid for every pot. However, it's only fair that you let the potential mate know well in advance what type of relationship you want.

Activity Suggestions – Think about how adventurous you are regarding sexual activities. Are there things you want and need to do? Are there things you refuse to do? How often do you wish to engage in sex? How important is sex to your future relationship?

63

MEN ARE FROM MARS AND WOMEN ... WHO KNOWS?

DATING HAS a lot to do with romance, sex, and every other want, need, and desire. It is imperative to recognize that men and women are vastly different. While that sounds trite, people forget that many problems emanate from these differences. Let us explore these differences as they relate to sex.

- The definition of *eternity* from the guys' perspective: the time from when he has an orgasm to the time she leaves.
- The definition of *eternity* from the gals' perspective: the time from when he starts begging for sex to the time he realizes you are not in the mood.

I don't think you need a treatise to figure out that men and women are different. However, there are certain differences regarding sexuality, as noted in the above definitions, that are very important. You must understand them when it comes to having a relationship. You can recognize some of these differences in these two poems that make light of the situation:

A Woman's Poem
Before I lay me down to sleep,

ROBERT M. FLEISHER

> I pray for a man who's not a creep.
> One who's handsome, smart, and strong.
> One who loves to listen long,
> One who thinks before he speaks,
> One who'll call, not wait for weeks.
> I pray he's rich and self-employed,
> And when I spend, won't be annoyed.
> Pull out my chair and hold my hand,
> Massage my feet and help me stand.
> Oh, send a king to make me queen.
> A man who loves to cook and clean.
> I pray this man will love no other,
> And relish visits with my mother.

A Man's Poem
> I pray for a deaf-mute gymnast nymphomaniac
> with big tits who owns a bar on a golf course,
> and loves to send me fishing and drinking.
> This doesn't rhyme, and I don't give a shit.

I don't mean to be overly simplistic, but the difference between men and women is well stated in these two poems. It's all about the difference between *romantic* needs and *sexual* needs. Yes, women need romance and men need sex! Don't tell me that we all need both. Of course, we do; however, when you look at priorities, the poems hold up.

Another difference between men and women is seen with postsex activity preferences, where the guy is ready to fall asleep after sex, while the woman wants to cuddle. Men and women usually have some of each of these traits, but the stereotypes predominate.

Generally speaking, women need much more time to feel comfortable with a man before they are willing to have sex. Once they get turned on, they need a good amount of time to reach climax and even longer to calm down. They want to cherish the moment for as long as possible by a process sometimes referred to as cuddling, also known as snuggling (these two behaviors are similar; however, the difference is in the amount of nesting the nose does upon the guy's neck).

Generally speaking, guys are ready to rock and roll rather fast, don't last very long, and are ready to go to sleep right after they perform their little trick.

These differences between the sexes account for a great deal of discontent and ultimately the failure of many relationships. It would be wise if both men and women learned a little about the each other and used this knowledge to please their mates, and thereby forge stronger relationships.

Here's how it can work to your advantage, guys: let's say after the act, your gal wants to snuggle and cuddle and have you hold her in your arms; just be a sport and do it. I know, after orgasm, most guys are ready to go to sleep. You see, we use up so much energy maintaining that erection that we can't do much more after it deflates.

You'd think just the opposite. After all, now that all that blood left the penis, it could go back to the other brain and allow us to recite poetry or perform other romantic gestures like cuddling. For some reason, it doesn't work that way. Instead, we are ready to call it a night. Understanding this phenomenon should allow you guys to put forth the extra effort to snuggle. After all, you don't have to cuddle all night.

I mean, in my case, I can only last 15 minutes before my arm goes numb. At that point, I gently pull my arm back to my side of the bed, and if she is still awake, I politely tell her, "My arm is falling asleep, and I want to retrieve it so that all my parts will be synchronized by the morning."

I do suppose if I could actually perform the sex act for the same 15 minutes that it takes for my arm to fall asleep, maybe she'd be worn out and want to roll over and go to sleep, too.

Now for you ladies: since you gals know it may take a bit more effort for you to get rolling, let him work on you rather than just telling him you're not in the mood tonight. And you know, there's a good chance you'll go along for the ride once you get to *that place*. If you turn him down too many times, he'll eventually start thinking about getting it elsewhere.

And when it comes to the snuggle/cuddle, just go along with us if we are trying our best. Don't expect an hour of cuddling after a two-minute exercise in sexual acrobatics. When we say we have lost all blood flow to our arms, cut loose and roll over.

Remember, *doggy style* shouldn't be 10 minutes of us begging, and then you roll over and play dead!

Activity Suggestions – On a scale of from 1 to 10, with 10 being the most important, how important is having great sex? How often would you like to have sex? While these questions eventually need to be asked of your potential mate, don't start off this way.

64

DO WOMEN HAVE AN ESTROUS CYCLE?

FIRST, let's be clear about this subject. For all of you bikers who ended up on this page thinking the "estrous cycle" has to do with Harley-Davidson, you have come to the wrong place. This is all about the *estrous cycle* that governs sexual desire as it relates to procreation.

Dating with an understanding of sexual desire (libido) will help both men and women find a compatible mate. Here you will learn why your date (or, for that matter, your spouse once you marry) is not always in the mood.

Humans have a number of vestigial parts, mutations, and formations found in early man (gender neutral) and found even more commonly in other lower animals. For example, today we have fewer people born with wisdom teeth, as their need to chomp on gritty food diminished over eons with the development of chocolate pudding and Dairy Queen. We retained the little toe for no real reason, as it is not needed. We do not have a tail like our monkey brethren, since the advent of the wheel, and the subsequent invention of the bicycle, made swinging through the trees by one's tail an outdated form of transportation. And most certainly we have lost the need for a multitude of functional designs still present in birds, apes, and a host of lower creatures. Even the advantages of the species we call sharks were no longer needed once we created law schools and lawyers.

One primitive function said to be lost to humans in the course of evolution is called the estrous cycle. Estrous is defined as a recurring cycle of sexual *receptivity* and *fertility* in many female mammals. We often use the term "heat" when referring to animals when they desire sexual activity. Who hasn't heard the neighbor's cat roaming the hood late at night squealing and screeching while engaging in sex with tomcats that have waited patiently for this moment? Horses, chickens, dogs, and a multitude of lower animals experience estrous. It's nature's way of making sure each species propagates and continues its lineage.

Biologists consider estrous to be something not experienced by humans. I take issue with that conventional line of thought. This theory of mine came about when I was on vacation and heard the lady in the adjacent room squealing and screeching much like my neighbor's cat. Realistically speaking, most guys have either heard similar sounds or actually experienced them in their own beds at night.

So, could female humans experience an estrous cycle where they are more receptive to sexual activities? Well, they sure can experience the opposite phenomenon – something we call the *premenstrual cycle*, a time in which there is a whole lot of squealing and screeching that sends the opposite message, that being, "Oh, you want sex? Well, not tonight, jerko!"

Logically speaking, why couldn't women have the opposite, complimentary cycle, a cycle of wanting sex more than usual (estrous)? Most every man and woman alike knows that there are certain times when women are more amorous and "in the mood," and there are other times when women are not. While you can't generalize, this phenomenon is usually related to an actual cycle that corresponds to the menstrual cycle. This means it is a hormone-based phenomenon – a biological process. Even though this is not a very new observation, scientists seem to ignore its existence and still say the estrous cycle is a process based in the lower mammals.

As humans evolved, the need for various primitive processes diminished. After all, we don't need to wait for that once-a-month moment, called estrous, to have sex. Humans have sex at will, assuming a willing partner. We engage in sex often in youth, and with diminishing frequency as we age. This pattern is also hormone dependent, though it is altered by our human traits, making sex much about mental processes that are *influenced* by hormones but not at all entirely hormone dependent.

Understanding that the human female does, in fact, have a form of estrous cycle helps to explain why women, more than men, may at times refuse sex, and at other times become very carnal – a euphemism for "horny." Because of a highly developed cerebral cortex, the estrous cycle can be evoked by such things as flowers, candy, and jewelry, which can encourage sexual activity beyond the effects of hormones or the lack thereof.

The next most obvious question: do men have an estrous cycle? For that answer you will you will have to read the next section.

Activity Suggestions – Do you notice a time when you feel more amorous? Is there a pattern? Have you noticed a pattern of sexual desire that came and went in your past relationships?

65

DO MEN HAVE AND ESTROUS CYCLE?

WE EXPLORED the possibility that women have an estrous cycle. In that section, I boldly stated that women most certainly do have an estrous cycle even though science states that the cycle is associated with female mammals of a lower order than humans. To understand women and estrous, you should go back to that section.

The next most obvious question is, "Do men have an estrous cycle?" After all, the scientific definition only mentions female mammals. If you examine the facts, men, too, have hormonal cycles that govern their sexual interest and activity. It's just a lot more difficult to identify male estrous as a result of such high levels of desire that men experience until they reach andropause in later life. Because men are so libidinous all the time while young, it is difficult to notice cyclic alterations in their desire for sex.

Men can get moody and not be interested in engaging in sex, especially when, for example, they are watching a ball game, playing golf, or going through near-death experiences. But generally speaking, men don't go through such peaks and valleys (cycles) in their libido compared to most women.

At certain times, men are actually hornier, if that's even possible.

Men, who are often considered horn dogs, may get more amorous at times, though the times are less cyclic, and more related to a generalized buildup of libido, probably the result of a buildup of their sex hormone (a.k.a. testosterone).

A sexually active male who has been without sex will have an increase in libido that grows stronger each day that goes by without sex. Most sexually active younger males will engage in masturbation when a mate is not present. As men grow old and their sexual libido diminishes in line with diminished testosterone production, they masturbate less, engage in sex less and less, and eventually lose interest in it.

There is, however, a period of time when most old men who have been less sexual will get horny, as fading hormones are still capable of building up to sufficient levels to get the old geezers interested again. For many older women, this can become a burden in that their husbands who have been behaving (not initiating sexual activity) suddenly want to hop in bed and *get it on*. In aging men, it is easier to see that the male libido is, in fact, cyclic. It may follow no *rhythmic* cycle, but rather every few weeks, months, or even years he will want to try again. Interestingly, when an older man's libido is up, he may actually be able to have an erection as the buildup of testosterone can make that happen.

How does this come in to play in the dating world? Young people will be less concerned with the issue of waning and waxing sexual interest, unless their mates have unbalanced hormones. But older folks may find that it is either a pleasure or a curse all depending on the receptivity of the woman at the later stages of her life.

66

PRAYING AT THE ALTAR OF THE JADE TEMPLE

THE *JADE TEMPLE* is the vagina for all of you who have not figured out creative writing. If you ask, or wonder, why the vagina should be a subject in a treatise about dating, then you don't understand the power of sex as it relates to interpersonal relationships.

Men do all sorts of stupid things to pray at the temple. They also do noble things at the same temple. The more you understand the power of sex in relationships, the better you should be able to navigate the dating waters, and, for that matter, all aspects of relationships from friendships to marriage.

What sorts of things do men do to go to the altar? Let's see. At a minimum, it motivates them to be social animals able to relate to women. I sometimes think if there were no Jade Temple, guys would just hang out with their guy friends. They may never take a break from work, sports, or television if it weren't for the temple visits. The primal need for sex gets men up and running. They actually have to hunt for sex much like they hunt for sustenance. Yes, men actually have to pick up the phone, or go to a club, or somehow figure out a way to get sex.

To maintain residence at the temple, men will agree to have children, learn to like them, and raise them to adulthood, often teaching them a trade, or paying to have them taught a trade in college. Men will settle down knowing that they have a temple at home and have no need to look for other temples. They shall become good men and know no others in the carnal way.

While primitive man (as well as some barbarians of modern times) forced themselves on women, today's man needs to use his cunning to find a mate. Notice I say *cunning*, which, for those of you who are astute, you may realize is very similar sounding to *cunnilingus*, which also sounds much like a *cunning linguist*. Guys who want to be successful at finding and pleasing and retaining their mates need to excel at all three of these skill sets.

Some men are so desperate for an altar to pray upon that they actually become whipped and do most anything the goddess presiding over the altar of the Jade Temple asks of them. These are the guys most devastated from a breakup, divorce, or loss through the deaths of their partners. There is probably some level of dependency, related to sexual dysfunction or psychological issues, that makes many of these desperate types cling to abusive relationships where they are totally controlled.

At the ultimate extreme, there are even those men who actually kill for their dedication to the Jade Temple. Yes, they actually become homicidal and end up killing their goddess, another man with whom the goddess may have let into the temple, or even people involved in the lives of the goddess and the disciple. These men should be avoided. It is, however, difficult to tell which men have this psychopathic personality disorder.

Women must understand that if they find a true disciple of the temple, this person will not stray, nor will his devotion ever fade. This devotee may shower the priestess with gifts, trips, and all sorts of good stuff. Depending on their personality type, some women actually like having control over devotees and the gifts. Others may feel contempt for such a wimpy kind of guy.

At the other end of the spectrum, there are "raiders of the ark" that resides at the Jade Temple also known as "players." These are the guys who like to go to the temple, but they are actually atheists who don't believe in the Jade Temple and would rather plunder as many temples as they can get into. Ironically, they like to be showered with gifts and trips and good stuff, too.

It is the lady's job to figure out the difference between the two. While there is no set way to make this determination due to such variability in personalities, psyches, and situations, you can get some hints. A guy who can't stay away from you and is always horny is the guy who will likely take out a membership in your temple – that is, he may want to make a commitment. The guy who is aloof and never really cares about being with you other than for sex is more likely a raider of the lost ark, or if he is seeing you and you alone, he is likely a fellow with a low sex drive, and that may be okay for those women who aren't interested in frequent sex.

It is best to identify the nuts and stay away from them, as they can only cause you grief. The deeper the relationship with a needy, nutty guy, the more likely you will end up in a frustrating relationship, or, worse, a violent circumstance, whether verbal or physical, or death.

It's pretty much like the Goldilocks thing: you want to find someone who is "just right"! That's not so easy to do. Do you settle? Great question!

Activity Suggestions – Describe some cues that tell you whether your guy is a raider or a disciple. What kind of guy do you want?

67

DO YOU JUST SETTLE?

YOU HEAR it all the time: "I don't want to just settle." It is as if these people are in search of perfection and will not compromise. I guess we can't really blame them, but realistically most people have to settle because there are only so many perfect people (like you and me) to go around. Have you ever thought about settling because it's difficult to find Mr. or Ms. Perfect? Do they even exist? Do we all just settle to some extent?

Do you settle for less than your ideal mate? Before we can answer this question, it makes sense to first look at the consequences of settling. If you don't settle, there are two outcomes: you may be the happiest person in the world or the loneliest. You end up happy if you find the perfect mate you have been looking for all these years. However, there is a good chance you will never find the perfect mate if you are unwilling to compromise at all. Then you end up with no one, and you get free membership in the Lonely Hearts Club along with Sergeant Pepper and all those other luminaries. Ironically, even if you do settle, you confront the same outcomes. So it's not whether or not you settle; it's how you go about settling or not settling.

Like most things in life, it is best to compromise to a moderate degree. But remember, you don't want to take any old mate for fear of being lonely, because if you pick the wrong person, you may end up wishing you were alone. You have to prioritize and establish what is important. Decide what you can live with and what you can't. All of the variables that go into a relationship come into play. The list is long: chemistry, looks, personality, common interests, intellect, socioeconomic background, personal interests, religion, moral values, activity levels, money or the lack thereof, even where you keep the thermostat. While these are some of the more important ones, you have to figure out what you want and need in a relationship. It's up to you to make a complete list to satisfy your needs.

Remember, you are going to be with this person for a potentially long time, or end up breaking up or going through a divorce with all the attendant hurt and pain associated with failed relationships. If you can't imagine being connected to this person both physically and emotionally for the duration, maybe you should look elsewhere, and don't just settle.

Too many people settle because of pressure from friends or family, the biological clock that keeps ticking, the need for security, loneliness, or even just the desire for sex. While things may work out when all is going well, there is a disaster waiting if the frequency of sex decreases, the money runs out, or whatever things you placed value upon fade away.

If you joined together for the shallower things in life, like sex, looks, or money, there is a good chance you will end up unhappy and vulnerable down the road. Of course, if you have a good divorce lawyer, you may end up rich ... and lonely – still not a pretty picture.

Another consideration of settling has to do with what you bring to the table. You have to be realistic. If you look like Chewbacca, you may have to settle for a Wookiee, unless you are very rich, in which case there are those attractive humans who will gladly live with Wookiees who will keep them.

The section on "Compromise and Compatibility" in Chapter 4 explores these two factors required for any discussion of settling.

Once you have that information, you'll be better able to decide if you should settle or not settle – *that is the question*. You knew the question all along, didn't you? You need the answer!

Activity Suggestion – Make your list of things you could settle for and the things you absolutely cannot live without.

68

PRAYING AT THE MOUNT OF THE CRIMSON MUSHROOM

WHILE MEN MAY PRAY at the altar of the Jade Temple, women may pray at the *Mount of the Crimson Mushroom*. To help out those who don't understand the poetry in these metaphors, just know the Crimson Mushroom is exactly what you think it is, so we don't need to spend time on silly questions. Just as men do foolish things in order to pray at the Jade Temple, so do women at the Holy Mount – maybe even more so at times.

Women "in the know" understand how powerful it is to shower affection on the mount. They understand how, when the mount is in the Vesuvius mode (i.e., ready to erupt), they can manipulate the high priest, as he is, at that moment, in a state of weakness and might just agree to anything, like buying jewelry and promising nuptials.

This is all said in jest, because everyone knows that as soon as the mount erupts, the last thing the priest wants to do is buy anything. He would rather turn over and go to sleep.

There are amazing similarities between the Jade and the Crimson experiences. Some women truly worship the Crimson Mushroom, and these women we call nymphomaniacs. It seems many priests like these types of women while they are dating, and they may even like them as wives as long as their libido can keep these women satisfied. Most men, however, do not want their daughters to be mushroom worshipers to this extent.

Then there are those women who only go to the Crimson Mushroom out of obligation or as a means to an end. These women are more interested in the security of a relationship and are willing to put up with the high priest's libidinal needs in order to experience the joy associated with having a companion (a.k.a. snagging a husband).

Then there are the women between these two extremes. What the guys want to find is the Goldilocks kind of disciple who has a good balance of "religious observance" and class. This is easier said than done because some of those who just pray out of necessity only reveal their true selves when they marry the high priest and tell him they no longer like to do certain things to the Crimson Mushroom. Well, by then it's too late!

Women who wish to succeed in becoming a member of the mount must show interest in the priest and his holy sacraments (a.k.a. his penis). The other option is looking for a priest who has no interest in the sacraments and prefers sermons, as this priest will be looking for a relationship devoid of the physical while embracing the spiritual (i.e., having fun discussing the meaning of life and other such topics).

Yes, there are many differences between men and women, and all of us have differing needs. This is why *compromise* is so very important in a relationship. This is why *compatibility* is so important in a relationship. We explored these two concepts, compromise and compatibility, earlier (Chapter 4).

Activity Suggestion – Ladies, on a scale of 1 to 10, where 1 is praying at the mount out of obligation, and 10 is praying at the mount because you love the ceremonies, where do you reside?

69

PERFORMANCE ANXIETY: IT'S MOSTLY A GUY THING

WE ALREADY DISCUSSED FIRST SEX. Go take a look at that material again to see how performance anxiety relates to this section.

Performance anxiety is generally thought of as a man thing. After all, without an erect penis, there's not much performance. However, this anxiety is widespread among women as well. Most of you folks in your forties, fifties, and sixties haven't been with another person since you were first married. This makes for a unique type of encounter: an encounter of a shy kind.

You find yourself worried about not only having sex and being good at it but also disease, reputation, and even how well you look naked. I prefer to wear my Viking helmet and to sound a ram's horn while standing naked at the foot of the bed. You'll have to decide how you would like to dress up for this encounter in a way that makes you look good. You know, something to hide the body like a barrel with a hole in the side.

For men, there is a real concern about performance. While men like to think of themselves as macho sex machines, the reality is that most are not, especially at this stage of life. Unless they've been having extramarital affairs on a regular basis, this first encounter may be fraught with fear. Once they get over the hump, by humping, they will usually be okay. If the first encounter is a disaster marked by *erectile dysfunction (ED)* or *premature ejaculation (PE)*, it could set the stage for difficulty. To remedy the problem, there are highly effective treatments, which include pills like Viagra, Cialis, or Levitra, as well as injections used to achieve erections that last for hours, even after prostate surgery.

Men who don't choose to remedy the problem by utilizing modern chemistry may consider psychotherapy (which could take a long time to achieve results, if ever), or they can work it out on their own by making several attempts until they get back their confidence. It may be best that they utilize the services of an escort or visit a prostitute to renew their sexual prowess. There are so many outlets for sex today that there is no need to lead a life of celibacy, usually the choice for those who let the anxiety rule.

Since many of the women you'll be dating aren't the "jump in the sack with anyone" types, they may be much more understanding if you have performance issues. And the nurturing type will want to do anything they can to get you back in the saddle. However, there are those women who are very aggressive sexually, and they are not likely a good choice for a guy having performance issues.

Ladies, you may have a different kind of problem. Women usually need some type of emotional attachment to engage in sex. Not all women fit this pattern, but those who have no problem engaging in sex don't really need to read this.

For those who do have a sexual anxiety problem, it can be a dilemma when you don't jump into bed and then don't get a casting callback. You don't want this kind of guy.

Many women have issues about their bodies, especially as they age. While they are often more accepting of their mates' flaws, they may be so hard on themselves that they will avoid dating altogether. That's not necessary. If you are that concerned about your body, consider working with a trainer and get yourself fit again. And there is even a chance you can hop into bed with your trainer.

If a guy is attracted to you, and you hold off sleeping with him, he'll try again – maybe not for ten dates, but for two or three. Some people may want to wait for ten dates, or even for a marriage commitment, before sleeping with someone, but that is sadly unrealistic in today's society unless you are a Quaker or looking for sexless relationship.

You have to remember that dating among older folks in this day and age isn't teenage dating. Most of you have been married, have children, or at least have had sexual relations for years. That teenager remark doesn't make complete sense here, because if you were teenagers today, you'd be hopping into bed with everyone.

If a guy is infatuated with you, and he isn't a player (one who has no trouble sleeping around), you may actually be able to get a commitment before engaging in sexual relations. You should realize that e-dating offers an abundance of opportunities to meet other people, so the rules have changed radically. If you are hot gal looking for a stud, he may not spend a lot of time courting you when there are others to go to easily for a sexual relationship.

Regarding actual performance, women do have it easier in that they can lay there and act like they are having an amazing time. However, many women have concerns about dryness and pain during intercourse, especially with advancing age. Many of you have, or are going through, menopause, a time when sex can become difficult in the best of situations. You may want to consider bringing your own personal lubricant to the bedroom.

Since you can't count on guys to be ready for safe sex, being that they think with their penises and not their heads, you also may be wise to bring your own condoms. Don't let the heat of passion be a reason to risk getting a disease that you may have for the rest of your life.

And, guys, don't be afraid to start off easy. Not many women will be upset if you don't jump into bed on the first encounter. You can do some petting initially and that may help to ignite the flames of passion needed to get you going. That may help get the woman going, too.

Sex is a very complicated physical, social, psychological phenomenon. It takes time and understanding. Be kind to those who may not be ready to engage.

Activity Suggestions – Develop a list of questions you may want to ask your mate about sex before you get to that point; include the following, and answer them for yourself: What are your religious and moral views about sex? Is sex an important aspect of a relationship? What is the wildest thing you have ever done sexually? Keep in mind that questions about sex can be a turnoff for some people or be thought of as too aggressive.

70

ASTROGLIDE, KY, VIAGRA ... OH, MY!

THERE IS a good reason these subjects aren't included in other books on Internet dating for the younger set who don't seem to need these remedies. I think you get the point, but if not, just remember that by fifty-something, the women have entered, or will shortly enter into, menopause and the men will or have been entering into andropause, the male equivalent – better in some ways and worse in others than what women go through.

Women may find they are drier than when they were young, making intercourse difficult and even painful. Assuming you are going to eventually enter into physical relations with someone, you may find the need to lubricate.

There are many products available to makes things glide better. It appears that some women already know about this stuff and they usually bring it with them once they are comfortable with the physical relationship.

Ladies, it's not a good idea to whip out your Astroglide the minute you get to his house, and certainly make sure it doesn't fall out of your pocketbook on your first coffee date. If the guy you are dating has 10 bottles of the stuff on his night table, it may be an indication that you aren't the only one in his life, or at least he's seen others with the same problems.

While it's never easy for either men or women to have sex for the first time with a new partner, ED can make it devastating, and it is much more common in one's fifties. ED makes first sex embarrassing at a minimum and just about impossible at its worst. That's why they made Viagra, the wonder drug that helps many men renew physical relationships. This drug has also allowed for lecherous behavior that was never before seen in impotent aging men.

Viagra and similar drugs are a double-edged sword in that they can make a guy great in bed and at the same time they may create a confidence that precludes the need for intimacy in a relationship. Suddenly, Viagra can make guys comfortable running around.

Some men cling to a relationship they feel comfortable in sexually, especially guys with ED who are more likely to be loyal to the woman with whom they feel comfortable. More cases like this exist than guys probably want to admit.

There are a couple of things you may want to know – or not. If your guy has an erection lasting more than 30 minutes he is probably on an ED medication – or he is a porn star, is from another planet, or has it wrapped in popsicle sticks and duct tape. Some of these medications will afford this otherwise mild-mannered guy with an erection lasting for hours and give him the ability to wear you out – literally. And if you are just getting back into the game with a sore, dry vagina, this is the last thing you want, even though us guys think you desire hard and long-lasting sex.

And you guys should know that if this *older* woman is flowing with love juice, it may be either that she prelubricated in the bathroom just before you engaged in lovemaking, she's experiencing an episode of incontinence, she is from another planet. Yes, us guys immediately think being wet is because you love us so much. Don't get too cerebral about sex, enjoy, and go with the flow ... or the lack thereof.

When deciding on the type of lubricant, consider that Astroglide sounds very chic and hip, much more so than KY Jelly, which sounds like something that you put on toast in the morning, or even like an ant killer you place around the corners of your kitchen. The truth is that both of these lubricants have their place in the bedroom.

Astroglide lasts longer for general lubrication during sex. KY Jelly is much more lubricating but doesn't last as long. If you need more protection from pain associated with penetration, use KY. If you just want to prevent irritation from a long sex act, especially if your guy is using Viagra, go with Astroglide and remember you can always add more as needed. Try to find lubricants don't include *parabens* in their ingredients. Some authorities claim that these chemicals can be toxic. Vaseline is an excellent lubricant, but being oil based, it can cause a condom to weaken and break.

There are a hundred, make that a zillion, companies hawking sex aids for men. They all claim to be better than Viagra and you don't need a prescription. Yes, they are all *natural* and *herbal*. It almost makes them sound like a sex tea of sorts. Be careful, as some of these herbal sex formulas can cause side effects. Generally speaking, none of them is as good as the prescription medications.

Activity Suggestions – Visit the section in your pharmacy that has sex products. This includes condoms, lubricants, and some vibrators. Purchase at least one lubricant and a package of condoms in preparation for sex. Do not purchase the extra-large condoms just to impress the cute cashier; they have to stay on to be effective.

71

SEXUAL INJURIES

THIS IS A RATHER unexpected topic for those who are young. While even a young stud or prom queen can get injured during the sex act, the types of injuries they experience are much different.

Young people are more likely to injure their sex organs, the result of overzealous sexual activity. Yes, a man can fracture his penis if a woman on top gets carried away. Most men may experience the snapping sound of their organs during vigorous sex, but most never actually see them break. Even a sudden bending of the penis hurts like crazy, so one would have to assume that an actual fracture is not pleasant.

The penis has no bones; it does have two chambers that fill with blood to make an erection firm and hard. If bent too far, one can experience a penile fracture, also known as "eggplant deformity." This odd name derives from the fact that your pecker becomes purple and huge. This injury requires surgery to repair.

As noted, young people have different kinds of sex injuries. They are more likely to have hickeys on their penis, scratch marks on their bodies, anal tears for those more adventurous partners, and even serious bites when passion becomes extreme.

Older people do not generally have the same level of passion and lust seen in youth. They are much more likely to experience injuries to major body parts. Who would have ever thought that in your sixties and seventies you would have pulled out your shoulder in the midst of a romp in bed? Sometimes lifting yourself off of your partner is all it takes to pull something. Any body part is susceptible to injury. It can be your knee, hip, elbow – really, any joint. These injuries can occur from something as simple as getting out of bed in the morning, so you can only imagine what sex can do to your body parts.

Considering the incidence of osteoporosis as you get older, a broken bone is not farfetched. You may wish to avoid adding any flying-entrance approaches to your sexual repertoire.

When you are older and aroused, your balance may be a bit off, so be careful that you don't fall out of bed altogether. If you do, when asked what happened, tell your lover that he or she is so hot that things like this happen.

As noted, lubricants are important, so use lots to prevent a chaffed penis and vagina. Don't be afraid to keep adding lubricant as necessary. Remember to ask for more if you are feeling the friction, as your lover isn't a mind reader. Worse yet, if you start moaning in pain, your partner will mistakenly think he or she is turning you on.

Be careful with your Viagra, or it's possible you may need to take a trip to the ER for priapism – you know, the four-hour or longer erection they warn you about on all those Viagra advertisements. This, too, requires surgical intervention. Waiting too long to get treatment can do irreversible harm.

If the worst-case scenario occurs, and you come home from the hospital wearing a large bandage resembling a diaper, and your neighbors are watching, they'll ask what happened. Don't mention sex. It's much easier to say you fell down the steps than to tell what really happened, unless you live in a ranch-style home.

Okay, there is something worse. You can die during sex. Sex accounts for a small number of sudden deaths each year. It happens way more to men, and especially when they are cheating. Cheating sex can be way too hot. Be careful and stay faithful to avoid being one of those Nelson Rockefeller kinds of stories. You know, dying in the saddle. What a way to go!

Activity Suggestion – If you are considering getting back in the saddle, talk to your doctor to make sure you are healthy enough for such activity.

72

100TH SEX

WE'VE GONE over the *first call*, the *first date*, the *first kiss*, the *first naked* and even discussed the tribulations of *first sex*. All these firsts are what makes the 100th romp in the sack so special. By now, you are not likely embarrassed to be naked with your new mate. After all, how new can it be after doing it 100 times?

If you are anything like most couples in this situation, and assuming that you both enjoy sex, it takes about 6 to 36 months to score the 100th-sex goal. Most people in their forties who have retained healthy sexual relationships that haven't gone south do it on average 69.2 times a year. In the fifties it's around 53.8 times a year, by the sixties it's around 32.5 times a year, and sex in the seventies happens around 16.2 times a year. So, depending on your age, and how long and active your honeymoon stage lasted, four times a week, early on, gets to 100 in around 6 months. As long as you do it more than average, you'll reach the 100th celebration, as noted, in 6 to 36 months. But wait! If you're in your seventies, it takes around six and a half *years* to have done it 100 times based on current statistics, assuming you haven't croaked. Perhaps you may want to set your goal a bit lower if you are older.

There's tremendous beauty in feeling close to someone sexually. There are no more worries about "dating" and going through all those stressful and embarrassing "firsts." It's time to sit back – make that lay back – and enjoy the ride.

If you ended up with your new mate because you didn't take care of your last one, you could get lazy and end up starting all over, dating ... *again*! I hope this realization keeps you on the path to eternal bliss, or at least until you just can't "do it" any longer.

73

FORBIDDEN FRUIT: THE KEY TO PERPETUAL LOVE

FORBIDDEN FRUIT – the formula for perpetual hot, romantic love, or why illicit love affairs and hard-to-get sex are so hot. Here, we'll be exploring a rather odd way to *keep it exciting*.

The quest for the elusive eternal, passionate love (a.k.a. endless desire combined with romantic love) can be understood through two concepts: wanting what you can't have, also known as the *forbidden fruit*, and *deprivation*, or not getting enough of your most precious desires fulfilled. Interestingly, both of these strong forces governing passion are the basis of illicit love affairs. Think about it: when one is involved in an illicit affair, the notion is clearly that of forbidden fruit and deprivation of the desire in that you can't freely see the person whenever you want – that is, you can't have the sex whenever you want. It works! After all, an affair must be pretty hot if people are willing to risk it all – their marriages, their careers, and their respect and dignity – for the sake of the affair.

Yes, have an illicit affair and you shall have perpetual passionate love! Well, not really. You see, someone is going to get hurt, hence the term *illicit*. Once this other person finds out about the affair and is hurt by it, he or she may leave you to be with your new lover. You suddenly find yourself much more available to this no-longer-illicit affair. It's no longer forbidden fruit, and there is no deprivation since you can be with your new love 24/7. And that's often when problems begin. This is like being able to have the best pizza each and every day. All of a sudden, it's not so special anymore, and you realize that which you thought was everlasting, passionate love (the best pizza) turns into the same thing you had yesterday – maybe worse, frozen pizza.

For truly endless, passionate love, it takes much more than an illicit affair. It takes something unique that can turn the mundane into the exciting, the everyday into the forbidden, and make the great things in life not so abundant that you no longer desire them (remember the pizza example). To accomplish this usually elusive goal, you need to put forth great energy and make sacrifices. And most importantly, you need to have integrity.

So how does this work? In your new relationship, you really just have to stop seeing each other every day so as to set up a state of deprivation and forbidden fruit in one fell swoop. You can't get it every day so you feel deprived, and because you made this new rule about not connecting at will, it is now forbidden. This is often the setup seen with couples when one or both are on the road a lot: the traveling salesman/woman who is away from home for days, weeks, or even months at a time sets up the right dynamic. The longer you are apart, the greater the deprivation and the more it feels like forbidden fruit. You can't wait to connect, and the sex is great.

This only works when there is *fidelity* in the relationship. If either of you is having an affair while you are apart, you may both be experiencing the forbidden fruit, but obviously the deprivation is only being felt by the honest partner, so that can't work.

If you don't travel, perhaps you can make certain times taboo for sex. If you go a week or two (two days for those with strong sex drives) without sex, and maybe sleep in different rooms, you now set up the forbidden fruit as well as the deprivation that may keep your relationship stronger by perpetuating the passion. You may even find that one of you sneaks into the bedroom of the other to get it on. Now that's passion that can last a long time if you keep the sense of deprivation and the forbidden fruit alive, the two components of human nature that are needed for the hottest sex.

This proposition may sound silly, inconvenient, and impractical, but if it works for you, so what? There are too many relationships that have left the realm of passion and fallen into disrepair. If relationships are neglected for too long, they fail, or at a minimum, your quality of life suffers greatly.

Occasionally withholding sex can create the forbidden fruit and deprivation paradigm; however, done too often, it destroys passion over time, as it produces frustration, anxiety, angst, and physical infirmity. While it may work for some relationships, it is more often destructive and great care should be taken before you make it a part of your mating behavior.

74

DATE RAPE

KNOWING the importance of safe dating and the potential for harm that exists, information on safe dating becomes ever more important. Rape is a very difficult subject for all the horror that it causes as well as for the continued psychological toll it takes on the victims; however, there are several areas of this subject that need to be explored.

What is the incidence of date rape? This is difficult to say because of the nature of the act. When a woman gets into a difficult situation because of an indiscreet choice, she often becomes embarrassed to report a rape. An example would be getting too drunk or too high in a guy's apartment, or doing anything that would look bad in a courtroom upon cross-examination: "So, you went to his room, drank way too much, and then you let him take off your clothing and you engaged in oral sex. What did you think was going to happen next?" You can see how embarrassing this could become. As a result, some states (New York and California) have enacted affirmative consent laws that say consent must be "ongoing throughout a sexual activity." New York takes it a step further: "silence or lack of resistance, in and of itself, does not demonstrate consent." These laws help take away the embarrassment factor in reporting rape. Without consent, it's rape. These laws help protect women who either by their own fears or by being drugged cannot consent to sexual activity.

According to former Vice President Joe Biden, "We know the numbers: one in five of every one of those young women dropped off for that first day of school, before they finish school, will be assaulted in her college years." Actually, there is no evidence that Joe's claims are true. Politicians, you know, are always looking for a cause to justify their existence. Actually, the rate of rape has been decreasing for decades. According to the US Bureau of Justice, 1 in 52.6 of college women will be raped. A far cry from one on five, but still a terrible travesty. The bureau goes further to say that women in college are actually safer from rape than those not in college. The streets are mean out there.

Date rape drugging is probably the most insidious violation. The victim never sees it coming, and the consequences can include psychological distress, pregnancy, and even death. Because the type and dose of drugs used in date rape are completely unpredictable, it's not unheard of that the victim can be overdosed and die from the drug. To better understand the gravity of date rape drugs, go back to one of the earliest cases involving Samantha Reid, who was given GHB (gamma-hydroxybutyric acid) and went into a coma, which led to her death. In another infamous case, Andrew Luster, heir to the Max Factor fortune, drugged his victims and recorded himself having sex with them. As a warning for any predator considering such vile activities, do know that Mr. Luster lost all of his family's fortune, had to declare bankruptcy after paying out $40 million to his three victims, and will be in prison at least until he's 64 years of age. In the Samantha Reid case, Joshua Cole and his three accomplices were convicted and given up to 15-year sentences. The consequences of such actions and the likelihood of capture should make any predator think before considering date rape using any of the drugs available on the black market. Your life will essentially be over.

GHB (a.k.a. Liquid Ecstasy) isn't the only drug. There is Rohypnol, or roofies, and ketamine, or Special K. These are the most common date rape drugs, but other hard-to-find drugs exist. Common alcohol, marijuana, and cocaine can put a person in a stupor such that they may perform acts, or have acts be performed upon them, that would never have happened with consent. Make every effort to maintain your ability to consent, or not, to sexual activity.

Besides drug- and alcohol-induced rape, sex can simply be forced in a violent attack. That guy you thought was really nice may get way too aggressive once he becomes stimulated, especially if he is under the influence of alcohol or drugs. Intoxication is no excuse for aggressive or violent behavior, but it happens all the time; stick with guys who are not abusing drugs or alcohol.

To defend against aggressive behavior, don't be afraid to emphatically state that you want him to stop. If necessary, you may want to scream, as this may wake him up, or at least may get someone to come to your aid. Sadly, screaming and fighting back could make some violent and aggressive men even more violent and aggressive. Once you say no, if the guy continues, he is committing rape. Keep in mind that we are not referring to an attack by a stranger. That's a whole different story and is not date rape.

Some people don't seem to have a good sense of understanding personalities and reading people. Some people get stoned on a first or second date. Sadly, those people are much more at risk. If you hold off any sexual activity until a few dates so you get to know your partner, you are much better off. You have to decide what works for you and learn ways to protect yourself. Everyone out there is not a predator, but it is a big enough problem that you can't afford to be oblivious.

Some guys think aggressive sex is something women like. Some guys actually think that when women moan, wince, squirm, or grunt, it's always from pleasure and the result of their incredible talents in bed. By this poor interpretation, they may push harder, reasoning that if the woman likes it so much, they can keep going. And the reality is that some women do enjoy aggressive sex with lots of moaning, groaning, and squirming around. However, all those sounds and movements of pleasure are the same found when enduring pain. Some women are too embarrassed to tell their lover, which is a big mistake. Make sure you make your feelings known early on so as to avoid getting into tenuous situations.

75

RECREATIONAL DRUGS AND DATING

IN THE WORLD of recreational drugs, there are several types of people that can be described and studied. For simplicity, the two groups of interest here are the *younger generation* and the *older generation*. Some like to call them *old school* versus *new school*. In this respect, the old school will be those from ages 50 to 75. This includes those who first experienced recreational drugs in the later sixties beginning when they were late teens. In contrast, the youngsters, aged 25 to 50, had the drug world all around them from grade school.

The old school mostly consisted of those who didn't get heavily involved in drug use. Many didn't take any drugs and only watched as they saw drug use proliferate around them in younger generations. This is not to say that there aren't any potheads or cocaine users today in their seventies. However, generally speaking, many in the older age group didn't have as many drug-related experiences. In contrast, in the younger generation, many have either tried recreational drugs or use drugs regularly. The younger the population, the more prevalent the use.

So, what makes recreational drugs so appealing, especially as they relate to dating? In a nutshell, drugs are another, yet more powerful method to let down sexual inhibitions and defenses. Drugs are the new alcohol used by men to seduce women. Drugs are often used to have sex with unwilling partners and result in many rapes that often go unreported.

While moral codes and sexual taboos have fallen by the wayside, generally speaking, there is still a reluctance for women to hop into bed with just anyone, while guys are much more promiscuous and need less motivation to have sex; however, the power one wields with drugs to obtain sexual favors in exchange for a high is enormous. Suddenly, some creepy guys can bed women they'd never have a chance with because both men and women will often do things they wouldn't have done if they were sober.

The heavier the drug, the more potential to become a slave to feed the habit. While this is common knowledge for a pimp, many regular guys have figured this out, too. Not that it took much thinking. They found out that the promise of "a great high if you want to come over to my place, because I've got some really great shit," to use the drug culture vernacular, works wonders. Now let's face it: not too many in the old school want to go to someone's apartment to see shit. To the contrary, this sounds rather perverted, though not to the new school. Combined with the high levels of promiscuity in modern American culture, getting high to let down the few inhibitions left might lead you to engage in strange sex with strange people. And who knows, you might even find photos on social-networking sites of yourself copulating with small farm animals.

So, what's the advice on recreational drug use and dating? If you do wish to engage in getting high, young or old, make sure it's with someone you know and trust. Just getting high, really high, in strange places with strangers can get you into a lot of trouble. While old-school people can't fathom the depths of depravity and decline going on in the new-school world, they might want to find a copy of *Kids*, a film by Larry Clark, that depicts the lives of teenagers circa 1995.

The movie is compelling and a good warning to the youth of America, many of whom are on a spiraling path to a world of suffering.

While God may have promised to never destroy the world by flood again, he never mentioned destroying us with STDs. Be safe, play safe, and stay safe.

VII

DATING, DISEASE, AND INFIRMITY

76

DATING AND DISEASE

NO ONE LIKES TO talk about this stuff, so I guess that means I have to be the one. This may be the scariest chapter in the history of dating self-help, so if you prefer to be an ostrich, skip ahead. All paranoid schizophrenic hypochondriac masochists who want to spend the rest of their lives suffering from some plague-like disease should also skip this chapter, and don't even consider dating. You may want to go for the inflatable doll, and even then, use protection unless you are sure it is made from virgin vinyl.

I feel sorry for all of us in the dating world. It's a scary and dangerous place. And it's especially difficult for the hypochondriacs. I knew this one hypochondriac guy who was dating just a mere six months when he died ... of hypochondria. Yes, I am trying to make light of this dilemma, but disease is very real and presents a very real risk.

We're not talking about getting a common cold from a good-night kiss. The diseases you have to avoid include all the old stuff, including the ones that did in the likes of Al Capone – gonorrhea, and crabs, syphilis. Those are the easy ones because today they are usually curable.

We live in a new world filled with diseases that can make you suffer for the rest of your life, and there are those that will kill you. We are talking about serious infections. We shall explore each of these diseases and see how likely we are to get them.

Some of the diseases we have to contend with today didn't exist years ago. These new diseases are related to the sexual practices of modern, free-spirited lovers. These diseases started as unexpected effects of the free-love phenomenon of the sixties. So in some odd way, I tend to blame the Beatles for the current problems encountered in dating.

Before the sixties, sex was taboo. It really was! Girls weren't screwing every guy they met, and guys, who would have liked to have sex with every girl they met, didn't either because those girls weren't screwing every guy they met. Those girls were the norm. They were called *nice girls*.

Back in the fifties, I couldn't discuss sex, condoms, STDs, or anything related to sexuality at the family dinner table, yet today they are showing kids in elementary school how to put condoms on bananas, which will probably account for some seriously odd sexual practices among the next generation, as well as even more exotic fruit-tree diseases yet unknown, like gonobanana.

When I was a kid, sex was taboo; today sexual behavior is found in young children. This free-love mentality produced a world in which both boys and girls (as young as 10 years old) have multiple sexual partners who perform sexual acts that there used to be laws against.

Oral sex, anal sex, and anal/oral sex among multiple partners breed and spread disease, especially the new diseases we encounter. Sadly, the medical establishment hasn't let the masses know or understand how all this happens. Yes, everyone's heard of the various diseases we fear, but most people don't fully appreciate how their behavior contributes to the plagues currently devastating many populations. Very bright people, both men and women, don't practice safe sex because they don't understand the dangers, or they let caution fall victim to passion.

If you think this section on sexually transmitted diseases (STDs) is just for the poor underclass, guess again. It is true that serious STDs are more prevalent in the inner city as a result of the higher levels of promiscuity, but if you think there's no way you'll fall victim to the modern plagues, think again. There is so much sex going on outside the purview of marriage that it's nothing if not predictable that the spread of diseases that were once found only in poor communities has come front and center. You really don't know who your partner has been sleeping with – and, at times, neither does your partner.

I knew this guy, who, when he first started to date, found out that the two lovely women he was seeing had hepatitis C and genital herpes, respectively. Could a guy be more unlucky? I guess he could have dated a leper with intractable TB, but *someone* was watching over him – not perfectly, but watching over him nonetheless. He was spared and moved on with a much more cautious view of dating. As a matter of record, he is now in the monastery practicing his vows of celibacy while soaking his penis in warm salt water.

And now for a treatise on STDs. This will be a shortened version, since details about each STD will be found in my next book, titled *Never ... Dating Again!* For now, let's look at a few words about each one.

Activity Suggestion – Do you know people who have contracted STDs? If they are willing to talk about it, see what they have to say.

77

THE STDS

CRABS ARE SMALL, wingless (thank God) insects also known as *pubic lice*. That is not a misprint – there is no such thing as *public lice*. Both men and women can get crabs from sexual contact, so I guess, in a way, they are public lice.

You can also get crabs from some really good seafood restaurants, as well as *non-sexually* from contaminated clothing or dirty bedding. That actually sounds worse than getting them from some illicit affair with a hot lifeguard.

The main symptom is itching of the groin, and it usually appears within five days of contamination.

Treatment involves using medicated shampoos or creams that kill the insects. You can get the medications *without* a prescription (thank God). If you aren't sure what you have, see your doctor. Just don't turn red when he tells you what you have. You may even break the tension in the room by saying something witty like, "Oh, I thought they were lobsters."

Activity Suggestion – Explore the pharmacy and look for an over-the-counter crab treatment. Better to be prepared.

Chlamydia is the most commonly reported bacterial STD in the United States and a leading cause of infertility among women. Its incubation period is one to three weeks.

Even though older people dating are less promiscuous and less likely to get STDs, the risk is still there; 50% of infected males and 80% of infected females have *no* symptoms. This is why it is known as a *silent* disease. The infection can then spread and cause other problems. If symptoms do occur, they usually appear in one to three weeks after exposure.

In women, the bacteria initially infect the cervix and the urethra. If you do have symptoms, you might have an abnormal vaginal discharge or a burning sensation when urinating. When the infection spreads from the cervix to the fallopian tubes, some women still have no signs or symptoms, while others may have lower abdominal pain, low back pain, nausea, fever, pain during intercourse, or bleeding between menstrual periods. Chlamydial infection of the cervix can spread to the rectum by itself and even more so if you help it along by engaging in anal sex.

Men with symptoms might have a discharge from their penis or a burning sensation when urinating. Men might also have burning and itching around the opening of the penis. Pain and swelling in the testicles could occur but are uncommon.

Rectal chlamydia (and we know how you likely got that) can cause rectal pain, discharge, or bleeding.

Chlamydia can also be found in the throats of women and men having oral sex with an infected partner.

Untreated chlamydia can cause complications leading to chronic pelvic pain and infertility. If you are dating and having sex with a lot of partners, you need to be tested for chlamydia *yearly*.

Twenty percent of men and forty percent of women with chlamydia are co-infected with gonorrhea. Nice company you are keeping!

Prevention involves making sure you are in a monogamous relationship with one who has been tested. You can use condoms to help reduce the risk of infection, but as you can see, with the many ways we can have sex today, you could still get infected in one place or another. Chlamydia is easily treated and cured with antibiotics.

Gonorrhea is a bacterial infection transmitted through vaginal, anal, or oral sex with an infected person. Often, there are no symptoms, while others have symptoms that appear two to five days after infection. Symptoms can take as long as 30 days to appear. If you do have symptoms, a white, yellow, or green vaginal or penile discharge, coupled with a burning upon urination or during sex, may be noticed. Sometimes men with gonorrhea get painful or swollen testicles.

In women, the symptoms of gonorrhea are often mild, but most women who are infected have no symptoms. Even when a woman has symptoms, they can be so nonspecific as to be mistaken for a bladder infection or a different vaginal infection. The initial symptoms in women include a painful or burning sensation when urinating, increased vaginal discharge, and vaginal bleeding between periods.

Symptoms of rectal infection in both men and women may include discharge, anal itching, soreness, bleeding, or painful bowel movements. Rectal infection also may cause no symptoms. Infections in the throat may cause a sore throat but usually causes no symptoms.

Gonorrhea is usually cured with one dose of antibiotics.

Syphilis is a bacterial infection that is spread by contact with open sores that may be present on the skin or mucous membranes. This means you can get syphilis from kissing, as well as all forms of sex.

Most people don't get symptoms early on, which means this disease can go undetected until it causes great damage to your heart, brain, and nervous system. Those who do get symptoms may notice rashes, especially on the palms and soles of the feet. Painless sores may develop on the penis, vagina, in the mouth, or anus.

Maybe you'll start to see a correlation here with the sex acts we perform and the sites of these sores. Yeah, I don't understand the soles-of-the-feet thing either. But who knows? Next thing we know, we will hear about athletes' vagina.

There are three stages of syphilis. The *primary stage* is usually marked by the appearance of a single sore (called a *chancre*). The time between infection with syphilis and the start of the first symptom can range from 10 to 90 days (average 21 days). It appears at the spot where syphilis entered the body. The chancre lasts 3 to 6 weeks, and it heals without treatment. However, if adequate treatment is not given, the infection progresses to the secondary stage.

Skin rash and mucous membrane lesions characterize the *secondary stage*. The characteristic rash of secondary syphilis may appear as rough, red or reddish-brown spots both on the palms of the hands and the bottoms of the feet. The rashes of syphilis don't usually itch. Other symptoms include patchy hair loss, fever, swollen lymph nodes, and fatigue. These symptoms usually last for several weeks and go away without any treatment; however, the disease does serious damage if not treated in the early stages.

In the *tertiary stage* of syphilis, the disease may damage the brain, nerves, eyes, heart, blood vessels, liver, bones, and joints. Signs and symptoms of the late stage of syphilis include difficulty coordinating muscle movements, paralysis, numbness, gradual blindness, and dementia. This damage may be serious enough to cause death.

Avoiding alcohol and drug use may also help prevent transmission of syphilis and most STDs, because these activities may lead to risky sexual behavior, like having sex with people you don't know, too many people at one time, sex with perverts and promiscuous people.

Syphilis *cannot* be spread through contact with toilet seats, doorknobs, swimming pools, hot tubs, bathtubs, shared clothing, or eating utensils. So that kills those excuses when people ask you how you got it.

Treatment is usually very effective as long as you start early. It usually involves getting a single-dose shot of penicillin.

Infectious mononucleosis is actually the Epstein-Barr virus (EBV), or mono. At your age, it is likely that you will not be bothered with mono because you've already had it; however, there are some concerns, so let's take a look.

About 95% of the world's population has been exposed to this virus. Most likely, they never knew they had it, as symptoms are not always present. When you do have symptoms, they include fatigue, sore throat, and swollen glands.

The incubation period is one to two months. Most people don't remember having contact with someone with a sore throat from that long ago, but it is probably smart to avoid kissing and having sexual relations with sick people. (Who would imagine?) While that sounds like good advice, sex-starved older daters don't always think with their heads, much like sex-starved younger daters. It's the sex-starved factor, not the age factor, that comes to play when you don't use your head in aspects of your sex life.

The virus is transmitted by intimate contact with body secretions, primarily saliva, thus the name "the kissing disease." You probably already had mono, as mononucleosis is often referred to, when you were a kid, so it's not likely to affect you now that you have developed immunity.

In the unlikely event that you do find a date or mate who comes down with mono, stop your intimate relations. That means no kissing and forget the sex, too, though they will not likely want to have sex the way they feel.

When you get mono over 35 years of age, there is the chance that a complication could include hepatitis, as the virus could attack your liver. If you get it at this age, you likely abused your liver by drinking too much, making it more susceptible to problems.

One thing that could be a consequence of the mono you caught when you were a kid is that EBV has been implicated as the cause of some cancers. While it's too late to worry if you've had mono in the past, this should give you a reason to do everything in your power to stay healthy: eat right, get plenty of sleep, reduce stress. You know the story. This way, your immune system can keep these viruses that lie dormant in your body at bay.

Many people get impatient with all this disease stuff. I ask that you bear with me (no silly, keep your clothes on!). Just a few more diseases and we shall be done. Then we can get on with the important things that will help you find your perfect mate.

Herpes (also known as herpes simplex virus or HSV) is a virus that most people know of as the common *cold sore*. Herpes is a very real issue for many daters, and just because you are older, you are not immune to getting this disease.

There are two types of herpes virus: *HSV-1* is the virus associated with *oral infection* (i.e., cold sores). It is also referred to as Type I herpes.

The first exposure to the virus is usually a bad case associated with multiple ulcers in the mouth and on the lips, fever, lymph gland swelling, and feeling weak and tired. Many times, this first exposure occurs in infants, so you probably had your first exposure and don't remember it. Subsequent outbreaks are usually not bad. They usually result in one or more ulcers that last a week or two.

Many people confuse another oral ulcer called an *aphthous ulcer* with herpes. Aphthous ulcers are not herpes and not likely contagious. Since you may not know the difference, pretend any mouth ulcer could be contagious and you'll be a lot safer. Aphthous ulcers do not form around the mouth on the face, unlike herpes.

HSV-2 is the herpes virus associated with *genital infection* (i.e., ulcers found on the penis, vagina, and anus). It is also referred to as Type II herpes. Like HSV-1, the first bout is the worst, with more ulcers, fever, and a generally crummy feeling.

HSV-1 can be transmitted to the genitals, and HSV-2 can be transmitted to the mouth. While these similar, but different viruses are usually found in their respective regions, they can jump the boundaries. This means that oral sex can result in your getting genital herpes from someone who doesn't have genital herpes and vice versa.

About 20% of Americans have genital herpes and about 20% of this group know they have it. Well, one out of five people you date could have genital herpes, and 80% of those with the disease don't know they have it. This means there is a good chance you may be exposed to this virus when you are dating lots of people. This means you should use protection when you have sex. Ideally, you should use barrier protection for oral sex, but most people just don't because it is not as much fun. Of course, having recurrent painful sores on your penis or vagina isn't fun either.

There is a real dilemma with regards to telling your mate about herpes. The stigma associated with genital herpes is staggering. Most people never give a thought to oral herpes, probably because it is usually associated with an occasional outbreak that isn't too bad. Genital herpes can lead to the same mild recurrences, but it just sounds dirty.

In either type of herpes, if you have bad recurrences, you could be rather miserable. Since herpes is a virus that never goes away, and because no one likes thinking about a chronically sore penis or vagina, the odds are good that if you list genital herpes on your Internet dating profile, no one will call you other than those similarly infected.

Do you have an obligation to tell a prospective mate about herpes? I guess you do, but it can make your pickings limited. Could you pretend you are one of the 80% who doesn't know they have genital herpes? I suppose you could. You have to decide what you want to do. Perhaps consider your case: if you have frequent outbreaks, you should tell, because you are more likely putting others at risk. If you haven't had an outbreak in years, ask your doctor what he or she thinks. Maybe you could let sleeping dogs lie (but think before you *lie*).

Taking Valtrex, an antiviral medication, may provide a solution to preventing the spread of herpes to your mate by reducing the chance of you having an outbreak. This is something you can discuss with your doctor. The drug manufacturer does state, however, that "Valtrex will not prevent the spread of genital herpes. Herpes infections are contagious and you can infect other people even while you are taking Valtrex."

Whatever you do, avoid any sexual contact when you have open sores, as you are more at risk to contaminate your mate, and you yourself are more at risk of contracting AIDS or other nasty diseases because of the open sores.

One day, when the medical establishment realizes that cancer is a viral disease, it will probably then be able to prevent or cure all the viruses that live within our bodies. Until then, you have to keep your immune system in top-notch condition by getting plenty of sleep, eating right, and avoiding stress.

The advantage of monogamous relationships is that if you both don't have any of these diseases, you can have all the sex you want anytime at all. The problem is that if you have or had a monogamous relationship, you may have already lost interest in sex, a sad reason that many of you are looking for dates in the first place.

Hepatitis is a virus that attacks the liver. There three main types are HVA, HVB, and HVC. Like many of these virus diseases, there is no cure. However, in recent times, the drugs used to treat hepatitis are rather close to eradicating HVC. Some say it's already curable.

HVA is transmitted by contact with contaminated *stool* and therefore can be contracted during sexual activity, especially if you need to use a stool to engage in sex. Oops, not that kind of stool. With better hygiene, there is less chance of contracting this disease. Less exotic forms of sexual activity will help to keep you safe. Keep your tongue where it belongs. Hepatitis A is the least problematic form of the disease and goes away on its own after approximately two months. It is unlikely to cause future problems, unlike HVB and HVC. You can get hepatitis A from eating uncooked, infected shellfish. Why anyone eats anything not cooked amazes me, but they do! Sushi, anyone?

HVB is transmitted by contact with infected *blood, semen,* and *other body fluids*. Having sex with an infected person falls into that category. This means you don't want to have sex with someone who has HVB.

According to the Centers for Disease Control and Prevention (CDC), among adults in the United States, hepatitis B is most commonly spread through sexual contact and accounts for nearly two thirds of acute hepatitis B cases. In fact, hepatitis B is 50–100 times more infectious than HIV/AIDS. Oral sex with strangers anyone? I don't think so.

HVC is transmitted by infected *blood*. Since the virus is not found in sufficient quantity in saliva and semen, it is not generally transmitted by kissing, sharing eating utensils, breastfeeding, hugging, holding hands, coughing, or sneezing. It is also not spread through food or water. It is not generally spread by sexual activity unless there is bleeding. As such, it is best to use a condom and avoid rough sex. If you don't know what rough sex is, you are probably going to be okay unless you meet someone who likes it.

There is a vaccine for HVA and HVB. If you are leading an active sex life, you should consider the vaccines.

There was a treatment for HVC that was difficult (lots of side effects and complications), protracted (injections and pills for up to a year or longer), and expensive. More recently, newer medications to treat HVC are being considered cures. They are very effective and not associated with such dire complications.

HVB and HVC can cause cirrhosis of the liver and even liver cancer years later. Treatment helps to reduce this risk.

Many people who contract HVB and HVC are current or past IV drug users. You may want to consider who you hang around with before you enter into a committed relationship with those who went down that path. The bottom line for all of these diseases is practice safe sex!

Human papillomavirus (HPV) is an important issue for all of us older daters. Since an illustrious former president seemed to regard oral sex as something innocent, too many kids today think of oral sex as a nonissue. Many of them actually think it is safer than having conventional sex. They may be mistaken, and so may you!

Genital warts are the most common STD caused by a virus. Here are some stats from the CDC: approximately 20 million Americans are currently infected with HPV. Another 6 million people become newly infected each year. HPV is so common that at least 50% of sexually active men and women get it at some point in their lives. About 1% of sexually active adults in the US have genital warts at any one time.

Genital warts are highly contagious. There is a 60% risk of getting the infection from a single sexual contact with someone who has genital warts. This means you probably have been exposed to this virus if you have had a number of sex partners. Fortunately, most cases heal on their own over time.

By having unprotected sex, you risk catching genital warts. And it wouldn't be so bad if all you got was warts. HPV (the wart virus) has variant strains (around 100 different types), some of which cause most cases of cervical cancer. Yes, cervical cancer is as STD. No one tells us this kind of stuff.

You get this virus from intercourse. Medicine knows this, yet they've done a poor job explaining it to a generation of people who are licking and sucking everything they see.

Recently it was discovered that this virus could just as likely jump from the cervix to the mouth or anus with all the oral and anal sex going on. If it can cause cancer in one mucous membrane, it most likely will cause cancer in others. Penile, anal, and oral cancer, along with cervical cancer, can be caused by HPV viruses.

The incidence of oral cancer is rising in young people, and while we used to think alcohol and tobacco were the culprits in oral cancer, a good 25% of patients with oral cancer don't drink or smoke. The medical establishment now realizes that HPV is a factor in oral cancer just as it is in cervical cancer.

Symptoms include one or more growths on the penis, testicles, groin, vaginal opening, and the vaginal canal, as well as the cervix, thighs, or anus. Warts may be raised, flat, or cauliflower shaped. They usually do not hurt. Warts may appear within weeks or months after sexual contact with an infected person. Men and women with genital warts will often complain of painless bumps, itching, and discharge.

Because genital warts often cause no symptoms, they may be left alone. However, because they are contagious, it is wise to talk to your doctor about having them removed. About 10%–20% go away with no treatment after around 3 to 4 months. You really have to be careful when having sex in the dating world. More and more people are looking to just have fun, and they don't realize the risks they are taking with their promiscuous behavior.

78

DOES DATING CAUSE CANCER?

AT FIRST, you might think the title of this section is scintillating so as to catch your attention. Sadly, it's not. Does dating cause cancer? The short answer is yes. Oh, my! *This author must be crazy*, you think. Well, that's not the case, and here's some proof.

It is well documented that most cases of cervical cancer are caused by HPV. This is not fiction. You can look it up and find references everywhere. Cervical cancer is actually an STD. This means that during sexual intercourse, the virus that causes this particular cancer is transmitted from the male penis to the female vagina and finds its way to the cervix where it causes pathological changes in the mucous membranes that may result in cancer.

If you do get exposed, and can't fight it off, it usually takes years for the process to advance to the point that you find out that you have cancer. This long incubation period –the long time for the virus to take its toll – is the reason that it is difficult for medicine to make determinations as to cause and effect when they study cancer.

Viruses have incubation times that can range from days to decades, and once the infection takes hold it, can take another number of years for symptoms to show up. This makes it very difficult to show the association with cancer, let alone its causation.

Using protection (e.g., a condom) is probably the best way to avoid this type of cancer other than avoiding sex altogether, or at least avoiding promiscuity that puts you at greater risk than if you limit your number of sexual partners. STDs are much like Russian roulette. The more times you take a turn (have sex with new partners) the more chance you have of losing.

There are many other cancers that may be STDs that we haven't yet recognized. Twenty-five years ago, they didn't know that HPV caused cervical cancer. Ten years ago, the association between oral cancer and HPV was not known, yet today medical science says there is an association, and very likely a causation, between HPV and oral cancer.

Though researchers haven't fully committed to the oral cancer issue, they are getting closer. The leading experts already know that HPV is an actual cause of oral cancer, but like much of science, they don't really want to go out on a limb until they are certain. Unfortunately, the media and the medical establishment seem reluctant to tell the masses that certain sexual activities can cause cancer. We've known the cervical cancer connection for years, yet most people (including women who have a cervix) don't know or don't understand the situation, which is why the disease spread so much until the advent of vaccines that help prevent HPV infection.

Interestingly, penile and rectal cancers are becoming much more common within the homosexual community. This, again, is HPV spreading from various sexual practices. When HPV vaccines were first made available, they were only for young girls to prevent cervical cancer. Now they are approved all young boys as well. That has to tell you something that the medical doctors are not talking about ... yet.

Now that we have established that dating *can* and *does* cause cancer, one might be inclined to ask, is there more bad news? In time, science will surely reveal more dangers that lurk in the shadowy corners of the genitalia.

79

DOES KISSING CAUSE CANCER?

WE LEARNED about the HPV and how, in certain circumstances, it is transmitted by sexual intercourse and can cause cancer if your immune system can't fight it off. So, what about kissing? Can such a glorious and pleasurable activity cause cancer?

Before you accuse me of being the Grinch who stole Kissmas, let me explain that the HPV virus can be in saliva, and, as such, should have the capacity to spread the infection by way of kissing. Certainly, oral sex is pretty much now known to transmit the virus and causes oral cancer and cervical cancer (i.e., penis/vagina sex isn't the only cause). While the kissing connection has not yet been proven – and even if it were to be – it is a much more difficult way to transmit the virus, so don't get in an uproar; however, understand that as science makes new discoveries, it is likely that they will figure this one out in time.

It makes perfect sense. After all, the incidence of anal and penile cancers has been on the rise with the increased practice of anal and anal-oral sex, especially in the gay population, and, as such, researchers now know that these cancers are caused by HPV and must be recognized as STDs.

It is this author's contention that cancer is a viral disease, and not just the HPV kind. Viruses have the ability to enter cells and mess with their DNA. They take control of the cells, causing them to replicate uncontrollably, resulting in unlimited growth, hence cancer.

There have been some rare cases of breast cancers being related to viruses. Even more disconcerting is the identification of mouse mammary tumor virus (MMTV)-like viral DNA in human breast tumors.

Many years ago, a rare leukemia with a 40-year incubation period was identified in Japan. Now, many years later, science has identified a human retrovirus (HTLV-1) that is known to cause adult T-cell leukemia.

How long until the world of science identifies more viruses that cause cancer and finally recognizes that cancer is a viral disease? The unusually long incubation periods of some viruses, as well as the difficulty in isolating viruses, makes the association between virus and cancer so difficult. Researchers are getting better, and in time we shall likely learn that cancer is a *contagious* viral disease. You read it here first! One day you may thank the Grinch who stole Kissmas for saving your life!

80

HIV/AIDS

HIV (HUMAN IMMUNODEFICIENCY virus) is probably the most studied virus of all time, and with this plethora of research, they still haven't been able to find a cure. HIV is the virus that causes AIDS (acquired immunodeficiency syndrome). This virus may be passed from one person to another when infected blood, semen, or vaginal secretions come in contact with an uninfected person's broken skin or broken mucous membranes.

Of the people who are infected with HIV (the virus), some, not all, will go on to develop AIDS as a result of their HIV infection. The only way to know whether you or your date is infected with HIV is to be tested. You cannot rely on symptoms alone because many people who are infected with HIV do not have symptoms for many years. Someone can look and feel healthy yet still be infected. In fact, one quarter of the HIV-infected persons in the United States do not know they are infected. Of course, don't meet on a first date and insist on an HIV test. You may come off as a bit of a nut.

Symptoms of early HIV infection include fever, headache, fatigue, swollen lymph glands, and rash. I know what you're thinking; you had those symptoms in the past. Yeah, these are the same symptoms as so many other viral illnesses, like the flu. HIV symptoms usually develop two to four weeks after exposure. These early HIV symptoms usually disappear within a week to a month and are often mistaken for other viral infections, like the flu. During this period, you are very infectious. More persistent or more severe symptoms of HIV may not appear for several years after this initial infection.

There are some things to be thankful for. HIV is *not* a hardy virus, in that it takes a large amount to cause disease, and it doesn't do well on countertops or toilet seats. It does, however, go to town when given the chance. It takes blood exposure to spread. Therefore, while the virus resides in semen and in vaginal secretions, as well as blood, you have to be inoculated by getting it into your bloodstream. Low and behold, that can happen when you practice rough, unsafe sex. Anal sex is a good start; anal sex by definition is rough sex. The mucous membranes of the rectum weren't designed to take a pounding. They tear and this results in an opening for the virus to spread.

While the authorities would like you to think all sex is the same regarding AIDS, it isn't. Plain old penile-vaginal sex is less likely to cause HIV. So don't be afraid to have sex, but practice safe sex. The vagina can tear, too, when sex is vigorous, when the vagina has atrophied from not having sex enough, or when the vaginal mucosa may be thin as is the case in postmenopausal women.

Don't have sex when you are menstruating. While most older women have passed that point, you older horny guys dating young women can get into trouble.

If you have any sores on your genitals or mouth, like those found with a herpes outbreak, or if you just had dental surgery, hold off on your sexual escapades until you heal. You can always use the "I have a headache" excuse to put off your sex-starved date.

If you have HIV or AIDS, it is a nice idea to tell your prospective dates that you do, so they can refuse to go out with you. Actually, that is a dilemma you have to decide how to handle. If you tell someone who is uninfected, the likelihood is high that he or she will not go out with you. This could mean your only dates will be with others who are also infected. Not to make light of the situation, but once you have HIV, you become a modern-day leper in regard to dating.

Take a look at some serious statistics from our government from 2015. According to the CDC, more than 1.1 million people in the US are living with AIDS, and of those, 15.8% don't know they have the disease. There are 50,000 new cases each year.

While we all know to practice safe sex, it is not always likely that in the fit of passion we use common sense. To be a little bit extra safe, consider where AIDS is most likely to be found. Again, according to the CDC, the highest incidence of new AIDS infection is found in white males who are MSM (men who have sex with men, i.e., gay or bisexual, at 11,200 new cases per year), followed by black MSM (10,600 new cases), Hispanic MSM (6700 new cases), black heterosexual women (5,300 new cases), black heterosexual men (2,700 new cases), white heterosexual men (1,300 new cases), and then IV drug users. This tells you that dating in certain populations puts you at greater risk for contracting AIDS. Be advised; according to the CDC, by race, African Americans face the most severe burden of HIV. Why is AIDS such a problem in the black community? There is a high degree of promiscuity and ignoring safe sex recommendations, especially in poor inner-city communities.

81

PREVENTING STDS WHEN DATING

THERE ARE some easy rules to keep you safe from catching STDs in the world of dating.

First and foremost, there is *abstinence*. Don't have sex with anyone other than yourself. Another option is virtual sex on the Internet (i.e., cybersex). Remember, virtual is nothing like the real thing.

At first blush, you may realize having sex with yourself, or avoiding it altogether, provides for a rather unexciting life: no blood tests, no trips to the doctor, no medicines that could make you sick, no shortened life-span, just no damn fun.

You want to have some fun, and you will want to date rather than wither away alone, so abstinence may not be the best way to go even if it is the safest. If you use common sense, you will reduce your chance of contamination.

Try a *monogamous relationship*. You don't want to sleep around. The more sexual partners you have, the more at risk you put yourself in.

Use protection. Condoms made of latex rubber help prevent STDs, but they don't protect you when engaging in oral sex, unless you use a condom to perform fellatio – try flavored condoms or use plain ones. You don't want to suck on lubricated condoms soaked in spermicides. Men can consider using a piece of latex rubber to perform cunnilingus. None of this is like the real thing, but it's better than getting a disease. Perhaps digital stimulation or the use of sex toys can become a good substitute for oral proclivities.

I actually don't know of anyone who uses latex protections for oral sex because it is not cool. I just can't picture a sexy movie star using a condom for a bow job any more than I can see James Bond using Saran wrap to perform cunnilingus. I don't know what to tell you other than make sure you know a little about those with whom you sleep.

Avoid having sex when you are drunk or on drugs, as your discretion and judgment may be impaired, resulting in sex acts you may not have otherwise considered. You don't want to wake up from an Ecstasy/mushroom experience to find yourself having sex with someone you don't know, involved in an orgy with people who speak little or no English, or find yourself on a movie set staring into a porn director's camera. Getting high leads you to make bad choices.

If you find someone who you consider spending much of your life with, get *tested* for STDs to make sure neither of you has any, and keep the relationship monogamous so you can engage in all sorts of sex without fear.

This series on STDs is not meant to scare you. It is meant to make you a bit more careful. As we now live in Sodom, it is best to be discrete and maybe skip that first-date sexual encounter with a person you don't know from Adam. Even Adam can't be trusted when you know he ate that apple after he was warned against it!

Activity Suggestions – If you have been sexually active this past year, get a blood test for STDs. This will hopefully give you a clean slate. You should ask a serious date to do the same if you like one another and both concur.

82

TUBERCULOSIS AND DATING

WHILE NOT CONSIDERED AN STD, tuberculosis is becoming a problem in many Third World countries, as well as in the developed world, the result of all the intercontinental flights between nations and the waves of immigration from poorer countries. If our government and the politicians who run things had a collective brain, perhaps they wouldn't let anyone and everyone enter our country without some type of screening for communicable diseases.

Most of you don't have to worry about getting TB while dating unless you go out with someone who contracted it in another country, is of low socioeconomic status, or who has exposure to many newly arriving immigrants. You could even go out with that nice doctor who just happened to contract a serious illness like TB from one of his patients.

For those of you frequenting houses of ill repute – how quaint a term for such an advanced society as we find ourselves living in – you may have an encounter with a provider (a.k.a. prostitute) who has recently come to America from a Third World nation where there was no testing for communicable diseases. More likely she came here illegally through our uncontrolled leaky borders. She is now turning tricks in some place you happen to frequent, and you can end up contracting a dangerous, difficult-to-treat disease.

If you find a provider coughing a lot, you may want to excuse yourself and go home. It is more likely be a common cold, but it could also be a serious illness. Granted, this same thing can happen if you happen to be sitting next to a person with TB while taking a flight or even while riding the subway in New York City. Yikes!

Stay away from coughing people. Be safe! Tell your politicians you'd like them to implement things like *quarantines* for suspected cases of serious illnesses, to prevent their spread, like they used to do years ago. Tell them to deal with illegal immigration.

83

CAN YOU CATCH EBOLA WHEN DATING?

WHY WOULD you even turn to this section? What is the chance that you could get Ebola on a date? According to our medical authorities, there is no chance that this could happen to you unless you fly to West Africa and go on that kind of date. But in America? No way. There aren't nearly as many Internet dating services to meet West Africans as there are services to meet people from China, Russia, and most every other country. You can even have your foreign date come to visit you here in the good old USA if you are willing to pay his or her expenses. And who knows what exotic diseases you might bring from foreign nations, including West Africa?

Actually, the whole idea of contracting Ebola on a date is farfetched for now. Could that change if we have an epidemic of this fatal virus that spreads throughout our country because we have terrible health policies in place? Let's take a look at what could happen that would make dating even more complicated and troublesome than it is already.

From the beginning of medical science, learned physicians understood the need for quarantine. This was the most effective way to isolate sick, highly contagious people to prevent the spread of disease throughout the general population. They soon discovered that quarantine can actually eradicate or at least control disease by preventing its ability to spread. Quarantine is a time-honored method that is still very much in use today. Diseases like typhus, cholera, plague, tuberculosis, and other nonpolitical infections have necessitated such medical intervention.

In the early 1980s, our esteemed politicians created a new, nonmedical approach to managing serious diseases. Contagious disease became a political issue and doing anything that might reveal the contraction of AIDS became forbidden. Quarantine was out.

This takes us to Ebola, an even more deadly virus that strikes faster (an incubation period of 21 days vs. AIDS, which is 2 years) and a very high death rate.

With regard to any type of dating, including Internet dating, the chances of contracting Ebola are remote. But that will change quickly if this disease is not contained through medical quarantine or finding a cure, and even more importantly, through sensible policies that prevent travel to and from the hot spots in West Africa – or anywhere insidious disease becomes epidemic.

If we do find that there is an extensive outbreak of Ebola, or if it were to become epidemic, there are some rules to help you in the dating world. First, stop dating, buy a hazmat suit, and stay home.

When meeting a new dating prospect by email, or phone, or at a museum, or anywhere, you may want to ask this person about their travel experiences. If they never go to exotic places, there is much less chance of contracting Ebola, that for now is more isolated in West Africa. Next, if anyone you consider dating is sick at the time of your date make sure you cancel. Unlike AIDS, Ebola is only contagious when symptoms are present, the most obvious symptom being fever. Even if you are offered a date with a nice person with the flu, stay away. You don't want the flu either.

While practicing safe sex by using condoms will help to prevent AIDS (no guarantees), with Ebola there is no such thing as safe anything other than a safe wave from across the room.

84

DEFORMITY, DISABILITY, AND DATING

AN INTERESTING THING happens in your fifties and sixties. You find that you and some of your contemporaries are much more likely than the typical youthful dater to have experienced diseases that resulted in deformity and disability.

By their fifties and sixties, there are many women who have had a bout with breast cancer or at least a breast biopsy. Sometimes there are disfiguring consequences. Other diseases result in people requiring feeding tubes, and now they have abdominal scars. There are certainly many people with old appendicitis, caesarian, or abdominal surgery scars. And by this age, others have had bypass operations that leave them with assorted scars of the chest. There are even those who have colostomy bags required to repair bouts with colitis or colon cancer.

It's not wise to include mention of these deformities on your e-date profile, unless you can do it with flair: "Happy person looking for a mate. Just purchased shoes to go with my bag (colostomy). Let's go on the town tonight!"

While you should forget that idea, the likelihood is that your new date will have no idea about your infirmity until you get intimate unless you tell him or her. Yes, there will come a time that your new mate will see you naked and realize that you have had problems in the past. This can result in worry that may translate into other fears, like performance anxiety in both men and women.

I would guess that it's best to let things happen naturally with a subtle heads-up. As you proceed with intimate relations, the revelation will take place. If a disability or deformity turns off your mate, you move on and recognize this wasn't the person for you.

Once you get to know and have a fondness for each other, deformity may be overlooked, as it should. Some will have the feeling that they need to be up-front with their dates before meeting them. They want to mention that they had breast cancer before the naked truth comes out. Others may want to wait until they have made out (do they even use that term anymore?). Some women may figure that if they stimulate the guy's sex brain, he'll be better with acceptance.

The conversation can go something like this: "I had breast cancer a few years ago, and I just wanted to let you know." This tells the guy that he may be in for something otherwise unexpected. A missing breast, nipple, or other assorted surprises maybe be better forewarned, but it depends on the person. If you are with someone who has trouble with the thought of any prosthesis or deformity, this isn't the person for you. It doesn't necessarily make the person shallow, as there are some people who can't handle certain medical issues, just like there are some people who faint at the sight of blood.

If there is a real issue, like you have no legs, or if you've had sex-reassignment surgery, you may owe this person a little detail before you undress. This even goes for a colostomy bag.

I wish I had the answer for you on these matters, but I don't. I guess there is a need for specialized sites like IHaveNoPenis.date.com or ColostomyBag.date.com. They would be able to deal with those types of personal matters. Your medical professionals would have ways for you to deal with your particular issue as they deal with them every day. Support groups are also a good source for how to deal with these issues.

Other ailments, like a bad case of psoriasis or leprosy, can be a concern as well. One of the reasons for such a comfort level with a mate who accepts you with all of your infirmity is that it makes for a loyal relationship.

Infirmity and deformity are serious subjects that keep many so inflicted out of the game altogether, and that is sad; there is nothing like a romantic connection. Eckhart Tolle said, "A romantic relationship is worth seven years of therapy." I think he said that, or maybe it was, "*After* a romantic relationship, you *need* seven years of therapy."

In any event, you may want to talk to others who have managed deformity and disability issues, because you really should be in the game. There are sites online that deal with all sorts of issues regarding deformity, infirmity, and dating.

Activity Suggestions – List any deformities or conditions you have that may bother others. List any deformities and conditions that would be a complete turnoff for you.

85

MENOPAUSE AND DATING

WHEN YOU WERE young and dating, ladies, this topic never came up. Now that you may be entering into, living through, or just past menopause, and dating ... *again*, there are some important issues to consider.

First, some women get so uptight about the effects of menopause that it keeps them entirely out of the game. For some, it was menopause that got them back into the dating game, as it could have been a factor in a fifty-something divorce.

Menopause may cause several changes that may adversely affect relationships. Almost all of these changes are the result of the actual cause of menopause: *decreased levels of hormones*. Hormones can affect sexual desire (libido), sexual performance, and mood and cause depression, generalized discomfort (hot flashes), and painful sex.

If you feel hot and sweat a lot, can't sleep very well, are moody, not interested in engaging in sex, and when you do it's painful, there is a good chance your marital relationship is not going to be all that good. Many couples get through this with the right amount of understanding, counseling/therapy, medical treatment, and other assorted remedies. For others, there is a downward spiral that ends in either living frustrated lives without the closeness of sexual contact or divorce.

The very first thing you must do, if you find yourself with a frustrated mate or without a mate at all due to this change in life, is recognize that there is a problem and then get help. If the problem is mild, you may be able to work through it without much difficulty, but if the problem is profound, you really need to talk to someone and get the appropriate therapy, which may be a combination of talk therapy and medication. This advice goes for the guys, too. You may need counseling to help you better understand your relationship.

Because there is such misunderstanding about *hormone replacement therapy* (HRT), many women have been frightened away from this remedy, which in certain cases is necessary. This book is not the venue to discuss specific remedies, but you should speak with a knowledgeable doctor who works with bio-identical hormones. For a good start, read *The Sexless Marriage Fix: Rescuing a Sexless Marriage and Making It All It Can Be*, by myself and Dr. Roberta Foss-Morgan.

If *depression* is the predominant effect of your menopause, it can easily become debilitating, or at a minimum it can make seeking treatment very difficult. Depressed people are often in denial, or they don't have the stamina, energy, or clear-headedness to seek care. Often their friends and families will not know how to address the subject, and it goes untreated.

I'd venture to say there are many women out there who have given up on relationships because they are too depressed to care. This is sad. If you know anyone like this, try to encourage them to get help.

If you want to meet a new partner through dating, being moody and sad all the time and having no interest in engaging in painful sex will limit your chances of finding anyone, and if you are depressed you won't care one bit. If you are able to maintain your mood and level of happiness, and the only problem you have is sexual discomfort, there are many sex aids, such as lubricants and toys, that may help you to fulfill your sexual needs, as well as his.

Women who have been out of the game for a long time may find sex with a new partner difficult both physically due to pain and dryness and emotionally due to morality issues (sex was a forbidden taboo), modesty issues (nakedness with a new person is not always easy), and image issues (feeling bad about your body and the changes that have taken place over the years). Again, these issues can all be remedied to different degrees depending on how much effort you are willing to put forth.

If your weight and body shape bother you a great deal, you may want to consider diet and exercise. Don't expect that to happen if you are depressed; even with the most positive attitude, too many years of neglect may make the task seem daunting. The other option is to use all of your other attributes: kindness, sexual prowess, and personality.

With advancing age, all the hormone-related effects seen with menopause continue, albeit less dramatically. As we approach old age, there is a lot less sex going on. Relationships evolve into companionships and friendships, so make sure you like this person you date, because it may eventually lose some of the sexual/physical spark seen in earlier years.

Activity Suggestions – List the changes in your body, libido, and energy level you are experiencing. Put a star next to the ones you think you can slow down with proper care for yourself. List the changes that may have affected your last relationship and that may have contributed to its dissolution.

86

ANDROPAUSE AND DATING: BUMMER!

ANDROPAUSE JUST MEANS YOUR TESTOSTERONE, the main male hormone, is fading, as it does with all men over time. Testosterone is what gives you your sex drive, your *libido*. It helps maintain your heart health as well as your mental health and has much to do with erections (the true meaning of life for many men and women). So, you can see this is an important hormone.

Guys, when you were young and dating, this topic never came up. Now that you may be entering into or just past andropause, and find yourself dating ... *again*, there are some important issues to consider.

Just like with the ladies who enter menopause, the first step is to recognize if you have andropause; the next is to consider treating it. Of course, if your libido is shot, you have erectile dysfunction (ED), and you're feeling depressed by all of this, you probably have no desire to date anyone, let alone have sex. Even worse, ED may be a problem associated with low testosterone. That is why you need to keep your mind and eyes open for these changes and don't ignore them. It is much easier to fix a hormonal imbalance earlier rather than later. If you fall too far, you may never have any interest in fixing the problem even though it is fixable – even in its later stages, if you can pick yourself up and go for treatment. By the way, it's the same for the ladies and their hormones. Don't wait until you are too far gone.

There is a fear that treatment with testosterone causes *prostate cancer*. Recent findings show this to be unlikely. Rather, it is the improper use of testosterone that can lead to cancer if you allow the testosterone to convert into female hormones, which are more likely the trigger for prostate cancer. This is why it is so important to find a good doctor who understands the intricacies of the treatment and who is willing to see you often enough to monitor your blood chemistry to make sure you are not at risk.

Besides the sex issues of andropause, there are the other negative effects of low testosterone, including weight gain, flabbiness, lost motivation, and decreased executive skills. Yes, all the things that make you a man are in decline. Is it any wonder they call these guys *grumpy old men*?

Again, just as with the ladies, if your weight and body shape bother you, consider a diet and exercise regimen. But don't expect that to be easy if you are depressed; even with the most positive attitude, years of neglect may make the task seem impossible, but you can fix yourself with proper guidance and motivation.

The other option to testosterone therapy is to use all of your other attributes, such as kindness and a stellar personality, to find and make a partner happy when dating. Don't expect a Victoria-Secret-model lookalike will have much interest in you if you have become Humpty Dumpty, a eunuch, or Jimmy Carter – unless, of course, you have a Porsche.

For those of you who are younger and vital, take heed, take care of yourself, or you, too, will become your father and grandfather *before* your time!

Another bit of important advice: be careful of what you eat! Much of the beef and chicken that you ingest has been injected with estrogen (the female hormone) to make them bigger, plumper, and more tender. Well, guess what? This estrogen exposure is making men bigger, plumper, and more tender. It is probably also putting all of us at risk for prostate cancer and the women at risk for breast, ovarian, and uterine cancer. Consider buying and eating organic, grass-fed beef and organic free-range chicken.

Activity Suggestions – Have you ever noticed those warnings in the gym to check with your doctor before engaging in any exercise? Well, it may be time for a full checkup with your doctor. Get medical clearance before you engage in dating, which may lead to much walking with your new date as you go on shopping sprees and have vigorous sexual activity. Make sure to get your testosterone levels checked, too.

87

WILL YOU STILL LOVE ME TOMORROW ... WHEN I'M SICK?

THIS HAS nothing to do with the feelings you may, or may not, have after first sex. That was the big concern when you were a kid. You slept with that guy who said he loved you, and now you worry that he won't call you again. The world has changed. For today's kids, if they don't have first sex pretty soon, they will, in fact, not love you tomorrow.

For you who remember the tune by the same name, it's not about the tune. What we are concerned with here is a very serious and somewhat depressing thought: what will you, or your new mate do, if either of you becomes seriously ill?

A spouse has the biggest obligation to stay by your side "in sickness and in health, till death do us part." Yet we all know someone who left before that death part. Plenty have left for reasons having nothing to do with health, but those who leave when the other one is down, and on the way out, are looked upon as immoral. If you take pledges, like marriage vows, seriously and believe in contracts (verbal or written), and if you are just a good soul, you should stand by your man or woman in most cases, but especially when he or she is ill.

In the case of dates, are we held to the same standard? It all depends. Things are relative. If you went out on one date and have plans for next Saturday night, your need to become a caretaker for this person should he or she become ill before Wednesday is limited to, "Gee, I'm sorry to hear you came down with Alzheimer's disease, and I'll be seeing you around." You hang up, and it's all over. Hopefully, they won't remember this conversation.

How about the case where you've dated for a year and set the date of your marriage? Now you have a tad bit more responsibility. However, there are many, and I would even venture to say a whole lot, of people in that situation who would jump ship.

If you're in a committed relationship, and your mate becomes terribly ill, you have some soul-searching to do, and it's not going to be easy. You are in love, we would suspect, and as such, you are supposed to be there for this person and not be as concerned with your own personal needs. Yet, there is no contract and you can walk away if you so desire.

I wish I had the answer and didn't just offer you a bad thought about a serious subject. When you fell in love with that other person (your ex), you never had any intention of leaving, nor did your ex have an intention of leaving you, but life went along a path that had you at each other's throats, and one of you jumped ship, didn't you?

Becoming a caregiver can be one of the most difficult challenges, yet also be a rewarding experience, depending on the way you handle the task. The actual decision as to whether you will stick around has to do with several factors based on how you respond to a calamity with your mate. It is a combination of the depth of your love, your capacity for dealing with adversity, your morality and sense of responsibility, your self-interests, the type of infirmity, your wealth or lack thereof that would allow you to provide care with less stress upon yourself, and the amount of time you have known your lover.

All of these factors come in to play, and it's never easy to think about how you would respond to a tragic infirmity. Many of you will have to deal with the likes of breast and prostate cancer, diseases that can be disfiguring and life altering. Some will have to contend with terminal illnesses that could can last for weeks or go on for years. Mental illness can drive you mad, and I'm not talking about the one afflicted with the mental illness.

These are just some things to consider. Don't dwell on the subject as it can be disheartening. And whatever you do, don't bring up the subject with your lover, unless you are going to tell them that no matter what happens, you will be by his or her side. If you can't tell your lover that, you will ruin your relationship, it will end, and you won't have to worry about this anymore.

One of the nice things about long-term relationships, as in 20 years or longer, especially when you're married, is that your mate usually stands by when an infirmity strikes.

VIII

THE MECHANICS OF DATING

88

GUESS WHO'S COMING TO DINNER!

YOU'RE THINKING, *A rather provocative title for this section.* You're probably wondering, *Who's coming to dinner?* Is this an interracial thing, like the movie? Actually, it's not related to race, and it's *you* who are coming to dinner *to meet the kids.*

There comes a time when you get to meet the children. This may vary depending on the age of your date, when she or he decided to have children, and what their personal philosophy is regarding such matters. And you may meet the kids in one of many settings, not necessarily at dinner.

Since much of this book is about older daters, meeting the kids at this stage is less stressful, since the kids are often adults by this time. Coming home to meet the kids is often unlikely at this stage because the kids may be living in their own homes, and they may have their own kids. So let's not worry about meeting the grandkids, though that, too, presents some issues we can discuss at another time (like when you are older).

The most difficult children to meet are those who are little, those under eighteen, and especially those under ten. If you are fifty-something or sixty-something and dating, you won't run into the young kids unless you start dating people ten to twenty years younger than yourself. Yes, dating a young person has some definite problems you may not have thought about until you find yourself doing their kid's homework and eventually paying for another college education.

Some parents want the children to meet their dates way too soon. They often introduce you as a friend, which is alright. Others want to call you "aunt" or "uncle," and this is not a good idea, especially since these kids usually end up having 20 or more aunts and uncles if their parents date around a lot. When they get old enough, they'll realize their parent is a slut or a womanizer.

If you have the luxury of holding off meeting the kids until the relationship is serious, that would be best. Ladies, if the guy has to pick you up at your home, it may be best to explain to the child, if they are mature enough to understand, that mommy is looking for a new husband. Of course, consultation with a psychologist is warranted if the kids are too young to understand, or if they are old enough to carry a firearm. If it's the guy who has to introduce his kids to the new woman, he can merely tell the kids he's looking to get laid (yes, this is supposed to be comedy).

There is much more chance of complications when the children are young. The psychological implications are varied and have much to do with the situation: divorce versus death, the maturity of the child, and the relationship the child had or has with either or both parents, to name a few.

Even your personality and looks come into play. If you are cool, beautiful or handsome, your dates' children may be more inclined to accept you, while if you are witch-like and scary looking, you may not have such luck being accepted as a replacement for their real mom or dad.

The best chance of a successful meeting has a lot to do with the preparation made by the child's parent. If the ex bad-mouths you, you may have problems being accepted by the kids. If the children favor the parent you are dating, you have much better chance of a good relationship. Since there are so many variables, a few rules may help you in your quest for peace.

Make sure you never bad-mouth your date's children even if your date does so. You are the outsider and blood is blood. The stressed parent may say things they really don't mean or believe, and when you agree or elaborate on the negative remarks, he or she may turn on you. If you really like this person, you have to accept his or her children to some degree based directly on how much your date wants you to.

Being complimentary about the children will ingratiate you with your date. That doesn't mean you have to be phony, but don't be afraid to praise them when in order.

Try to be personable and include the child in your conversation (i.e., don't brush them off). They can sense insincerity and condescension. The older the children, the less the hassle, as college-age kids have their own lives and probably care less about you, but you can still show interest in their endeavors.

While you may be more interested in hopping in bed (mostly the guys), or looking to buy a diamond ring (mostly the gals), you may have to spend some time with those little rascals belonging to your date. If you love kids, this will enrich your life, but if it's the bed hopping or diamonds that mean more, kids will be an imposition.

Control your expressions of discontent, or you may just lose this person. I know that if my potential lover and new life partner didn't like or want to be involved with my kids, she's no longer in contention. Most people feel this way about their kids.

If you really don't like kids, your date's in particular, and if he or she wants to dote on them incessantly, you may be in the wrong relationship. Recognize the reality and move on as required. Even good sex or big diamonds don't make living with a miserable family worthwhile.

It is nice to ask about your date's kids when you are in a real relationship or if you wish to move the relationship forward. Bringing a little treat for the kids is a great way to bond. It can be as simple as a candy bar or a dime bag of cocaine, depending on the interests of the children. Not only will the kids like you, they may even get you naked pictures of their parents.

Since, as noted earlier, many of you are older and dating older folks, and the kids will mostly live out of the house, either away at college or on their own. Opportunities will arise that will allow you to meet them. Don't be afraid (or too cheap) to take them to dinner with you. Not only will you ingratiate yourself with your date, you may get new insights that can help you close the deal or move on.

If you find that your prospective mate is overbearing, controlling, spoiling his or her kids, you may find yourself experiencing the same things once your mate hooks you. Keep your eyes open, and use all of the information you glean to help you make informed judgments about this potential new life partner. The way potential mates treat their kids is often a good indicator of how they will treat you.

Activity Suggestions – Give some thought as to how you feel about children at this stage of your life. If you are definitely not interested, consider mentioning this in your profile, or pay particular attention to the profiles of prospective dates.

89

THE MAGIC OF DATING - THE MAGICIAN

YES, the Amazing Crisco is appearing tonight. From near and far, the townsfolk gathered to see his performance. There is much in common between the Amazing Crisco and your new love interest. The analogy is quite strong, but most people never make the association.

If you know anything about magic, and even if you don't, you must have seen how one or another magic trick works. Once you learned the secret, you pretty much ruined the illusion for yourself and realized that the trick wasn't such a big deal. It was like when you found out there is no Tooth Fairy or Santa Claus. There's a reason that all the great magicians have a code of honor to never reveal their tricks. It's because they know, well, that once you know the trick, *the magic is gone*. Now, let's try to relate this simple, easy-to-understand concept to love and relationships.

When you first meet someone with whom you find that special thing we call *chemistry*, part of the magic is that you don't really know him or her very well. Your new partner is a mystery, like the metaphorical magic trick, not to be confused with the trick you picked up in the bar the other night.

The element of mystery makes new love interests desirable because all you see are the things that you like ... the things related to your immediate chemistry. Once you get to know them, you see all sorts of things from behind the curtain. Notice we continue with the metaphors, in this case taken from *The Wizard of Oz*.

The things you learn about new love interests are often mundane and even border on the not so great. Let's face it: if you met someone who kept picking his or her nose and passing gas, you wouldn't give the person another thought. That's why it takes time for your mate to feel comfortable enough to let it all hang out – and start nose picking and farting – and when he or she does, *the magic is gone.*

The point of this section is to better understand why relationships are so much more difficult as they move forward, allowing the magic to disappear along the way.

In order to maintain the fire, the passion, we all have to work hard to hide our magical secrets, like picking our noses and playing pull-the-finger, something all men learn from their fathers. There are so many behaviors that are repulsive, and yet we seem to think that just because someone makes a commitment to us, we can show this all these secrets (secrets here being a euphemism for disgusting behaviors).

You have to take stock of yourself, and try to think of all *your secrets*. Let's list a few. For the guys, we already mentioned two. Other guy *secrets* include not listening to our mates when they need to vent, leaving our dirty clothing laying around, missing the bowl and never noticing, leaving hairs in the shower that could easily be washed away if we kept a magnifying glass with us in the shower, and turning over to go to sleep within two minutes of our orgasms with little or no cuddle time. We forget birthdays and other assorted important moments, like the anniversary of the day we met. And let's not forget that especially good *secret* we seem to have acquired genetically because it is so universal ... leaving the toilet seat lid in the up position. I could go on and on for the guys, but you get the point.

The women have an equally good bunch of *secrets* up their

sleeves as well. They might try to hide their arguing over every little thing, crying for no apparent reason, hounding their men with long stories of gossip and bullshit the moment husbands get home, spending hours to put on makeup and do their hair, and shopping whereby they spend more than a small Third World country's gross national product. Again, I could go on and on, but you do get the idea.

Part of the inspiration for this section has much to do with the idea that dating is fun, whereas more involved relationships tend to degenerate into not so much fun. You see, when we are in the dating stage, the honeymoon phase, and the early period of any relationship, we don't show our lovers the secrets behind our tricks. They only see us in the light of pure, amazing grace. They feel the magic, and, oh, how good it feels.

It takes a lot of work to keep the magic alive. If you don't think you can do it, maybe you'd be better off keeping a little distance and retaining a great dating relationship rather than entering into a marriage that may end up the same way around half of them currently do.

Activity Suggestions – List three bad secrets that you should never show to your mate. Become aware that these secrets can ruin relationships over the course of time. Are there any secrets you could work on improving now?

90

MONOGAMY OR NOT MONOGAMY ... THAT IS A QUESTION

YOU HAVE to decide what you require besides simply the traits of the person you want to meet. Do you want a monogamous relationship, or do you want to date many people? Do you want commitment like in the institution of marriage? The answer to these questions has a lot to do with your personal experiences, your desires and your view of the world. It even has a lot to do with your sex, and I mean that in terms of both your gender and level of promiscuity.

From my observations, it appears that more women are looking for marriage or at a minimum a monogamous relationship. Can you blame them? After all, they are the smarter sex – to an extent. You see, monogamy is safer from a disease standpoint and more secure from a "take good care of me" security standpoint. And it has the potential to afford deeper spiritual and emotional connection.

It is not that all women want or need to be taken care of, but if they can get a chance at an easy life, why shouldn't they take it? It's called marrying for money, and don't ever think this doesn't happen. And don't for a second think there aren't guys out there with the same motivations. They, too, would love to hook up with a Splenda Momma. (That's the female version of a Sugar Daddy without all the calories. Don't think too much about that one; it's just a joke.)

Considering that many males have that insatiable sexual appetite, they may not be ready for a monogamous relationship. Evolutionary psychologist David Buss, among others, says "men are simply wired to seek out as many female partners as possible."

Now here's the part about how those "smart women" aren't really all that smart. You see, there is much to be said about the expression "Why buy the cow when you can get the milk for free?" We wouldn't be having this discussion if a woman held back sex until the guy made a commitment. People seem to forget (or in the case of those under 40, they never knew this stuff in the first place) there was a time guys could not get sex unless they made a commitment. There may have always been a floozy (loose woman) or two floating around, but for the classy girls, us guys would not get to sleep with them until we made a commitment.

The world has changed for the better according to those who subscribe to pop culture. Yes, we have free love, lots of strange diseases, and all sorts of sexual crimes and perversions that may have never surfaced and made their way into daily conversation had we maintained some level of taboo associated with sex. Instead, we took the "anything goes" attitude, and, yes, anything goes.

If you try to withhold sex in our uninhibited, cool society, you'll come off looking square, not hip, and you will probably not get many dates – unless you are drop-dead gorgeous or you don't mind dating nerdy guys who are just happy to have a date. You can, however, at least be a little discrete and not jump into bed with everyone you meet on a first date. Yes, there are some nymphomaniacs out there who do jump into many beds, but they are usually not looking for monogamy any more than many of the libidinous guys.

I venture to say that women's need for monogamy and men's serial dating are universal, as much as you might like to think I am off base. Just look at *konkatsu*. You may have never heard of this, but it is the latest thing to hit Japan (not counting that earthquake from a few years back). *Konkatsu* is marriage hunting and all the rage in Japan. Marriage rates in Japan have plummeted. From 1975 to 2005, the unmarried population went from 14% to 47% for men aged 30 to 34, and from 8% to 32% for women in the same group. Some argue that these societal changes are related to money troubles, uncertain jobs prospects, and the disappearance of traditional matchmaking. Bull! The women are giving away the milk, and the guys don't need to make a commitment to fulfill their ever-present lust. *That's* why marriage rates are falling!

The women's desire to be taken care of is present in Japanese society, too. It was best said by a 35-year-old office worker, Yuriko Akamatsu, who told the *Wall Street Journal* interviewers, "I want to get married because I sometimes feel like quitting my job. Marriage is like permanent employment."

Right on, baby! I just wish I could have pulled that off in my first life. It is true; women still have the opportunity to become the homemaker and be a stay-at-home mom if they are fortunate enough to have a husband who can support them that way. Many gave that up with the feminist movement. The *konkatsu* movement sees more women than men running to meet for the purpose of marriage, and again I think this all has to with the dairy industry.

You really can't date more than one person at a time if you want any kind of decent relationship. Everyone wants to feel loved, and if you are seeing two or more people, one or more partners are going to get jealous, and you can't blame them.

It is up to you to decide how you want to deal with the person who won't make a commitment toward monogamy after a few months. You have every right to tell this person that you care for him or her, and if he or she expects the relationship to move forward, you need to be going steady. You can even take this further and insist upon marriage. Just realize this person may walk out of your life if you push too hard, and if your partner is not ready for any commitment at that time, or ever, that being his or her prerogative. You should try to figure this out rather soon in a relationship, before you get hooked and it becomes very difficult to break up.

Of course, you never know; perhaps if the two of you are really good for each other, treat each other with kindness, and engage in sex as much as each desires, your partner may have a change of heart and want to live with you for eternity. You never know!

Activity Suggestions – For those desiring matrimony, how long are you willing to wait? For those wanting a single life, what would it take to change your mind?

91

MARRIAGE ... WHEN DATING GOES TOO FAR!

- IF YOU want someone who will eat whatever you put in front of him or her and never say it's not quite as good as mother's, then get a dog.
- If you want someone always willing to go out, at any hour, for as long and wherever you want, then get a dog.
- If you want someone who will never touch the remote, doesn't care about football (or can't do without it), and can sit next to you as you watch romantic movies or the most recent action flick, then get a dog.
- If you want someone who is content to get on your bed just to warm your feet and whom you can push off if he snores, then get a dog.
- If you want someone who never criticizes what you do; doesn't care if you are pretty or ugly, fat or thin, young or old; who acts as if every word you say is especially worthy of listening to; and loves you unconditionally, perpetually, then get a dog.

But, on the other hand, if you want someone who will never come when you call, ignores you totally when you come home, leaves hair all over the place, walks all over you, runs around all night and only comes home to eat and sleep, and acts as if your entire existence is solely to ensure his happiness, then get a cat!

If you expected more from this book, sorry. Sometimes you need to have a sense of humor!

92

THE HEART, THE BRAIN, THE SEX GLANDS

UNDERSTANDING RELATIONSHIPS REQUIRES UNDERSTANDING the interrelationship of three organs, the *heart*, the *brain* and the respective *sex glands* (penis/testicles, for the men and clitoris/vagina/ovaries for the women). While the heart is, in this case, being used symbolically to represent *emotion*, the brain represents *reason* and the sex glands represent *physical desire/lust*.

For centuries philosophers, poets, and behavioral scientists have, at times, left out the sex part of the equation (probably because of the general taboo on anything sexual), and it is for that reason I posit that we are all misguided.

All too often we try to reconcile our understanding of ourselves and others by analyzing the heart and brain: Why did she leave me? Why does he drink? Why do we argue all the time? Why does he do all those jerky things? Why does she worry about money? Why does my mate cheat? Why do I have to put the toilet seat down? Any question you can imagine can best be explained by understanding the motivations and interactions of the heart, the brain, *and* the sex glands.

This is profound but also probably boring, so don't feel bad if you move on to another chapter, but also don't complain when you can't figure out why your life and the lives of your loved ones are evolving the way they do with seemingly little rhyme or reason.

Everyone knows that we should think with our heads, followed by our hearts, and particularly not with our sex glands. However, one special thing about our humanity is that we do have hearts and sex glands and should try to use them to make lives and conditions better. That is a noble goal and quite often it makes the world a better place. However, everyone knows of one case or another, either from personal experience or friends and family, where the use of the penis or vagina, over the heart and over the mind, had disastrous consequences.

You should have left this relationship long ago, whether you were putting up with an addicted personality, living with a gold digger; the list is long. They are all examples of where using the brain instead of the heart and sex glands may have led to a better outcome.

We can also count the many examples whereby, when we use the heart over the brain, we changed lives, enhanced our own, and made the world a better place. It is using a balance of the three immense forces of glands, heart, and brain that helps us navigate through the currents of life.

When we can't figure out why things turn out the way they do, or why people act the way they do, it is because we often forget to include sex in the equation. Many may think they include sex in the analysis, but all too often we count emotion as the sexual component of human behavior.

If you don't understand that love and lust are wildly different, you miss the point. Don't feel bad, because while it is easy to understand the difference between love and lust when looking at the words from a definition point of view, we can easily mistake love for lust and vice versa, and thus fail to understand certain behaviors.

So far, we looked at the easy stuff that everyone knows. It's the subtler reasons that come into play that make relationships difficult, and sometimes impossible, to understand.

Many of the complexities of human relationships have much to do with the sex glands – or, shall we say, sexuality. A glaring example has to do with older male daters who would have a generation ago been content to be in a sexless, coddled, lapdog relationship because their sex glands were no longer functioning. Once Viagra landed upon the shores of dating, they no longer had to be frustrated. The advent of ED medications brought forth what can be described as the *third sexual revolution*, the first being society accepting the promiscuity of the sixties/Woodstock era, and the second being the liberation of women, which very much coincided with Woodstock but had much more to do with the advent of birth control pills.

The liberation of women, along with the loss of sexual taboos, has allowed them to engage in just as much promiscuity and infidelity as men. This revolution has not necessarily led to a better environment in which to foster intimate relationships because it is no longer necessary to work out problems when one knows they can get satisfaction and sex elsewhere.

When you try to figure out what the hell is going on with your mate's behavior, just remember to include the sex glands in your analysis, or you may miss something important. They sometimes don't think with their brains.

Activity Suggestion – Think of a time when your head, heart, and sex glands were not working in unison. How did you resolve the conflict?

93

THE ODD COUPLE

THERE IS a certain curiosity when we see a 10 with a 1. When you see a hot woman with a nerdy guy, you have to wonder. No, not if he has a big wiener; rather, what the ...? How did this guy get this woman to hang on his arm?

The first thing we think is that she must be an escort. I know that's what you think, so don't deny it. Really, how many of you think, *oh, she must love him for his intellect.* Yeah right! Only if his intellect is how he made lots of money. About the only freaky-looking guy to have hot women longing for his intellect might be the Maharishi. But even in that case, I figure it's the size of his wiener.

I was walking around a very wealthy town in Silicon Valley. Lots of technology-money guys live around here. I had the opportunity to observe several of these odd couples. Yes, it's mostly hot women with nerdy men, not the other way around. It's like the porn thing and the prostitute thing. Most times, men are the participants in such activities, not women. It doesn't mean you won't see some cases of homely women with hulks; it's just the exception. And what are you thinking in those cases? *Yeah right, he appreciates her intellect.* Actually, it could be that she is good in bed, or he has a sexual hang-up and is dependent on her for the erection he can't have with others. Yes, the psychology of sexuality is a vast and interesting subject and may account for many unexplained phenomena.

More often than not, men who are kept will hang on to the arm of whoever keeps them the best. To this guy, it's a job, and when he gets off work, he usually is on the town with some hottie, complaining about how he can't be with her all the time because he is held on a leash.

Women who are kept exhibit similar behaviors. They hold on tight, and some are happy to live in luxury, while others want excitement they may not get from their dorky mates. So they play around with the tennis coach, the gardener, or the plumber.

And, yes, you never question the perfect couple, because they look like they belong together – think Brad Pitt and Angelina Jolie. Yet they have the same issues as the couples who don't seem to match, and look where they are now.

94

YOUR EX THINKS YOU'RE A JERK!

IT'S UTTERLY AMAZING how many great men and women are on dating services – at least based on their descriptions of themselves. They often start out by telling us how their friends would describe them. They use terms like *loyal, sweet, loving, kind, caring,* and *nurturing*. Add every conceivable nice quality, and you get the picture. Now here's the part that's difficult to comprehend. Most of these folks are divorced. Why would anyone in their right mind let these people get away? There's got to be something wrong with this picture.

Maybe we should have a "Truth-In-Dating" website where the *ex* writes the profile for each person. Then we might get a different picture. He's a lazy bum, drinks too much, can't hold a job, and cheats at the drop of a hat. Or maybe she's a real bitch, keeps a lousy house, and cooks things that can't be eaten.

In spite of all the negative ways your ex may think of you, there is a lid for every pot. Someone out there may find you just as charming as all your friends think you are. So, if your ex thinks you're a jerk, how is it that your new love thinks you are so great? This is an almost absurd reality of life and love. No matter what a jerk your ex was, there are going to be those out there that will not know it or see it right away. If he or she is really a jerk, in time it will be found out. Yes, once the honeymoon (lust) is over, the real person shines through.

There could also be some jerky traits that drove you crazy that may be admired or ignored by someone else who is actually nice. It's all relative. If your ex was a controller, and this new mate prefers to be controlled, now that's going to work, while it didn't work for you.

Some women think I am really nice, romantic, helpful, and all sorts of other things that would probably make my ex's blood boil. She could tell them a thing or two.

The reality is that we can get sick and tired of each other over time because we take each other for granted, we lose the passion, we are disrespectful when speaking to each other, and we forget why we fell in love. We show *contempt*, the prime source of failed relationships according to Dr. John Gottman, who has studied marriages more than most anyone.

Different needs and tastes explain it all! This is best explained by the expression "one man's trash is another man's treasure." I do hope this metaphor helps when you think of your ex ... that piece of trash.

It is probably best to find peace with your ex, especially if you have children and want to be able to sit in the same room and be civil. Perhaps your ex was really a good person, and for one reason or another you grew apart. There's even the highly unlikely possibility that *you* are the jerk. Always give the benefit of the doubt, and remember you are no longer with this person, so don't let them continue to hurt you. Think of the good times!

Activity Suggestions – Rate your current relationship with your ex from 1 to 10, with 1 being absolute contempt. Is this relationship warm and friendly or you can't stand this person? Is there anything you could do to fix this?

95

THE BATTERED MAN AND DATING

THERE'S no question about the lives of battered women. They are well documented, and there are treatment centers available to provide protection and counseling. What about men? Have you ever heard of a shelter for men? Not likely.

What does the battered condition have to do with dating? Well, you can't get into a destructive relationship unless you meet someone, and dating is how all relationships begin.

It's important to understand there is a major difference between battered women and battered men. Even the automatic word finder in many word processing programs associate the word "battered" with women and doesn't offer the word "men" as an option. It's obvious that as a society the battered man is *invisible*. The big difference with the battered man is that he is often battered mentally, not physically. It's more difficult to see his wounds.

In conversations, with several battered men, it seems that they let their women both run and ruin their lives. In one example, the fellow had been married three times and was at it again on one of the common Internet dating sites looking for *controller* number four. It's not likely that he wants to be controlled and battered psychologically, but that seems to be the pattern that played out in his life.

With wife number three, the beginning of the relationship, like most, was cordial. Somehow, over a period of a few short years, this woman moved her children into his house, yet wouldn't let his children visit. Now there may be a backstory that wasn't revealed, like maybe his children were ax murderers, but it's more likely that he was in a relationship with a controller at a minimum and more likely a sociopath with some type of borderline personality disorder.

Next, this unfortunate gentleman, desperate to find Ms. Perfect, decided to seek out an old flame who just so happened to live three thousand miles away. He dated her for a few months before that, too, fell apart. What's the point? This shows a pattern of desperation. Who dates someone that far away? Sure, there's the star-fated lovers who actually make long distance relationships work, but looking at the pattern this fellow followed, it's more likely that he's rather desperate to find love. This gentleman was battered in the most horrific manner: not physically, but in a way that ruined both his relationship with his children and his honor and self-respect.

How can this story help you in your dating life? The most important point is that you should open your eyes to red flags. If someone begins controlling you (it's subtle at first) stop it early, and if you can't stop it, get out. Run as fast as you can, or you might end up losing half your house, money, and pension along with all of your dignity.

Controlling sociopaths will not stick around if you don't become submissive. When you think you're in love and having great sex, it's easy to fall prey. Sadly, the personality type of some people actually makes them more vulnerable. Strong personality types are more difficult to control, and it requires a really good controller to get the job done.

Ladies, beware! Falling under the influence of a controller and becoming a psychologically battered woman happens all the time. It's probably even more prevalent than in men. Heed the same advice and save yourself from a life of misery. There are those who become so controlled and so dependent on the controller that they are drawn away from family and friends to the point that the only one left in their lives is the controller. And that's the goal: to have complete domain over your life.

IX
DATING BEHAVIORS

96

WHERE TO GO, WHAT TO DO?

97

DIRTY DANCING AND DATING

DATING and dancing go together like Ginger Rogers and Fred Astaire. Women, often more so than men, like to dance. If a guy is a good dancer, he's a hot commodity in social circles. And because it seems so many men can't dance well, those that can are going to get the hottest women.

However, dancing is much more complicated than a couple trotting around on the dance floor. Dancing is an art form, a recreation, a hobby, and a pastime for starters. Many people do not realize that dancing is integrally tied to sex and fertility. How, you might ask, is dancing all about sex? How can being a good dancer get you into the bedroom?

From the early days of humanity, dance has been part of the primitive experience. Check out YouTube to watch a real Zaouli African dance if you are looking for some new steps. Even back then, dance was much more than a social pursuit. Early dance was all about sex. Primitive man used dance to attract the better, more fertile women in the tribe. Those better women wanted the *smooth* dancer, figuring that his genes would help make their sons cool; a woman who was able to snag him could someday be mother to the tribal chief. Next time you go to a wedding, look at all the people on the dance floor, and you will see some interesting anthropological events playing out. You should easily be able to pick out the next chief and his queen.

First and foremost, you will notice the bride dancing somewhat wildly with her girlfriends. This is the *fertility dance*, and they are getting her ready to dance with the groom, also wildly. This is a prelude to the bride and groom going to their room, tent, hut, or whatever, and at the end of the night throwing up all the alcoholic drinks they thought were going to let them have a good time in bed after their wedding – which will be forgotten by morning and replaced by a headache. Fortunately for premarital sex, the bride will probably have a child in a little less than the usual nine months in spite of the failed fertility dance.

Next, notice the bridal party and all the young people dancing up a storm. Like primitive peoples, they are all trying to find a good mate. You know, one that can keep a beat and dance up a storm. As the evening goes on, and the more they drink, they start looking pretty cool on the dance floor. The only problem is they don't look so cool to the rest of the guests who aren't drinking.

Now a logical leap is required to understand the dancing done by the old people in attendance. These folks no longer need to attract a life partner. They have their mates, who are rather obedient and captivated; the wife says, "Would you like to dance, dear?" "Yes, your highness," the husband responds.

Onto the dance floor they go. What you would see coming from this group are more likely moves to encourage a bowel movement. Yes, at some point in life, a good doody takes precedence over the need to attract a fertile mate. They step to the left and to the right; they shake their booties and wave their hands in the air. Now look closely. If you see any of these old people crouch down as if to perform some hip-hop dance move, that's the exact moment they pooped in their pants. Keep watching, as they will make a sudden exit for the bathroom while walking that walk required to keep the contents within their underpants.

Dancing is rather fun if you know how. If you don't, consider some lessons, or have a friend show you a basic step. It's actually easy, and you will make your mate happy. The next time you go on a dancing date, either to go dancing just for dancing's sake, or to celebrate at a party or a wedding, consider why you are there, and dance accordingly. Oh, forget eating prunes on the morning you plan to go dancing.

Activity Suggestion – What was the last dance you could do well? It may be time to take a formal dance lesson. This is also a great way to meet a future partner – who likes to dance.

98

MEETING THEIR FRIENDS: WHO PAYS?

AT SOME POINT, you may want to introduce your lover to your friends. The more you like your lover, the greater the temptation to share the good news with your friends and family. There is also the *yenta factor* (a.k.a. the busybody factor) that involves everyday asking and talking on and on about things going on in other peoples' lives.

If you have a lover, that subject sure beats the mundane things in life, and this means your lover's friends already know a lot about you, and your friends know a lot about him or her.

Assuming you really like this person, you are probably not ashamed to have your lover meet your friends. You can't wait!

Unless you or your lover are antisocial, you would expect your date to put on a good show for all to see. This is much like the first date when you went all-out to impress. Now you are trying to impress the friends of your lover to gain further acceptance. If you just act like yourself, which is what he or she fell for in the first place, you should do just fine.

When it comes to meetings and meals, there are several scenarios that may arise. You could be the guy meeting your girl's girlfriend. In this situation, it is nice if you would pick up the check for any meals you have. It is the gentlemanly thing to do. If you are the girlfriend in this situation, it makes you feel proud that you are going out with the type of guy who can afford three Starbucks coffees without taking out a mortgage.

If you are going to meet your girl's guy friend, you can still pick up the tab on this first meeting. It shows that you're a sport. If there is a whole group of girls, I would still pick up the tab, but if your girl has you meet a bunch of people, both guys and gals, you can split the check with the guys or the whole group depending on what they usually do. If they offer to treat you and it's a mixed crowd, you can be humble and let them treat you. When in Rome ...

You girls have it a whole lot easier. If your guy introduces you to anyone, you just have to be your nice self and let him pick up the tab.

That covers the "who pays" etiquette of meeting friends. For much more detail on what to do and how to behave, see the next section, "Introductions."

99

INTRODUCTIONS

THERE COMES a time when you want to introduce your new date to your friends, parents, siblings, and other such people in your life, like your parole officer. One of the first and usually easiest introductions is to acquaint your lover with your friends, including married friends. It will likely involve a dinner in a place in the hood, because they, too, don't want to spend any more time with you than you do with them. You, especially, as a new dater, want to go home and make love. They, as a happily married couple, want to go home and watch the *Tonight Show* and get to sleep. Oh, the benefits of dating!

Dating introductions can be made for your casual dates; heavy, serious contenders; or even your first dates, though that can get tricky and you shouldn't try that unless you are a professional.

Your date will likely be on his or her best behavior so as to impress your friends or family. However, if you notice too much of a change in how your date acts compared to when he or she is alone with you, you may want to take note. The more a person is the same in all situations, the more likely you are seeing the real person. If your date is phony with others, he or she may be hiding something from you as well.

This is your chance to showcase the new person in your life. The whole reason to take time away from having good sex to introduce your date to your friends is to get another opinion about this person, unfettered by your obvious lack of clear vision, which results from all that good sex. Yes, sex blinds reason. I do hope that phrase is attributed to me when it becomes popular, like "love is blind." And hopefully, it, too, will become a saying of enduring worth.

Your friends are not likely to tell you what they think while you are with them, other than the possible thumbs-up sign you will get if your date comes off as a real winner. You should respond with a thumbs-up to acknowledge that you, too, think this one is a winner.

After the date, like the next day, you can call your friends to see what they really thought. If they are compulsive, opinionated types, you can expect to get a call, and they may not wait until tomorrow. So, if your phone rings late that night, and you are in the middle of wild sex, ignore the call. Better yet, turn off your cell.

Don't get offended if your friends or family members criticize your choice of mates. You must remember, they are either concerned about your well-being or jealous that you are with this person you perceive of as a winner. Listen to what they have to say, and thank them for their thoughts. Then you can cross them off your list of friends.

While I jest, they really are either concerned or jealous; don't forget that. If this person is also single and looking, they may be jealous that you found someone that threatens his or her relationship with you. After all, if you find Mr. or Ms. Right, you won't be hanging around with your friend as much once you tie the knot. You may even have some married friends who love you so much that they don't want to share you, and they, too, could criticize your new lover due to jealousy and possessiveness.

If you get consistent criticisms from friends and family regarding your new love, you may want to heed the advice, at least a little bit. When you hear enough people tell you that your lover is a predator, user, controller, or asshole, they may see something that sex blinded you to. Remember, sex blinds reason. Where did I hear that before? Great expression! I wonder who said it first?

Like all seemingly good relationships, there is a honeymoon stage that lasts from a few minutes to around two years. Any longer than that and you are probably needy, nuts, or an aberration. Sure, you're going to tell me about the couple who have been married for 50 years who still hold hands and smooch all the time in public. Like I said, they are either needy, nuts, or an aberration.

Most long-lasting couples treat each other like family after all that time. Yes, they yell at each other, show great intolerance, or take each other for granted. Then there are many couples who treat one another with dignity, respect, and love, combined with exciting, frequent sex. I even knew one like that once.

After the honeymoon is what really counts, and just know that it may not be all wine and roses, so heed the advice of others, not blindly, but rather buyer beware.

Try to avoid your being needy. If you have been without that connection for a long time, you could become desperate, which is a bad combination. If you are too needy or too desperate, you may tend to be blind to the flaws that are readily apparent to your friends and family. As a matter of fact, desperation dulls the soul. That's a great expression, and you were here to witness its creation.

So, what if your friends and family love your new lover? This is a good sign, but don't let their approval disarm you to what may be lurking in the heart of others. Remember, your date is more than likely on his or her best behavior and may be masking some traits that are less than conducive to a good relationship and saving those bad traits all for you.

When all is said and done, you are responsible for your choices. Use all the information you have at your disposal. The opinions of your friends and family, what you see, and your intuition are tools to help you make choices. You will have to pay the consequences both good and bad.

Activity Suggestion – Look back on your life's experiences and try to remember when friends or family had a negative opinion about your friends or love interests. Did their opinions turn out to be valid?

100

GETTING TO KNOW YOU ... ON THE VACATION

THE BEST WAY TO get to know someone is by the passage of time. Over the long haul, each of us acts more like our real self as various defenses and cover-ups go by the wayside.

Having to go through a year or more of dating to find out more about the true person you are deciding on spending the rest of your life with may be an unnecessary burden. You can learn much faster by dating more regularly in an exclusive relationship, but there is an even speedier process that takes the relationship to a new level, and it's called *the vacation*.

The sleep-away can really speed up the process of getting to know someone. Going away with someone allows you the time to see behaviors that may be more difficult to hide on an hourly dating basis.

Even beyond merely sleeping at your date's house, a vacation to a faraway place gives one the opportunity to see beyond the surface behaviors and get a glimpse into the heart of the beast.

It is hard to hide neuroses, psychotic behavior, OCD, and general maladjustment for too many days of constant intimate contact. This makes the road trip an important part of getting to know your new partner. And while vacations are usually based on relaxation and bliss, the mere activity of packing and traveling and unpacking and deciding what to do each day has enough stress built in to cut through all the layers of civility, allowing you to meet your new mate – the ogre or the witch, depending on which gender you take on this vacation.

If you have the opportunity to see this person pack, you get a good idea of how practical, efficient, and able to handle stress he or she is.

Generally speaking, men pack in a most efficient, albeit ridiculous, manner. Watching a man pack, or at least looking in his suitcase, reveals much about him. Usually, the clothing is thrown into the abyss in a haphazard manner, unless your guy just so happens to be a neat freak, in which case he will have everything folded to perfection, neatly placed in a well-thought-out pattern. Right off the bat, you can tell more about this guy by a mere glimpse into his packing traits than a year of dates.

The same applies for the ladies, only they tend to be the more organized and fastidious packers. The thing you don't see in just looking at the opened suitcase, unless you look carefully, with a magnifying glass, is how many frustration hairs she pulled out of her head in creating this neatly organized baggage.

The truth is that women usually have more clothing than men, and that means many more options when it comes time to go away. Think about it: you men have one pair of black shoes to go into the suitcase. It doesn't involve an internal discussion or a debate. It's that easy. While the dirty soles of these black shoes may seem strategically placed on top of that nice white dress shirt, it was probably not intentional.

Now look at the average woman's closet. There are 80 to 100 pairs of shoes in all the shades found in the premium Crayola crayon box set. Deciding on which shade of purple shoe goes best with the dark purple bag could be difficult and actually require putting the six purple shoes on the floor in various lighting situations to best determine which ones to take. And if they look good in the fluorescent lighting, but not the natural lighting, she may have to take several of the purple shoes and bags so she won't appear mismatched when on the town. While this is much hyperbole, there is truth lurking, too.

Deciding where to go, what things to do, and where to eat gives you a look at many of the qualities and nature of your partner. Be on the lookout for bossiness, always wanting his or her way, an inability to make decisions about going anywhere, and stressing over every little thing that happens.

Be prepared for at least one argument, and maybe more, depending on how good a judge of character you are that got you together with this person in the first place. The argument can be divisive and result in you never seeing this person again. If you see an argument brewing, and you think it could lead to the demise of the relationship, stop it at all costs if you aren't the one in possession of the car keys or plane tickets. You don't want to find yourself on the street begging for fare for a Greyhound ticket.

Some of the traits you may discover include being *pushy, controlling, indecisive, stubborn, oblivious, overbearing,* or *stressed* (and how your mate handles it), as well as *complaining* and all sorts of other negative behaviors. On the other hand, you may see great qualities, such *being in control, being decisive, handling stress well, being spiritual,* and just about any of the many good human qualities and behaviors known. It is your job to weigh the good and the bad and see if this person could be a match for you. The vacation could help you determine whether it is time to pass on a relationship or move it forward toward a union of eternal bliss.

101

THE CRUISE

THE CRUISE IS EVEN BETTER than the mere land vacation to really get to know your new mate. All of a sudden, you are thrust into close quarters in a closed biosphere with the person you are dating on a regular basis, and may even be considering for a life partner.

It's the close quarters that make this situation so touchy. If you were smart and took a full week-long cruise, you get the whole effect. A two- or three-day voyage won't always cut it. Of course, if you do the whole week and this person is driving you nuts, you may want to toss him or her overboard. Conversely, if you are driving your lover nuts, you may get tossed overboard, so watch your back ... and wear water wings.

Putting away clothing and deciding who gets the most closet space is usually gender based (yes, the girls get more space because they have more stuff). If your mate is unusually greedy about how much space he or she gets, this is a good foreshadowing of what you may have to pay out in the divorce settlement. While that was supposed to be a joke, it is very true.

If you see a dark side to your mate, in any circumstance, it is going to come out big-time when conflict arises, and there aren't too many conflicts more contentious than a contested divorce. That is why you have to read the soon-to-be-released book, *Covering Your Ass in Divorce*.

A cruise also offers a great opportunity to see your mate's stamina, because cruises offer so many activities that take place in such a multitude of locations under the intense weakening effects of the Caribbean sun that you will learn a great deal about how much this other person can handle as the days go by.

Watch for eating and drinking habits. You may be able to pick out the alcoholic or the future blimp by observing how your date behaves in the midst of unlimited free food and alcohol.

Being in close quarters and having certain romantic expectations, you may have sex every night (remember, you're dating; if you're married and on a cruise, sex may not be as important any longer). If you picked any longer than the seven-day cruise, you may both need to see a urologist by the end of the vacation.

102

THE DINNER DATE

WHEN DATING, most people are looking for cool things to do. That makes sense. However, many times they overlook the vast variety of eating establishments that may very well take up the entire date. No longer do you have to find a dinner-plus-something-else kind of date, such as those that involve a movie, theater, or other venue. In actuality, if you fill up your date night with too much to do, you and your date may be too tired for a nightcap of rolling under the covers. A date night with too much to do, especially for older married couples, will often end with the two of you dozing off to the monologue of the *Tonight Show*. For way too many people, the sexless marriage revolves around being too busy in all aspects of life, including date night. You don't want to fall into that trap.

Once you decide to do a dinner date, you want to pick something special. A chicken sandwich and a burger at McDonald's may cut it for a quickie dinner, but tonight the entire purpose of the dinner-only date is so that you don't end up with a quickie. Picking a proper place has a lot to do with many personal variables, taste being just one.

When going on a dinner date, there are certain food choices that don't fit well. For example, you may want to avoid Los Angeles's popular The Stinking Rose, where garlic is rather popular. It's even in their ice cream. Garlic breathe is not good for a date, even if it's with your spouse. Difficult foods that tend to stick with you should be avoided. Onions are a no-no, too, lest you have breath that's just as bad as garlic breath.

Dairy intolerance is a big problem for many people. Stomach bloating and gas can be rather uncomfortable, especially if you do manage to get in the sack. When it's just the two of you, it's difficult to blame the dog for that smell, especially if you don't have a dog. And forget about the ride home, which can become toxic for your date should a gas leak happen before you make it there. You pretty much know what does and doesn't agree with you at this point in your life. Don't be a glutton and think it won't happen again, because it will.

Other foods to avoid on first dates include Indian food, Mexican food, any food that may not digest well, or those that tend to result in body odor, such as that seen with curry. As with onions and garlic, curry odor may exude from the pores of your skin resulting in a less-than-desirable dating experience.

Activity Suggestions – Make a list of some different and special places to dine. Refer to this list when you and your date are trying to decide what to do. You will look very organized!

103

ON THE ROAD AGAIN: DATING WHILE AWAY FROM HOME

YOU GUYS MAY FIND yourselves away from home and horny. I don't think e-dating will help you in this regard because mature women aren't looking to jump into bed without a commitment that includes at least six emails, three telephone conversations, an informal meeting for coffee, and a subsequent dinner.

Ladies, the guys are looking for a commitment, too. They just want you to show up. You see, the guys don't need much of a commitment, so if you women find yourselves away from home and horny, get in touch with a guy on an e-dating service, be very forward, and you'll likely score.

Seriously, you may find yourself away from home in a place you go to often for business or family visits, and there is no reason you can't find a companion. Who knows? It could turn into a romance if all the stars are lined up just right, a friendship, or it could just be casual sex.

Do a dating-site search for people in a radius of a few miles from where you are staying, and bingo! You get pictures of hundreds of people looking for some type of connection.

You have to approach these people a bit differently than if you live in their neighborhood. I'd suggest a sob story: *I'm here in town on a business trip and find myself feeling very lonely. I realize a faraway relationship is not likely to blossom, but I sure could use a friend to talk to. If you would be so kind as to accompany me to get a cup of coffee, I would appreciate your indulgence.*

Who could resist this type of request?

If you really want to spice it up, add something like this: *In my state of loneliness, I found your picture on the dating site and felt an almost immediate attraction. You are so pretty, and you remind me of my mother! How about that cup of coffee?*

This is the way to a woman's heart. It works for guys, too. If I got a request like that from a nice woman, I'd start grinding the coffee beans and boil the water.

This type of relationship is not usually going to be much, but if all you want is a fling, go for it. However, there actually are sites where you can find casual-sex companionship while away from home, and they are for swingers and all sorts of men and women looking for nothing more than sex. This can be as blatant as sites offering prostitution, or as simple as some very liberated people looking for a casual hookup.

Flings involve many risks, the most lethal one being killed by a psychopath, followed by death by disease. Then there is the chance you'll get caught in a police sting, or you could even get rolled (that means beaten up and robbed). Be careful out there, and try to avoid getting involved in dangerous relationships just to satisfy your lustful needs.

Activity Suggestions – Would you consider e-dating for a casual fling? How would you feel if your potential date was into this type of relationship? Does it cheapen the potential for a real relationship?

AFTERWORD

If not yet, soon; if not soon, eventually you may find yourself alone and interested in finding a new partner. It's never easy to make this major adjustment in your life. It was the first goal of this book to help you make it happen once again. This comedic look helps to ease the anxiety and fear of dating again. The second goal was to let you know that you are not alone. We all have the same concerns and apprehensions.

Whether to begin dating – in addition to your choice of partner – is one of the most important decisions you ever have to make, besides what to have for dinner next Thursday. Most people go it alone and survive the process. However, when looking at the failure rate of relationships, it's easy to see that lots of mistakes are made along the way. Perhaps, by following some of the advice herein, you will find that dating again can be both enjoyable and life changing ... for the better.

ABOUT THE AUTHOR

Dr. Fleisher has a BA in psychology and a DMD from Temple University. He then earned a specialty certification in endodontics at the University of Pennsylvania. After building the largest endodontic practice in his tri-state area, he left practice to devote time to his passion for writing. Having published professional articles, he later moved on to publish five self-help books: *Forty Something*, *Fifty Something*, *Bedside Manner*, and *From Waiting Room to Courtroom: How Doctors Can Avoid Being Sued* by Jay Pee Medial Book Publishers (February 2016), and *The Sexless Marriage Fix*, by Basic Health Publications (August 2016). Dr. Fleisher is now excited about his novels, *The Devine Affliction* and *The American Strangler*. He looks forward to finding them many new homes.

ALSO BY ROBERT M. FLEISHER

Forty Something

Fifty Something

Bedside Manner

From Waiting Room to Courtroom

The Sexless Marriage Fix